The Great Cartoon Directors

The Great Cartoon Directors

by

Jeff Lenburg

Jefferson & London : McFarland

Library of Congress Cataloguing-in-Publication Data

Lenburg, Jeff.
  The great cartoon directors.

  Bibliography: p.
  Includes index.
  1. Moving-picture producers and directors — United
States. 2. Moving-picture cartoons, American.
I. Title.
PN1998.A2L44 1983   791.43'0233'0922   82-23923

ISBN 0-89950-036-6

Manufactured in the United States of America

McFarland & Company, Inc., Publishers,
  Box 611, Jefferson, North Carolina 28640

To Tex, Friz,
Bob, and Walter
— this one's for you!

Acknowledgments

Film studies are a culmination of blood, sweat, and tears. Those who think that it is just a matter of viewing a few films should leave the room immediately. But seriously folks, it took several years of patience and dedication to research, write, and complete this film study.

The task was made easier because of the untiring assistance of three gentlemen featured in the book—Bob Clampett, Friz Freleng, and Walter Lantz. All reviewed their chapters for accuracy and provided fantastic revelations for others as well. They were just a part of the overall "team work" that helped made this book a reality.

Supplementing the workload was another team—the secondary, which included: Mike Lefebvre (who deserves an eternal "thanks" for his contributions), Bob Nelson (for loaning a fine array of Warner Brothers illustrations), Steve Schneider (for furnishing some nice candids of Warner Brothers' directors), John Field (for offering a rich collection of wonderful frame blow-ups), and David R. Smith (the lone archivist at Walt Disney Productions who answered every question).

Also, special thanks to Mark Kausler, Dan Beck, Joe Adamson, Robert Miller, the Museum of Modern Art, Don Glut, and Glenn Dyckoff.

Then, of course, there were the front linemen, two men who are true film devotees—Greg Lenburg and Randy Skretvedt. Both contributed much time in researching the book, and fulfilled every request without complaining. Thanks fellas!

And, finally, to all who have given me constant support and encouragement—thanks!

Table of Contents

Preface

The Great Cartoon Directors is dedicated to the most prominent cartoon short directors from the 1930s and 1940s, many of which are still popular today. Not included are foreign, feature-film, or television cartoon directors (with the sole exception of those who branched off into television). Subjects were selected on their popularity, their innovations, and their significant achievements in the field of animated cartoon shorts.

Covered will be such men as Friz Freleng; a five-time Academy Aware-winner; Dave Fleischer; the brilliant other half of brother Max Fleischer; William Hanna and Joseph Barbera; seven-time Oscar winners for their MGM *Tom and Jerry* cartoons; Tex Avery, whom many credit for inventing the "comedy cartoon"; Chuck Jones, a three-time Oscar honoree; Bob Clampett, the mastermind behind such cartoon characters as Tweety and Sylvester; Walter Lantz, for his numerous technical and supervisory contributions; and many, many, more.

The intent of The Great Cartoon Directors is to single out these directors' finest cartoons, analyze their style of cartoon-making, and provide valuable insights and biographical material as well as complete filmographies. Illustrations for the book were culled from many of the directors' own private collections. Chapters also feature exclusive interviews with some of the directors themselves.

Chapter 1

Friz Freleng

Chuck Jones has described veteran cartoon director Friz Freleng as "stimulating, irritating, loyal, cynical, wise, funny, stubborn, pragmatic, explosive, intelligent, impatient with stupidity, and generous with everything he could think of to improve another director's cartoon."

The man Jones speaks of is the creator of such cartoon luminaries as Speedy Gonzales, Yosemite Sam and the Pink Panther. If the name doesn't sound familiar, maybe I. Freleng does, as he often billed himself under the name of Isadore Freleng in earlier cartoons. Many, including his former Warner associates, consider Freleng an all-time great in the field of cartoon animation — because he is.

Born in Kansas City, Missouri, on August 21, 1906, Friz's career began when he first had some cartoons published in a monthly employee's magazine by the Armour Packing Company, where he worked as an office boy. The cartoons he drew usually centered on safety hints, or working problems. Cartooning had always interested him and he wanted to be a part of it.

During his days at Westport High School, he entered a contest sponsored by the Kansas City Star newspaper. Open to kids over the age of 16, the contest offered a $50 first prize for the best editorial cartoon. There Friz ran across the name of Hugh Harman (later an animator at Disney and a producer at Warners and MGM), who had also entered the contest.

Says Freleng, "I was fortunate enough to win first prize, and Hugh was awarded runner-up. It wasn't until I came to work at United Film Ad Service that I met Hugh. It was the summer after I graduated from high school [in 1924] that I read an ad in the paper asking for a young man to act as an office boy who had the ability to draw."

Freleng responded to the ad, but when he approached the front steps of the studio, he suddenly got cold feet. He was afraid he wasn't yet qualified to call himself "a professional artist." So he turned around and went home and suffered. "I knew deep down I was a coward," he recalled later. A short time later, Friz got another chance when United Film Ad Service ran the ad again in the same newspaper. This time he answered it and was hired. The company's animation staff at the time numbered just two, Hugh Harman and Ub Iwerks. Walt Disney, who started his career at the film ad company, left for California to set up his own cartoon studio.

Friz credits Hugh Harman for teaching him everything he knows about

1

animation. A book by E.G. Lutz, *Animated Cartoons*, was also a helpful aid to Friz. Up until that time, his knowledge of animation was drawn from what he saw in movie houses, mainly Paul Terry's *Aesop's Fables*.

When Harman and Iwerks left United Film Ad Service in 1924 to join Disney in California, Freleng stayed behind as the lone animator. He also worked as in-betweener, background artist, inker and painter, and sometimes he even handled the camera work. When Freleng first joined the company he was earning $27.50 a week. Now with his added responsibilities, his salary increased to the unheard of $40 a week.

Not long after Disney left, Friz heard from Walt who asked him to join his staff as well. Disney's decision was prompted by Hugh Harman, who told Walt that Freleng had unlimited potential. Though Freleng was reluctant to leave his post at the film ad company, he accepted Disney's offer — with a substantial raise. His salary now climbed to $50 a week.

Friz took on the job because Disney had expressed in many letters to him that he had the patience if Friz was willing to learn. This meant that Walt realized that Freleng was inexperienced, and was willing to help him develop into a top-notch animator. With this commitment, Friz took the next train for Union Station in Los Angeles. Walt greeted him at the station and drove his new employee to the Walt Disney Studios on Hyperion Avenue.

There Friz was introduced to the entire animation staff: Ub Iwerks, Hugh Harman, Rudy Ising and Walker Harman, an inker and painter who was Hugh's brother. Friz became the fourth animator, replacing Ham Hamilton, who had quit because he couldn't stand being abused by Disney.

With this group of animators, Disney produced and animated Oswald the Rabbit cartoons. Usually Walt came up with the basic storyline for the cartoons, with all four animators providing the gags.

In time, Friz discovered that Disney didn't have as much patience as he had previously expressed in his letters. Whenever Friz made a mistake in animating a scene, Walt would harass him to no end. Freleng soon became upset and discussed the situation with Disney. When they met, Freleng remembers that Disney told him "he appreciated me having enough guts to tell him what was on my mind."

Walt evidently forgot about the discussion a few days later, because he continued to harass Friz. Finally, one morning Freleng was so tired of this treatment that he skipped work and instead caught a movie at the Carthay Circle Theatre on Wilshire Boulevard in Beverly Hills. Since he had no transportation, he took the bus to town. During this period, double-decker buses were running down Wilshire Boulevard on the hour. The upper deck had no roof, so passengers had a panoramic view of the city.

That morning when Freleng caught the bus he seated himself in the upper deck. To his surprise, directly behind the bus was Walt, driving his Moon-roadster. Friz was certain that Walt had seen him. When he returned to work the following morning, his suspicions were confirmed. His desk had been cleared; everything he had been working on was gone. Concerned about his job, he told Disney how he truly resented his attitude and treatment of him.

Freleng remembers, "We both lost our tempers, and I threatened to quit, giving him two weeks' notice. He said he didn't have to have any notice and that I could leave any time." Several days later, Friz picked up his final paycheck from Disney and returned to Kansas City in 1929. There he went back to work for the film ad company at his old salary. He joined a staff that included two other animators, Ben "Bugs" Hardaway (later a director at Warners, where he provided the name for a certain rabbit) and Tubby Millar.

Shortly after he left Disney, Freleng was told by Hugh Harman that Walt's entire animation crew likewise quit for similar reasons. They all went to work for producer Charles Mintz, who had taken over the Oswald the Rabbit series. At Harman's recommendation, Mintz hired Freleng as an animator as well. So for the last time Friz quit his old job at the film ad company and returned to California to animate Oswald cartoons in late 1929. He performed a variety of jobs for Mintz, everything from cleaning up drawings to writing story ideas. When Mintz sold out to Walter Lantz and Universal several months later, Freleng and other animators were put out of jobs.

Friz discussed the possibilities of forming a studio with Harman and Rudolph Ising. They all agreed to the plan and rented space in the Otto K. Olson building on Vine Street, just south of the Brown Derby. There they produced a cartoon which served as launching pad for their careers. Entitled *Bosko the Talk-Ink Kid*, it was produced as a pilot film to be shown to potential backers interested in distributing a series of Bosko cartoons. The film starred a black minstrel boy, Bosko, and his girlfriend, Honey. The pilot had no story; it was a plotless revue with the characters tap dancing and singing.

Good as the film was, no one expressed interest in the series. Freleng took on the job as animator for Charles Mintz, who was now producing Krazy Kat cartoons through Columbia Pictures. Meanwhile, Harman tried to find a distributor for the Bosko series. One of the last persons he visited was producer Leon Schlesinger, head of Pacific Arts and Titles Company, who had connections with Warner Brothers. His firm had provided titles for practically every Warners feature film since the early 1920s.

With Schlesinger's help, Warners offered all three animators contracts to head a new animation department. Harman and Ising became directors and Freleng was appointed head animator. His highest salary had been $50 a week at Disney; it now became a whopping $200.

In 1930, production got under way on the first Bosko cartoon and the first Looney Tunes release, *Sinkin' in the Bathtub*. All of the Looney Tunes released through 1933 starred Bosko. Most were directed by Hugh Harman, with Freleng codirecting and even directing a few. Shortly after the start of this series, Warners put Ising in charge of a new series, Merrie Melodies. The Melodies series used a structure similar to Disney's Silly Symphonies cartoons. They had no main character and stories were shaped around hit songs of that day.

Actor Carman Maxwell was contracted to voice Bosko, and luscious starlet Rochelle Hudson supplied the voice of Honey. In addition to *Sinkin' in the Bathtub*, four more Bosko cartoons were released in 1931: *Bosko's Holiday*, *Bosko's Shipwreck*, *Bosko's Doughboy*, and *Bosko's Soda Fountain*.

The first batch of cartoons were received so well that Warners called for the release of 15 more Bosko cartoons in 1932. By then, the cartoon division had expanded and more animators had been added: Robert McKimson (later a director of Warners Foghorn Leghorn series), his brother Tom, Larry Martin, Ham Hamilton (whom Friz had replaced at Disney), Norm Blackburn, and a young man by the name of Bob Clampett.

When Friz wasn't directing, he worked in different classifications — animation, layout, story — wherever he was needed. When Harman and Ising left Warners in 1933, Schlesinger made him a full-fledged director. His first project was a series that Leon had created, Buddy, a boy character that resembled Bosko. Warners had been forced to abandon the Bosko series because Harman and Ising owned the character. Later, they produced additional Bosko cartoons at Metro, but without the success of the former series.

Freleng's job was to salvage two cartoons that Tom Palmer had been directing: *Buddy the Gob* and *Buddy and Towser*. Unhappy with Palmer's work, Schlesinger fired him. Palmer found a job as director of a cartoon fables series called Rainbow Parades, produced by the Van Beuren Company. As Freleng recalls, the Buddy series had its share of problems: "The whole thing was devoid of humor, and there wasn't any warmth to the characters." He saved these cartoons by rewriting the stories and retiming the animation. Much to Leon's delight, Friz salvaged enough material to make three cartoons out of two. The third cartoon was *Buddy's Trolley Car*.

Leon next assigned him to direct his first Merrie Melodies, *Beauty and the Beast*, the studio's first Cinecolor cartoon. Friz did an excellent job on this plum assignment. A reviewer for the *Motion Picture Herald*, a trade paper, said: "The subject should be found cleverly entertaining by both adults and youngsters. The little girl eats too much and too widely before going to sleep and has a disturbing nightmare, landing in a toyland where the wooden soldiers march. She is pursued by the great spider, and is being triumphantly rescued by the captain of the soldiers when she wakes with a bump. Smart and well executed."

The cartoon turned out to be a splendid effort for Warners and for Freleng. The studio was so elevated over his work that they offered him a permanent post as director of Merrie Melodies. He accepted the job, and Earl Du Vall took over his position as director of Buddy cartoons.

No matter what Friz directed, he always made the most of it, especially when he supervised the Melodies cartoons. He gave his gags maximum precision by timing his films on musical bar sheets. Other directors preferred to time scenes on exposure sheets, but Friz believed he got a much better feel of movement by using musical bar sheets. Timing the action this way made the problem of doing the musical score to the picture much easier for Carl Stallings, who scored most of the Warners cartoons.

Most importantly, Friz knew how to give even the weakest story inventive direction. His cartoons never failed to provide laughs; he was a master at setting up slapstick. This even holds true in his earlier cartoons, which relied primarily on musical scores and visual humor.

Friz also proved he was excellent at directing a cartoon that used a lot of dialogue. Such a cartoon was written by Bob Clampett, *I Haven't Got a Hat*, which was released in 1935. The cartoon marked the film debut of Porky Pig.

Originally the character was created by Clampett as part of a team called "Pork and Beans." Freleng discarded the pickaninny character, Beans, but kept Clampett's pig character and renamed it Porky.

Friz remembers what inspired the name: "I called him Porky because as a kid I had two playmate brothers, who happened to be very fat, and one was nicknamed 'Porky,' and the other, the younger one, 'Piggy.'"

Porky's first cartoon takes place in a schoolroom, where his teacher is having her students recite nursery rhymes. First up is a little girl who recites "Mary Had a Little Lamb." The next students the teacher calls on are twin puppies, Ham and Ex. They likewise recite a poem to the plaudits of their classmates. Finally, Porky is asked to recite "Paul Revere's Ride." He tries repeatedly but his constant stuttering thwarts his efforts.

Long before the cartoon went in production, Freleng held auditions to find a suitable voice for Porky. Producer Leon Schlesinger suggested that Freleng audition actor Joe Dougherty, a bit player under contract at Warners who actually stuttered. Obviously he was right for the part, so he was immediately hired as the voice of Porky.

Freleng has noted that Dougherty's speech impediment did cause some problems, however. When he delivered his lines, he used up excessive amounts of soundtrack film since he couldn't control his stammering. As a result, soundmen who worked on the cartoons sped up the recordings to make Porky a fast-moving stutterer. After a few years, it became virtually impossible to keep Dougherty from stammering wildly, so he was let go. Instead the studio decided to hire someone who could fake it. At the advice of Warners story editor Treg Brown, actor Mel Blanc was auditioned for the job. Once Freleng heard Blanc, he was convinced he had found his new Porky and signed him to a contract in 1937. Blanc remained at the studio and went on to voice practically every Warner Brothers cartoon until the demise of the animation department in 1963. Since then, Blanc has voiced additional cartoons and specials starring Warner Brothers cartoon characters that were released through the parent company and produced by DePatie–Freleng Enterprises.

When director Tex Avery was hired in 1936, Freleng was put in charge of the color Merrie Melodies; Avery supervised the black-and-white Looney Tunes starring Porky. The Merrie Melodies that Freleng directed served as a starting point for the development of possible starring characters. Although no new cartoon stars resulted from his early Melodies, some fine cartoons did. Some of Freleng's best cartoons between 1936 and 1937 were: *Bingo Crosbiana* (1936), *Boulevardier from the Bronx* (1936), *Coo-Coo Nut Grove* (1936), *She Was an Acrobat's Daughter* (1937), *Sweet Sioux* (1937), and *Streamlined Greta Green* (1937).

In 1938, Freleng lit up the screen with a couple of gems: *My Little Buckaroo* and *Jungle Jitters*, in which a salesman stumbles upon an African native tribe and almost marries the tribe's queen, and in *A Star Is Hatched*, Freleng burlesques the Janet Gaynor epic, *A Star Is Born*.

A Star Is Hatched was released on April 2, 1938. It was Freleng's last cartoon at Warners, at least temporarily. In August 1937, Freleng had received a call from producer Fred Quimby at MGM. He wanted to discuss the possibilities of having Freleng supervise a newly formed cartoon studio. Friz said he was flattered but he was under contract with Schlesinger until October of that year.

Says Freleng: "Quimby painted a beautiful picture for me, telling me I could hire anyone I saw fit, and that money was no object; when MGM set their minds to do something, it had to be the best, and they were going all out. Quimby also told me I could use any character I saw fit. I felt at the time I would probably have to produce a number of cartoons until I discovered a main character, much on the order of the Merrie Melodies at Warners."

Quimby hoped that Freleng could create a character along the lines of Porky Pig. Animal characters seemed to endure and have greater success in movie cartoon situations than human characters.

When Freleng's Warner Brothers contract expired that October, he had two options: renew his present contract or sign with MGM. Metro made Freleng an offer he couldn't refuse, so he left Warners.

Once at Metro, he found that things had changed since he last talked with Quimby. The vivid picture Quimby painted had suddenly become abstract. The board of directors had recently made a deal with United Features Newspaper Syndicate to produce a series of cartoons based on the Captain and the Kids comic strip. This eliminated Freleng's chance to invent new cartoon characters of his own, as Quimby had promised. He also learned upon his arrival that the studio had already hired all its animators and directors. They included: Carman Maxwell, Mel Shaw, Robert Allen, Bill Hanna, Joe Barbera, Mike Meyers, Dan and George Gordon. Quimby's default on his promises certainly disturbed Freleng, but Quimby told Friz he had no control over the studio's decisions.

In recent years, Freleng has called the Captain series "a mistake" and wished he never made it. He believed the Katzenjammer Kids weren't the right type of characters for animated cartoons. It was, as he says, animal characters such as Mickey Mouse and Porky Pig who had a broader audience appeal than human characters.

Though he thought the series would fail, Freleng gave it his best effort. The third cartoon of the new series and his first at Metro, *Poultry Pirates*, was released on April 16, 1938, two weeks after his last Warners cartoon. The story centers on the Captain's growing problem with chicken thievery in his garden. One Hollywood trade journal said the cartoon "drew quite a few laughs and was sure to entertain."

Following the success of *Poultry Pirates*, Friz went on to direct two more Captain cartoons in 1938, *Pygmy Hunt* and *The Winning Ticket*, and another in 1939, *Petunia National Park*.

About this time MGM signed Hugh Harman and Rudy Ising to produce and direct a new cartoon series. There was a controversial reason for their hiring. There had been a power struggle among animators at MGM. Everyone wanted to produce and direct. Previously these animators had ousted Jack Chertok, producer of the Captain series, and had pushed for the dismissal of Harry Hirschfield, Chertok's replacement. Now they were conspiring against Harman and Ising. Because of these internal problems, Freleng resigned from his post at MGM. He thought of calling his former boss Leon Schlesinger to see if he could have his old job back, but Leon called him first. During Freleng's absence, Leon tried to fill his position with several Warner directors — Bugs Hardaway, Cal Dalton, and Norm McCabe — but they didn't come up to his standards. He not only offered Friz back his original position as head director and animator, but gave him a bonus in salary. Friz now earned $250 a week.

During his first year back at Warners, Freleng turned out ten cartoons, several of which rate among his best. In *You Ought to Be in Pictures* (1940) Porky is induced by the glib talk of Daffy Duck to have producer Leon Schlesinger release him from his contract, so he can pursue work as a dramatic actor. Another good cartoon, *Porky's Baseball Broadcast* has filmdom's popular pig announcing a baseball game between cross-town rivals, and in *Shop, Look, and Listen* Jack Bunny invites hundreds of celebrity guests to his beach party, but they all desert him when he plays his violin.

Though these cartoons were hilarious, his best cartoon since his return to Warners came in 1942: *Rhapsody in Rivets* stars a collection of animals who build a skyscraper to the rhythm of Liszt's "Second Hungarian Rhapsody." Friz's penchant for timing his films out on music paper serves him well, since music took the place of all dialogue in the film. *Box Office* magazine, a daily Hollywood trade paper, said: "What develops is a delight to the eye and ear. A schmaltzy musical score is one of the ideal mediums for animated cartoons and not a single bet was overlooked in writing this one. Recommended unreservedly for next year's Academy Award consideration."

Rhapsody in Rivets was nominated for best cartoon in 1943, but it faced one very difficult problem: strong competition from Metro-Goldwyn-Mayer. Rival studio producers Bill Hanna and Joseph Barbera had likewise animated a cartoon shaped around the music of Liszt, *The Cat Concerto*, which starred Tom and Jerry. Freleng claims his cartoon was finished long before Hanna and Barbera originated a similar idea. Animators at Warners back up Freleng's claim. On the contrary, though, Joe and Bill have accused Freleng of stealing their idea.

No matter who produced their cartoon first, the final decision as to which cartoon was the best would be up to the Academy's voters. The night both pictures screened for Academy Award consideration, Freleng believes MGM maneuvered the program so its cartoon was shown first. Thus, when *Rhapsody in Rivets* followed, it received a less favorable response and audience members thought Freleng had copied MGM's cartoon, instead of vice versa. The winner ended up being *The Cat Concerto*. Freleng says of the loss, "I was broken-hearted at the time, but time heals everything."

In spite of the loss, Freleng continued to grind out superbly animated cartoons throughout the 1940s. A quick scan of his filmography at this point reveals he was primarily directing Bugs Bunny cartoons. Of all the cartoons he directed in the mid-1940s, two especially are of great historical value.

The first came in 1945, *Hare Trigger*, and thrilled moviegoers with Bugs Bunny antagonizing Freleng's latest screen arrival, Yosemite Sam. Bugs' cunning ways were too much for Yosemite's boorish behavior. As one movie critic pointed out: "Sam pulls no punches in his attempt to prove he's all the sheriff's notices claim. There are a good many entertaining situations, with a surprise finish, in which our friend the rabbit smugly announces his victory over the pocket-sized badman." One additional element became apparent as the film concluded: Yosemite was the perfect adversary for Bugs. Unlike Elmer Fudd, his character and motives were defined from the outset.

Explains Freleng: "I found Yosemite Sam to be the perfect opponent for Bugs, as there are no subtleties in Sam's character. The moment he appeared on the screen, there was no doubt about his character, or motives. He was an absolute villain. When another adversary appeared, we would have to build a motive for the unknown character. I really thought Elmer was the wrong guy to oppose Bugs, because he was weak and stupid. He could have been outwitted by a chicken. But who am I to argue with success?"

Although Elmer ranked as the favorite adversary for Bugs, in time more of the spotlight was given to Yosemite Sam. Freleng avoided using Elmer in his cartoons as much as possible. Though Yosemite made fewer cartoons than Elmer, he made a distinct impression that he was not to be outdone.

A good example of Sam's determination can be seen in the 1947 cartoon, *Bugs Bunny Rides Again*. The film opens with a long shot of a saloon in the Old West. Inside the saloon a noisy bunch of cowpokes are mingling at the bar and having a few rounds of drinks. The celebration ends, however, when a series of gunshots ring outside the door. This is followed by three frightened cowpokes screaming repeatedly: "It's Yosemite Sam, run for your life!" The saloon door swings open and there standing in its way is Yosemite Sam, the toughest hombre ever to invade the West.

Everybody clears the saloon when Yosemite flatly states: "Any varmit here to tame me?" A slight pause and silence. "Well, be there?" Standing in the far corner of the saloon, rolling a cigarette is Bugs, dressed up like Gary Cooper. He is seen sporting a ten-gallon Stetson and armed with a six-shooter.

The cartoon quickly becomes a spoof of all the lousy B westerns that moviegoers were subjected to in the 1940s. Every line of dialogue Yosemite delivers has been heard in one B western or another. Freleng, of course, plays up these lines for big laughs. In one scene, Sam warns Bugs: "This town ain't big enough for the two of us." Bugs tells Sam: "Don't worry Sam, I'll take care of that." He goes off screen and in record-breaking time builds a replica of the New York skyline right in the center of town! Exasperated by Bugs' antics, Yosemite tells him in another scene, "Okay you wise guy, dance!" (Now how many times have you heard that line in a western?) Bugs begins to dance but not to the music of Yosemite's gunshots. Instead he puts on a straw hat and twirls a cane to the rollicking sounds of Carl Stallings' ragtime musical score. Following his successful display of dancing, Bugs provokes Sam to do the same. He does and quite a few bellylaughs come from watching the stern-faced Sam act as if he's enjoying his fling at dancing.

Though the cartoon was another excellent Warner Brothers entry, it was never nominated for an Academy Award that year. Instead another Warner cartoon directed by Freleng earned the nomination. It starred a character that director Bob Clampett had introduced in the 1942 Warners cartoon, *A Tale of Two Kitties*. His name was Tweety. This time that good old canary bird retur-
to star in the 1946 tale, *Tweetie Pie*, which costarred a newcomer to the screen,

Sylvester the cat. A reviewer for the *Motion Picture Herald* said: "It's an old story about the cat vs. the bird and, as usual, the bird wins out." As one can see by the review, the basic structure of the Tweety and Sylvester cartoons was much like Metro's Tom and Jerry series. Each character tried to outwit (or destroy) the other. It was also similar to Chuck Jones' later Roadrunner/Coyote series for Warners; the unending conflict between the two characters sustained the series.

As Freleng stated in an interview with the author: "When I made Sylvester cartoons, the only restriction I had was to be sure to keep him as an alley cat with vicious intent. I think that he was really responsible for the success of the Tweety cartoons. Tweety was used in a very minor role. If you analyze his cartoons, he only served as a foil. But he received all the credit, much the same as the Roadrunner cartoons; the Coyote was the real success of the pictures, and the Roadrunner got the credit."

When *Tweetie Pie* won the Academy Award in 1947, it gave Freleng his first statuette, the first to be won by a Warner Brothers cartoon director. The victory had special significance for Freleng since he had beaten a perennial tough competitor, one that had beaten him out of a gold statuette several years before: the MGM–Hanna and Barbera Tom and Jerry series. The Metro series had dominated short subject competition for the past four years, winning every year.

Some of Freleng's other first-rate Tweety cartoons include: *Home Tweet Tweety* (1950), *Putty Tat Trouble* (1951), *Bird in a Guilty Cage* (1952), *Tweety's Circus* (1955), and *Tweet and Sour* (1956). Friz also directed another Oscar-winner in 1957 starring Tweety and Sylvester, *Birds Anonymous*, in which Sylvester tries to swear off chasing canary birds.

In the mid-1950s, the entire complexion of cartoon animation changed. With the advent of television, studios began to suffer terribly at the box-office and tried to save money by cutting production costs. One way for cartoon units to save money was to adopt a new technique in cartoon animation that United Productions of America (UPA) first implemented in 1948: limited animation. Instead of using 24 cels per second to animate one movement, the number was cut in half. Backgrounds, which had previously been fully detailed, became simple and stark.

In spite of this restrictive animation technique, Warner Brothers' directors managed to turn out top-notch cartoons starring new characters. One such character, created by Freleng in 1953, was the fast-running, mischievous Mexican mouse, Speedy Gonzales. Speedy added a new dimension to the already well-stocked stable of Warners characters. He had the speed of the Roadrunner, and the quick wit of Tweety bird.

Speedy had all the right physical elements for comedy: his innocent, impish grin and naive remarks in times of trouble provoked laughter. The trouble was mainly caused by Sylvester the Cat, Speedy's costar and adversary in the series. Casting Sylvester opposite Speedy provided a firm foundation for comedy situations. Without a strong personality like Sylvester, Speedy's characterization was weak, almost lifeless. Not that Speedy wasn't lovable on the screen; he just couldn't carry a cartoon without having someone to antagonize.

Freleng's first Speedy cartoon, *Speedy Gonzales*, was first shown publicly on September 17, 1955. *Box Office* magazine, a major Hollywood trade publication, had this to say: "Speedy Gonzales, the fast-moving mouse tangles with Sylvester the Cat and becomes a hero to the other Mexican mice by foiling all the cat's attempts to prevent him from raiding the cheese factory. No matter what Sylvester tries to catch Gonzales, the mouse is too fast for him. In the end, the cat delivers all the cheese to the mice and quits his job as watchman." Although this was Freleng's first Speedy cartoon, it did not mark the mouse's film debut. Speedy was introduced to the world with a supporting role in a 1953 Warners cartoon directed by Robert McKimson, *Cat Tails for Two*. The Academy of Motion Pictures Arts and Science accorded its approval of *Speedy Gonzales* by naming it best cartoon of 1955. Thus Freleng won his second Oscar and the Speedy series was on.

Freleng continued to direct Speedy cartoons up until the late 1960s when his company, De Patie–Freleng Enterprises, animated a series of new cartoons for Warner Brothers starring Speedy and Daffy Duck. Just before this series began, he developed another character as Speedy's sidekick: Slowpoke Rodriguez. Slowpoke made occasional guest appearances in the series, mainly as the comic relief, but his lethargic personality never caught on.

Besides supervising Speedy cartoons, Freleng remained active by directing Bugs Bunny and other cartoons at Warners. One of his 1957 cartoons, *Show Biz Bugs*, ranks as a masterpiece. The cartoon plays for laughs from beginning to end, with Daffy Duck providing most of them. In this Looney Tunes adventure, Bugs is emceeing a variety stage revue. Every time he goes on stage to introduce his next act, egocentric Daffy Duck tries to capture the spotlight instead. He fails miserably and has to battle a raft of boos from the audience.

Daffy tries to upstage Bugs by doing something so spectacular that not even Bugs can equal it. If Bugs does a super job of dancing, Daffy hoofs one step that's better. This competition continues until Bugs does his finale. Confident that he can top Bugs, Daffy rambles on stage and informs the audience he will take a stick of dynamite, light it, and swallow it. He does, and the result sends the spirit of Daffy rising above his crumpled body.

The audience goes berserk. They just love the act. Bugs remarks to the new ethereal Daffy: "Gee, Daffy, that was great! They want you to do it again." Daffy sadly replies: "I know, I know. But I can only do it once!"

Oddly enough, a cartoon of this caliber didn't earn Freleng his fourth Oscar. Instead it was another Bugs Bunny cartoon, *Knighty Knight Bugs*, released in 1958, that did. With a story by Warren Foster, the film offers little new innovative material and relies heavily on timeworn gags. Freleng's direction is sharp as usual, but it does not save the cartoon from rating about average.

The story concerns King Arthur's knights of the round table and their efforts to retrieve a "singing sword" from the Black Knight. King Arthur asks for volunteers to recover the sword but nobody steps forward. He bemoans, "What are you, a bunch of chickens?" As expected, they all cluck together, supporting the same answer, they are *definitely* chicken! Bugs Bunny, the court jester, enters laughing hysterically at the knights' cowardice and quips, "Only a fool would go after the Black Knight!"

King Arthur believes Bugs is that fool, and awards him the job of tracking down the Black Knight (Yosemite Sam). Bugs, no longer laughing, exits crying as other knights breath a sigh of relief.

The film segues to a scene featuring Yosemite Sam feeding his dragon coal to fuel his fire. The dragon, oafish and clumsy by nature, is the perfect sidekick for Yosemite. He causes more harm than good for his pint-sized boss. The dragon is guarding the sword but misplaces it long enough for Bugs to steal it. Thus, the chase begins! Swiping the trusty blade arouses Yosemite who whips the dragon for sleeping on the job. The dragon reacts by burning Yosemite to a crisp!

The chase results in some typical Yosemite Sam–Bugs Bunny situations. Chasing Bugs to a moat, Bugs pulls up the drawbridge once inside the castle, and watches Sam and the dragon plummet into the algae-filled waters below. In other quintessential gags, Sam falls off cliffs, acts as a human catapult (crashing into the castle's brick wall instead of over it), and fails on all counts. The dragon is a real thorn in the side for Yosemite.

The last scene finds Yosemite and the dragon locked in an explosives room of the castle (chased there by Bugs). Searching for a way out, Yosemite looks for a light but the dragon beats him by blowing flames and igniting the explosives instead. Thus, the castle's pointed wing turns into a rocketship, and fueled by the dynamite, blasts off for parts unknown. Again, Bugs gets the last laugh, and returns with the sword to his homeland.

With cartoons and movies passing into a new decade, the 1960s, the quality of motion pictures began to decline. The same went for cartoons. Thus it came as no surprise in 1962 when Warner Brothers announced closure of its cartoon division. The board of directors, one report said, made the decision to shut down the department because it was losing money. As one producer said, "There was just no money in short subjects."

Director Chuck Jones was one of the first to leave Warners after the shut down, joining MGM to direct a new Tom and Jerry series. Soon the others followed, the last being Freleng. He was assigned to direct animation and assist on direction of live-action sequences for Warners' feature-length movie, *The Incredible Mr. Limpet* (formerly *Be Careful How You Wish*), starring Don Knotts in the title role. The cast also included Carole Cook, Jack Weston, Andrew Duggan, Larry Keating (famed for his role as Roger Addison on the *Mister Ed* TV show), Elizabeth MacRae, Paul Frees, Charles Meredith, and Oscar Beregi. Freleng left the production after he finished storyboards for the film and sought his future elsewhere.

He joined Hanna-Barbera Productions as head animator for the studio's cartoon feature, *Hey, There, It's Yogi Bear*. Assisting him on the film were his story man at Warners, John Dunn, and layout man Rich Hobush. They completed the storyboard on the feature.

Back at Warners, Chuck Jones and David De Patie were discussing the possibilities of forming a new animation company. They didn't want to do so without Friz, so they contacted him to see if he's join in as a partner, and as he says, "I had nothing to lose." And so the animation company, De Patie–Freleng, was born. Jack L. Warner, long-time president of Warners, rented out all the facilities including an animation camera (and even paper and pencils) to them for $500 a month. The first year, 1963, the new cartoon studio produced several television commercials and a film for the armed forces.

Shortly after the success of these films, Freleng signed a deal to animate titles for Blake Edwards' *Pink Panther* feature, which starred Peter Sellers. Friz worked up a storyboard and some time after that he presented it to the Mirisch brothers, Harold, Marvin, and Walter; Blake Edwards, the director; and producer Martin Jurow. Remembers Freleng: "They all flipped with laughter. Of course, the title itself initiated the creation of the character, which was only natural, but the character's personality and material was quite innovative, and created a lot of positive comments."

Harold Mirisch, head of the Mirisch Corporation, was so elated with the Panther titles that he proposed that Freleng animate a cartoon series based on the character. Mirisch was so eager to see the series develop that he took the idea to United Artists' board of directors. It was unanimously decided to pursue such a venture, and thus the Pink Panther was born.

Though the character didn't talk, he provided laughs by reenacting sight gags that Charlie Chaplin and Buster Keaton first made famous in the 1920s. Who said that silents were dead? The Panther cartoons were just that, purely visual cartoons accompanied by a lively ragtime musical soundtrack.

The Panther made his theatrical cartoon debut in *The Pink Phink* on December 18, 1964. It premiered along with Billy Wilder's *Kiss Me, Stupid* at Grauman's Chinese Theatre in Hollywood. Besides directing the cartoon, Freleng assisted story man John Dunn in writing the cartoon and those that followed. Besides getting his first laugh, the Panther also won for Freleng his fifth Oscar and first under his new company. Consequently, the cartoon's success set the stage for a series of Panther cartoons to be produced through 1975.

Production budgets for Pink Panther cartoons ranged from $25,000 to $35,000 per one-reeler. This was quite inexpensive in comparison to the budgets directors were allowed in the 1940s, which ranged from $35,000 to $45,000 for an eight-minute cartoon. Freleng was able to work within the smaller budgets by using limited animation and simple backgrounds. He employed a small staff of animators, including some specialists, to produce the cartoons.

Prior to launching the Panther series, Freleng was commissioned to produce a new series of Warner Brothers cartoons, starring Daffy Duck, Speedy Gonzales, Foghorn Leghorn, and Sylvester and Tweety. On a scale of one to ten, these newly animated adventures rate at least a five for effort. Pure unadulterated slapstick was lacking in these 1964 theatrical offerings and animation was not up to par. Even the voice characterizations by Mel Blanc had lost some of their zing.

In recent years, Freleng added more cartoon series as the company grew, such as *The Tijuana Toads* (later distributed to TV as *The Texas Toads*), *The Ant and the Aardvark*, *The Dogfather* (spoofing *The Godfather*), and half-hour animated specials for ABC starring the Pink Panther. In all, the studio has produced nearly 275 cartoons since its formation in 1963, something Freleng is most proud of.

De Patie–Freleng Enterprises discontinued its production of cartoons when on March 15, 1980, it was announced that Friz Freleng and David De Patie, his associate for 17 years, were splitting up. De Patie accepted a job as president of a new animation company owned by the Marvel Comics Corporation, producers of comic book characters like Spiderman and The Hulk. All of De Patie–Freleng's existing program commitments to television networks were completed in "a timely manner." After these productions were finished, Freleng returned to Warner Brothers to head up another cartoon department — the studio's first since 1962. His first project will be *The Second Bugs Bunny Movie*, a collection of his best cartoons. At age 76, Friz is not about to quit: "I'm very much involved in creating new thoughts, new ideas for TV. I love it too much to ever dream of quitting."

It's a good thing, too, since not many movie cartoonists can direct as masterfully as Freleng. He truly has earned the title of "great movie cartoon director."

Chapter 2

Ub Iwerks

For more than fifty years his tools were a pen and an inkwell. He found prominence as Walt Disney's top animator, later formed his own production company, and still later, returned to Disney. In his prolific career, Ubbe Ert Iwwerks created several amusing cartoon characters and contributed many outstanding innovations in animation. (He shortened his name to Ub Iwerks when he became a commercial artist in the 1920s).

Ub was born, of Dutch extraction, in Kansas City, Missouri, on March 24, 1901. There he attended Ashland Grammar School where he graduated in 1914. Not particularly fond of scholastics, he became a part-time apprentice at Union Bank Note Company while attending Northeast High School. After Ub dropped out of school, in 1916, he worked full-time for one year at the Bank Note Company.

When Ub was 18, the Pesmin-Rubin Commercial Art Studio hired him to do lettering and air brush work. It was a minor job, but a start in commercial art, nonetheless. Another budding young artist, who had just returned from a wartime stint as an ambulance driver in France, soon joined the studio staff. His name was Walt Disney. Iwerks and Disney became friends and discussed the idea of going into business for themselves.

The two artists got their opportunity when Pesmin-Rubin laid them off after the pre-Christmas rush in 1919. They discussed the probabilities of becoming partners in a joint commercial art studio. When they agreed in terms, Disney rented office space and opened a small commercial art business at 31st and Holmes streets. Art facilities were adequate for doing lettering, animation, and air brush work. The fact that there were larger, well established firms in the area presented a problem. They just couldn't compete. Walt searched for other jobs to supplement their studio's meager profits.

Because his weekly salary was modest, the meticulous Disney landed two more positions doing lettering for the *United Leather Workers Journal* and *The Restaurant News*, owned by Walt's friend Al Carter. In the meantime, Iwerks managed the business while Disney invested his hard-earned dollars to keep the commercial art studio afloat.

However, salvation was not far away. One day, Disney read in the *Kansas City Star* newspaper's classifieds that the Kansas City Slide Company (later called Kansas City Film Ad Company) was looking for an experienced commercial artist. In quest of financial security, Disney applied at the company and won the job several days later, enabling him to quit moonlighting. Where Disney went, Iwerks followed. Walt saw that Ub was hired as well since he appreciated Iwerks' efficiency with a pencil. He was a remarkably fast animator.

The Iwerks-Disney commercial art studio was shut down when Ub joined the film ad staff in 1922. He was paid $40 a week for producing crudely animated commercials that were shown at local theaters. Ub's duties included lettering, animation, and even sporadic live-acting spots in the company's movies. The firm offered the first real exposure to film animation to the two artists.

Infatuated with animation techniques, Disney and Iwerks borrowed a company animation camera to film a cartoon consisting of comic vignettes. The end result was a half-reel film, *Laugh-o-Grams*. The Newman Theatre, a local movie house, bought the initial pilot from Disney for a theatrical screening and became coproducer of the series. Hence the films were billed as "Newman Laugh-o-Grams" from 1922 to 1923.

The films, featuring numerous comments about Kansas City events, were so profitable that Disney and Iwerks left the Kansas City Film Ad Company to form their own production company, Disney-Iwerks Studios. Disney staffed a handful of animators at first, including Ub Iwerks, Hugh Harman, and Rudolf Ising, all of whom were paid $50 a week.

Fortunately, the first crop of cartoons enjoyed modest success and enriched Disney's pocketbook. Laugh-o-Grams cartoons, for the most part, showed that Disney strived to present a look of quality in his films. The animation was basic — using wash tones and tremendous amounts of background details — which was something missing from competing studio cartoons. Probably the most well-remembered cartoons from the series were those spoofing famous children's fairy tales like "Cinderella" and "Puss 'n' Boots."

The series halted production in 1923 when Disney's studio folded because of unsuccessful business deals, forcing it into bankruptcy. Disney packed his brushes and inkwells, moved to Hollywood and set up shop in his uncle's garage to produce a new series, "Alice in Cartoonland, which combines live action footage of a little girl with the antics of her animated playmates.

Caught in the shuffle of Disney's move to California, Iwerks remained behind in Kansas City. He considered making a living in the Golden State but preferred the simplicity of Missouri. Instead he returned to his old job at the film ad company, doing lettering and air brush work until Walt persuaded him to move west in 1924.

For three years Iwerks was paid a weekly salary of $120 for doing animation and drawing lobby cards and other promotional artwork for Disney cartoons such as *Oswald the Lucky Rabbit*. Disney embarked on the Oswald series after the popularity of the Alice films had begun to fade. The new character, whose Universal releases were produced by Charles Mintz, bore more than a passing resemblance to Disney and Iwerks' later cocreation, Mickey Mouse. In later cartoons, Oswald wore short buttondown pants and pure white gloves, which was a Mickey Mouse trademark.

When Disney finished editing the final Oswald cartoon, *Sky Scrappers* in 1928, a contract dispute arose between producer Mintz and himself. Mintz owned the rights to the Oswald character, and in an attempt to squeeze more profits from the series for himself, Mintz asked Disney to accept a lower-paying contract. Walt refused, and the series was turned over to a new director, Walter Lantz.

Now what to do? Disney had just lost his most financially successful cartoon character. Again, salvation was not far away. Ub came to the rescue by designing a new character, one that has gained international prominence since its screen debut in 1928. The character's name was Mickey Mouse. After Ub's creation, Disney contracted with Pat Powers' Celebrity Pictures to distribute Mickey Mouse cartoons. The character made his debut in two 1928 films, *Plane Crazy* and *Gallopin' Gaucho*.

Ub animated the first cartoon, *Plane Crazy*, all by himself. To do so he had to work at tremendous speed. He began the last week of April 1928, and by the second week of May the cels were ready to be painted. Friz Freleng, who got his first job as an animator at Disney in 1927, said that Iwerks "was a genius when it came to the mechanics of animation." According to Walt Disney Studios archivist, David R. Smith, Ub turned out about 700 drawings a day. Today in cartoon animation, an animator is lucky if he puts out between 80 to 100 drawings a week! In an interview Ub once remarked, "I've always had a competitive nature. I'd heard that Bill Nolan, who was doing 'Krazy Kat,' had done five hundred to six hundred drawings a day, so I really extended myself."

Extend himself Ub did. His long and prestigious career as an accomplished animator and innovator had just started to take off. The beginning of his technical wizardry came in 1928 when he animated another Mickey Mouse cartoon, the third in the series and first sound picture, *Steamboat Willie*. Mickey's first talkie was released for public exhibition on November 18, 1928. It utilized a synchronized sound process that Ub had renovated, called Cinephone, which adapted the method of frame-by-frame movements for animated figures. The idea of casting Mickey in a sound cartoon was just the shot of new life the series needed. For when he appeared in the first two cartoons, exhibitors said he didn't catch on with moviegoers. Faced with this problem, Disney decided to animate sound cartoons to show off Iwerks' new sound process. It not only spelled money at the box office but prompted other cartoon studios to produce sound cartoons as well.

While Disney cashed in on the success of *Steamboat Willie* and its star, the studio's musical director, Carl Stallings, suggested an idea for a series that would become another long-running hit: "Silly Symphonies."

The good fortune of the Disney Studios marked a turning point in Iwerks' career. He was promoted from animator to director in 1929. During the next two years, Iwerks asserted himself as one of the great cartoon directors. All of his films are inspired works, and several have moments of genius. While at Disney, he directed only five Silly Symphony cartoons, a series he animated before he was promoted.

His first cartoon as a director, *Hell's Bells*, was released to theaters in the spring of 1929. Iwerks knew his future as a director for Disney depended solely on the outcome of the film. Either he continued to direct because the cartoon met Walt's rigid standards, or it was back to animating films instead. When all the critics' notices were counted the results were clear: Iwerks impressed them greatly with the cartoon and his work. The animation had strong shades of gray and was as surreal as Ted E. Powers editorial cartoons, "Joys and Gloom." Each movement was timed well and no flaws in animation were apparent. Iwerks followed his first success with four additional Silly Symphony films: *Arctic Antics, Springtime, Summer,* and *Autumn.*

David Iwerks, Ub's son, illustrated how essential Ub was to the Disney organization. "Proof of Dad's importance to Walt lies in the fact that in 1930 he earned $150 a week; Walt collected $75. Reason Dad got twice as much was because Walt wanted to keep him there at all costs. He understood his value."

So did Ub, who had a desire to produce cartoons independently. Ub felt a deep sense of loyalty towards Disney for getting him started in cartoon animation. But no amount of loyalty could hold Iwerks from advancing his career elsewhere. Thus when Pat Powers, Walt's distributor, offered to finance Ub in a studio of his own in 1930, he resigned from his post at Disney. Walt couldn't match Powers' offer; Iwerks received both a studio and $300 a week. Burt Gillett, later to become a two-time Academy Award-winner at Disney, took over for Ub.

Under the banner of Celebrity Pictures, Iwerks produced three series from 1930 to 1936: Flip the Frog, Willie Whopper, and the ComiColor cartoon fables.

The star of Iwerks' first Celebrity series was originally named Tony the Frog, but Iwerks disliked the name (perhaps reasoning that frogs weren't usually Italian) and named him Flip instead. Flip's debut was a film called *Fiddlesticks,* released August 16, 1930. The cartoon was made in two-strip Cinecolor, two years before Disney produced the first Technicolor short, *Flowers and Trees.*

With the aide of a small staff, Iwerks animated most of the cartoon himself. The first season of cartoons, including *Fiddlesticks,* had Flip designed after a real frog. He had webbed feet and hands and was humanized by large button-eyes and a bow tie and buttons on his chest. Flip doesn't speak in *Fiddlesticks,* but instead entertains other forest animals by dancing on stage and providing piano accompaniment for a mouse who plays a violin. The cartoon wasn't strong enough in the eyes of Iwerks' producer, Pat Powers. He wanted something with more zest and punch behind it since Powers planned to sell the series to a distributor. Based on Iwerks first two cartoons, it looked doubtful that any distributor would take a chance.

Before additional cartoons were animated, Powers asked Iwerks to modify Flip to make his character less *froglike.* Iwerks did and movie audiences were astonished when the *new* Flip the Frog starred in *The Village Barber* in September 1930. Flip had gained human qualities; he was now dressed in plaid pants, white shoes, hand mittens, and he was taller. These changes both strengthened Flip's character and enabled Powers to sell the series to MGM for distribution. Flip became Metro's first cartoon venture and hopes it would attain worldwide success was never fulfilled.

Once Powers signed the MGM pact, Iwerks sped up efforts to bolster his animation staff with a fine array of veterans. His first catch was musical director Carl Stallings, who first scored Disney's Silly Symphony series and later Warner

Brothers' Merrie Melodies and Looney Tunes cartoons. Iwerks began his search for top animators in the field of movie cartooning, veterans with profound cartoon experience. After scouring both coasts he hired people like Irv Spence, Grim Natwick, Max Fleischer, Rudy Zamora, Al Eugster, and Shamus Culhane. Fred Kopietz, later a director for Walter Lantz, was another new addition as well as Chouinard Art School graduate Chuck Jones, who was employed as a cel washer.

Such talent was never properly used by Iwerks, who tended to stifle their creativity. And it shows in his cartoons. The Flip cartoons had their share of problems. First, the films were actually silent cartoons supported by an added musical soundtrack. Moviegoers wanted something else besides music and a frog doing handstands. They wanted characters to talk and act funny, not just look funny. Flip didn't do either. Iwerks selected visual gags rather than verbal ones for Flip. Visual comedy was commonplace in silent films where the leading man would overreact for laughs in farcical melodramas. The same parallel can be found in Flip's reactions, because he too exaggerates his gestures for comedic effect.

Flip's predominantly visual comedy was one reason why writers had problems in developing a complete story of sight gags starring a frog. The first Flip cartoons had one major plotline and several subplots, because writers were unable to develop stories that could supply Flip with enough gags for an entire film.

Another area of improvement was animation. The first few years, animation was inconsistent in the vintage Flip cartoons. For instance, the opening scene in *Fiddlesticks* had obvious animation flaws: the background veers upward as Flip hops across a pond. Animated backgrounds were also primitive, lacking the standard full animation that distinguished later cartoons. Of course, shoestring budgets contributed greatly to the many technical flaws of the Flip cartoons.

Once Iwerks modified Flip, however, his films did gain one essential element previously lacking: personality. Flip had blossomed — matured — into a character full of charisma. Unlike other cartoons characters, Flip wasn't the catalyst of his comedy, but an individual caught in the middle of situations. His romping search for life's virtues always reversed course, with Flip entangled in spots that the other characters created for him. Since Flip didn't talk, his frantic gyrations and gestures of desperation had to create audience empathy.

Flip reached his peak in popularity in 1932. By far it was the series' most successful season, with Iwerks producing an all-time high of 15 Flips for one season. Some of the films made that year were clever and not typical Flip the Frog fare.

The Bully, the sixth cartoon released that season, is bizarre but entertaining. Flip is challenged by a burly boxing champ. Once inside the ring, the champ punches Flip so hard that his spirit leaves him to walk amongst the cheering throng. When the spirit leaves his body, Flip regains consciousness only to be punched around by the champ. The final blow by the champ sends Flip soaring around the earth; a technique combining live footage of a globe as a backdrop with animated footage of Flip whirling around the planet.

Another good entry that season was *Funny Face*, which has Flip trying to impress his girl friend by changing his appearance. He goes to the office of Dr. Skinnum to check out what kind of new face he can give him. On the wall in the waiting room is a collection of faces that laugh in unison when Flip walks up to investigate. They make fun of his "funny face," but Flip isn't laughing. Shortly after this scene, Flip chooses the face he wants: one of a handsome boy. The doctor grafts the new face onto his own, and presto-chango, Flip is a new frog...a new man! He struts out of the doctor's office proudly and is anxious to show off his new kisser to his girl friend. But first he must save his girl friend from the clutches of a burly bully. Flip grabs the man but the bully punches his new face shattering it. In the end, the villain loses out and Flip wins the girl without his new face.

Around this time, Iwerks devoted more time overseeing production and supervising all his cartoon productions. Nothing was filmed unless it met Ub's approval. He was much the same as Disney; a very meticulous man who wanted everything just right. One of his animators, Shamus Culhane, remembers how he once drew the wheels for a stagecoach but didn't worry much if the ovals were neatly round. "I would just draw wheels and if they came out oblong, it wouldn't matter," Culhane recalls. "It mattered to him—he blew his stack, and he sat down and drew them like an engineer. Perfect ovals."

In 1933 Flip starred in only seven cartoons, including the second Cinecolor release, *Techno-cracked*. The cartoon received poor reviews and Flip's future as a cartoon star looked dim. Iwerks began looking elsewhere for a replacement for Flip. He was afraid that if things didn't improve he might just lose his distributorship at MGM. With Leo and Lion restless, Ub intensified efforts to create an endearing character who could take Flip's place. The series he ended up with was animated adventures of the accomplished liar Willie Whopper.

The first cartoon, *Play Ball*, was released on September 16, 1933. It opens with Willie standing in front of a Looney Tunes–type oval, saying to the audience: "Say, did I ever tell you this one?" This acts as a clever segue to Willie's telling a story about the time he was a great baseball player, the status of Ty Cobb or Lou Gehrig. The cartoon ends with a caricatured Babe Ruth and Flip the Frog being feted in a New York ticker tape parade.

Willie went through some physical changes before his next cartoon. Iwerks wasn't completely satisfied with the character yet and decided to make him more "cartoonlike." Before production began on *Stratos Fear*, the second cartoon in the series, Iwerks put some last minute touches on Willie. The extra effort paid off as his latest cartoon adventure was greeted by nothing but praise, and put a smile on Leo the Lion's face. Willie was far more convincing after Iwerks made changes in his appearance. He was now roly-poly with freckles on his face and a wave of red hair that complemented his wide impish-grin.

Stratos Fear was a turning point for Willie; his cartoons were accepted and he was likewise more appreciated. In this black-and-white subject, Willie's tooth is giving him horrible pain. He visits Dr. A. King, a local dentist, to have the tooth pulled. The doctor gives Willie so much gas that he bulges into a large blimp and floats through the roof of the dentist's office. The story itself is paced well, with Willie later waking from his gas-induced slumber.

Other Willie's worth noting include *Davy Jones' Locker*, the first Cinecolor cartoon in the series, and *Jungle Jitters* (1934) in which Willie is shipwrecked on a desert isle but escapes when he finds out the native cannibals have him in mind for dinner.

Just two months after Willie debuted on screen, Iwerks introduced his third series to the movie going public, ComiColor cartoon fables. These fairy tale lampoons became a profitable venture for Iwerks from 1933 to 1936, starting with *Jack and the Beanstalk*.

It was one year later, in 1934, that Iwerks unveiled his most prestigious invention: multiplane animation (which Max Fleischer used later in Paramount's two-reel Popeye cartoons). The multiplane camera, adding three-dimensional foreground and background to cartoons, was capable of shooting through layers of animated background, moving either forward or backward, to project on film elaborate backgrounds and a great feeling of depth. It also resulted in fuller animation and brighter colors in this Cinecolor series.

Iwerks experimented with his multiplane invention in *The Headless Horseman*, based on the famous Washington Irving story, *The Legend of Sleepy Hollow*. Scenes in which the horseman rides are almost three-dimensional. The background colors are vivid and all aspects of the multiplane system dazzles the mind. But dramatic these ComiColor cartoons are not. Instead these films are predictable and obviously intended for juvenile audiences.

Two cartoons that deserve more than a passing mention are the 1934 releases *Jack Frost* and *Don Quixote*. Iwerks presents a lively and amusing tale of Jack Frost not seen before in any medium. The story, of course, is the same as all others. Jack comes down to warm the animals at play in the midst of the snow that fell the night before. All the animals listen and come to Jack except a bear cub who thinks his fur is thick enough to keep him warm. That is when Old Man Winter shows the bear he is in error, blowing out blistery winds and whipping up a snowstorm, leaving the cub frigid. In many ways, the cartoon reminds audiences of Iwerks' best Silly Symphony cartoon for Disney. It is full of fun and frolic and good animation.

Don Quixote is genuine cartoon entertainment and one of Iwerks' best ComiColor films. The story opens with an insane asylum inmate reading about the knights of old. He too wants to become a legendary knight so he escapes from his padded cell to become a Don Quixote. Throughout the film he does all sorts of knightly deeds, everything from attacking a windmill to saving a lady he thinks is in distress. The lady turns out to be elderly and unattractive, so he is glad to return back to the sanctuary of his padded cell at the asylum.

Not all ComiColor cartoons were produced using the multiplane camera, but even those films that weren't shot in multiplane retained quality animation and story; the standards of cartooning remained superb. Iwerks must have remembered his work for Disney when he made the ComiColor series, because most of them had distinct similarities to his Silly Symphony cartoons.

By late 1934 Willie Whopper faded from the screen, since the series never lived up to Iwerks' expectations. He had hoped Willie would become a greater cartoon character than Flip. He didn't. About half of his cartoons were amusing, the rest subpar. Willie had some great fibs over the years, but not even his best fib could convince Metro or Iwerks to continue the series. It was a mutual parting both sides never regretted.

In the meantime, Iwerks' ComiColor series ran just two more years before it was cancelled in 1936. *Happy Days*, released on September 30, 1936, marked Ub Iwerks' final production for Pat Powers' Celebrity Pictures. The last cartoon, incidentally, was a *pilot* for a new series Iwerks was proposing to animate based on Gene Byrnes' famous newspaper strip, "Reg'lar Fellers." Original plans called for the series to be produced in addition to a fourth season of ComiColor cartoons already scheduled for the 1936–37 season. The plans never materialized.

One reason Iwerks' studio folded was because of strong competition from such major studios as Warner Brothers, MGM, and Paramount. With as many as 15 or more series produced yearly by competitors, it made the going rough for Iwerks and other cartoon independents. Ub didn't stay out of a job for long, however. He met with Leon Schlesinger, producer of Warner Brothers cartoons, to discuss the possibilitites of directing. Schlesinger, overwhelmed at the prospect of having Iwerks, offered him a contract. Iwerks' arrival left some bitter feelings among some Warner animators, notably Bob Clampett, whom Schlesinger promised would take over the next directorial post. Leon told Clampett to be patient as he expected Iwerks wouldn't be around for long. Schlesinger's predictions were accurate as Iwerks directed just two Looney Tunes, both Porky Pig cartoons which received good trade reviews and pats on the back from Schlesinger. But neither glory nor accolades could keep Iwerks at Warners; he was finished. Iwerks' reason for leaving Warners isn't exactly known, but Clampett believes he left because "his heart just wasn't in it."

Instead Iwerks accepted an offer to direct Columbia Pictures' Color Rhapsodies series. These cartoons were color fairy tales that have some resemblance to Disney's Silly Symphonies, but that's as far as the comparison goes. Columbia's animation was the weakest of all major cartoon studios, and so were the cartoons. Iwerks' first cartoon at Columbia, *Two Lazy Crows*, was released to theaters on November 26, 1936. This Technicolor short received good trade reviews, partly because of Iwerks' superb direction. Two crows relax in the hot summer sun while neighboring animals prepare for winter. Everybody feathers their nests except the crows. When winter arrives the crows are left out in the cold and pretend to be ill, hoping one of the animals will take them in. A friendly squirrel extends an invitation to these crows to sleep in his bungalow, but when Mrs. Squirrel returns home, the two lazy crows find themselves out in the cold once again.

Another excellent Rhapsody cartoon directed by Iwerks was *Skeleton Frolic*. This 1937 Technicolor cartoon stars a group of skeletons who head up a swing band late at night in a deserted old haunted house. Iwerks applies a time-worn cliché here—music loud enough to wake the dead—but brings a different dimension to it. The cartoon has a loud ring to it that makes it eventful and worthwhile. In some respects this film is as jazzy and entertaining as Lantz's Swing Symphony cartoons. Overall the cartoon had a slight edge in production to Iwerks' previous best, *Two Lazy Crows*.

Iwerks continued to turn out about a half dozen cartoons a year at

Columbia until he finally grew tired of the studio's rundown condition. Iwerks was presumably as unhappy to be working there as his colleagues were. One esteemed animator who worked with Iwerks described the studio conditions as "the pits." Facilities were poor and office space was "the size of a two-car garage"; Iwerks' meager salary offered no consolation. After four years of hit-and-miss cartooning, Iwerks left Columbia in 1940 after the release of *Wise Owl*, his last animated subject for the studio. The cartoon was not one of his best; a critic for *Motion Picture Herald* called it "repetitious ... recommended for juvenile consumption."

Iwerks produced two independent cartoon series in England later that year. Gran-Pop Monkeys was a short-lived series featuring the misadventures of three monkeys. It was animated at Cartoons Limited and released through Monogram Pictures. His second independent series is the least known of the two, The Way-Out series. Research has been unable to uncover much on this series, other than that it was a comedy-travelogue similar to Tex Avery's travelogue spoofs for Warners.

Later that year, in 1940, Iwerks wound up back at Disney and became Walt's creative technical director for the studio's new Optical Print Department. While in his new post, he developed new techniques and improved existing sound techniques. Walt later promoted him to technical researcher in the Special Processes and Camera Department, where he perfected techniques for color traveling matte composition cinematography. He won an Academy Award for this in 1964. He had previously garnered an Oscar in 1959 for his design of an improved optical printer for special effects matte shots.

It has been said that Iwerks was responsible for the success of *20,000 Leagues Under the Sea*, in which he modified the fascinating special effects process of combining live footage with animation. He was later in charge of special effects in a non-Disney film, Alfred Hitchcock's 1963 classic, *The Birds*. Ub also expertly assisted in the development of xerography for Disney's animated feature, *101 Dalmations*. This technique is used by all studios today. Basically, it eliminates inking by photocopying the animator's pencil sketch directly onto the cel.

Ub's string of credits reflects many hours of hard work. More importantly, they show his special effects innovations and his importance to Disney. When a Disney animator once asked Iwerks about the evolution of Flip the Frog, he answered suspiciously, "Shhhh! Don't ever mention that around here."

Iwerks was not bitter or embarrassed about his years as an independent producer and director, but he preferred not to remember the past. He was proud of all his achievements as an independent producer and as a member of the Disney studio team.

Ubbe Ert Iwwerks, creator, director, innovator, died July 7, 1971, leaving behind for students of the art a legacy of fine films and many innovations.

Chapter 3

Chuck Jones

Whenever the film characters Bugs Bunny, Daffy Duck, or the Road Runner are mentioned, movie audiences easily recognize who they are. They are just as much a part of American folklore as Moby Dick, probably more so. Yet often lost in the creation and development of these cartoon superstars is due credit to the genius behind them. Such has not been the case for the man who entertained filmgoers with these and other characters. He is considered an institution in cartoon animation. His name is Charles M. Jones, or as he prefers, Chuck Jones.

A nominee 14 times for an Academy Award and the winner of three, Jones has been called "the most important cartoon director America has produced next to Walt Disney." He did the main drawings for some 250 films and through them made moviegoers laugh as often or as well as Charlie Chaplin and Buster Keaton could. Most of his cartoons are pure unadulterated slapstick. Slapstick Jones learned from watching Chaplin and Keaton comedies as a teenager.

Chuck first became infatuated with the movie business at the tender age of six. It was several years after his birth on September 21, 1912 that Jones and his parents moved from Spokane, Washington, to Hollywood. They lived on Sunset Boulevard right across from Hollywood High School. It was here that Jones learned about movie making. Just two blocks down from his house was the Chaplin Studios.

Jones has a snub nose, he says, from pressing it too hard against the fence in front of the Chaplin Studios to watch how comedies were made. As he recalled, "I learned a great deal about timing from watching Chaplin. Father came home one day and said he saw Chaplin film a scene he'd done 52 times to get it right for fifteen seconds on the screen. It had a lot to do with timing." The bit Chaplin was trying to perfect was his famous one-legged turn.

It was from that day forth that Jones yearned to get into the movie business. Exactly what position he would pursue he wasn't sure of yet. But it didn't take long for him to find out. When Chuck attended Franklin High School as a senior, he became actively involved in drawing illustrations for the school yearbook and newspaper. Upon graduation in 1930, Jones continued his art education at the Chouinard Art Institute. There he learned about color composition, pastels, pencil, and pen and ink drawings.

When Jones graduated he engaged in various enterprises before actually landing a job in animation. For awhile he was a sailor, sketch artist, puppet designer, and commercial artist. His first job in animation was as a cel washer for Ub Iwerks at Pat Powers' Celebrity Pictures. There he worked on a couple of Flip the Frog cartoons before leaving to join Warner Brothers Cartoon Division in May 1933.

Jones was offered the same position at Warners that he held at Iwerks' studio. Eventually he worked his way up from the bottom rung of the ladder to animator, writer, assistant director, then director. Animators have said that Jones was always full of "enthusiasm" at *Termite Terrace*, an inside designation for Warners' cartoon unit. Every day he'd come to the studio with a stack of story ideas, which he presented to producer Leon Schlesinger for consideration.

One might say that Jones was anxious to prove to his employers his true value, maybe as an assistant animator or possibly as a director. Schlesinger was indeed impressed by Jones' creative story ideas, so much so that he didn't have to wait much longer for that promotion.

After five years as an animator on Merrie Melodies and Looney Tunes, Jones wasn't far from becoming a full-fledged director. He did so with a little luck involved, thanks in part to his old friend Friz Freleng. News had spread that Freleng was leaving his position as head director at Warners to take on a similar position at Metro-Goldwyn-Mayer's cartoon department. The announcement left Warner Brothers' animators stunned as Freleng had been a leader since the cartoon division's inception in 1930. For days animators were anticipating a promotion from within. The obvious choice was Jones. Everybody else who had joined Warners before Jones were already directors by now, including Bob Clampett.

In May 1938 the long awaited promotion became a reality when Schlesinger announced that Jones would assume the duties vacated by Freleng. As a director his first cartoon assignment was one of his own, featuring a star character he created called Sniffles the mouse in *Night Watchman*. The cartoon was on the same line as the cute Hugh Harman and Rudy Ising cartoons that were being produced at Metro. Needless to say, however, Sniffles was far from Jones' best creation. Funny he wasn't; cute he tried in vain to be. He was cuddly, complete with button eyes, and sported a bellman's cap on top of his fuzzy head. In some respects, he bore a striking resemblance to Hugh Harman's ungodly mouse star, Little Buck Cheeser. Actress Bernice Hansen supplied the voice for Sniffles, and the character itself became one of the screen's most forgotten luminaries. He faded as quickly from the screen as Flip the Frog did in 1932 and Willie Whopper in 1933.

Despite Sniffles' weak on-screen character, Schlesinger and Warner Brothers executives believed Jones had done an impressive job his first time out as a director. And, because of it, Jones stayed on as a director and Sniffles' career was prolonged that much longer. Jones frequently returned with Sniffles cartoons, as he did in 1939, with *Naughty But Mice*, *Little Brother Rat*, and *Sniffles and the Bookworm*.

Of all the Sniffles cartoons produced, not one stands out. All of them were equal in mediocrity. The 1939 *Bedtime for Sniffles*, is an example: Jones gives no reason for Sniffles' actions. Instead it's as if the character is just wading through the motions until the alleged plot unfolds. The film is set during a season as cheerful as Christmas Eve, but Jones turns the season to be jolly into the season to be yawning.

The cartoon is about as action-packed as a turtle race. The pace is slow and the dialogue not sharp. A good deal of Sniffles' lines in a large portion of this cartoon include, "Gosh! Gosh!! Gosh!!!" That's exactly what the audience is thinking: gosh, how bad can a cartoon get! Such dialogue is his response to the wonders of Christmas and the gorgeous snowfall outside his mouse haven. Even so, those are about the only lines Sniffles speaks during the first half of this eight-minute cartoon. Unfortunately, Sniffles is about as unfunny as a comedian pulling down his pants, straining for laughs. The clever gags exploited in later cartoons by Jones do not appear in these earlier films.

In years to come, Sniffles became an insignificant part of Jones' annual cartoon production schedule. He focused his energies instead on other characters who had broader appeal. One of them had such a pronounced impact on moviegoers that Warners immediately requested more of the same. Jones is not credited for originally unveiling this wacky screen hero, but for refining and making his character grow. The character's name is Daffy Duck, and he was first brought into the world on April 17, 1937, as costar in a Tex Avery cartoon, *Porky's Duck Hunt*. Although Daffy was already two years old by the time Jones directed him, his first Daffy cartoon is considered the duck's first star-billing effort: *Daffy and the Dinosaur* (1939).

Some clever moments are provided in this cartoon and many great visual gags that seem inspired by one of Jones' contemporaries, animator Bob Clampett. It is a good example of how different was Daffy's character in earlier cartoons; he was zany and unrestrained. In this film he matches wits with a caveman who resembles Jack Benny. The starving caveman proclaims to moviegoers at the beginning, "I'm famished!" as he looks to his pet dinosaur for sympathy. Maybe his dinosaur can fetch him some morsel of food before the night's out. Precisely at the moment Benny delivers that line, he spots a duck ("Yum, yummy — my favorite vegetable — duck!"). Daffy is swimming gracefully across a pond in the foreground. As he wallows above water the caveman pulls out a slingshot and loads it with a rock before letting it go in the direction of Daffy. With the rock approaching fast, Daffy suddenly becomes a traffic cop and directs signals — stopping the rock dead in its tracks while he waves on a school of ducks in the other lane. After the ducks pass, he drops his hand and the rock zooms by — forgetting momentarily that it's supposed to hit Daffy. Just as it remembers, it makes a quick rebound and heads back after Daffy, who ducks just before the caveman does, smashing the dinosaur in the noggin. Scratching his head, the caveman remarks, "That duck acts as if he's crazy!" Daffy responds wisely: "That's it — you're absolutely correct — 100 percent correct!" finishing his sentence before he goes off merrily springing handstands and the like.

The cartoon builds to a simply marvelous ending by Jones. It all begins when the caveman proclaims he's getting hungrier. This gag comes after Daffy has just fooled the caveman by painting a replica of himself on a boulder. The caveman, thinking it is Daffy, crushes his club against the rock — leaving him vibrating for the longest time. Once he returns to normal, Daffy hands him a card which says he can find the most luscious duck just about 200 yards away. The caveman, believing a big feast awaits him, takes off for the site. Signs are posted strategically along the route, reading, for example, "Duck is brainfood!" or "There are more costly ingredients in Duck!" Arriving at his destination, the card proves true. There standing directly in front of the caveman is a colossal blimp-size duck (which Daffy has blown up with a bicycle pump). The caveman pulls out a knife and prepares to dig in, resulting in a phenomenal explosion that sends all three characters to cartoon heaven, with the caveman closing out the film in typical Benny fashion by saying, "Good night, folks!" A critic for the *Motion Picture Herald* trade magazine, citing the film's hilarious conclusion, said: "The finale is a bust for hunter and hunted alike. The gags and situations are appropriately matched to the zany personality of the duck."

Notice the word "zany" is used to describe Daffy at this stage of his career. He lived up to his billing in this and other cartoons directed by Jones. It wasn't until the dawn of the 1940s that Daffy became more of a foil in Warners cartoons, rather than the offbeat comedian. In earlier films, he reminded audiences of a tightly wound spring unleashed on screen, doing acrobatic bits of business like handstands and somersaults.

Daffy's comedy was further exemplified on the screen by his exasperated lisp, which took form in the late 1930s. Jones has said the lisp was stolen from Warners producer Leon Schlesinger. Says Jones: "I believe it was Cal Howard who said once that Leon's voice would make a great voice for a character — he sounded just like Daffy. At the time Tex Avery was doing the first Daffy, *Porky's Duck Hunt*, he did it with the same lisping voice as Schlesinger's. Then after we finished we were scared to hell, because we had to go in and Leon had to look at it. Then he would fire us all for sure. So he looked at it and jumped up — and we thought, here it comes. Instead of that he said, 'Hey fellas, that's a wonderful voice — where'd you get it?' He never knew. If he has any claim to immortality it won't be because he's rich, it'll be because he inadvertently supplied the voice of Daffy Duck."

Like other Warner Brothers characters, with the exception of Elmer Fudd, Daffy was brought to life by the brilliant voice of actor-comedian Mel Blanc. (Blanc didn't voice Elmer until his creator, Arthur Q. Bryan, died in 1959). Blanc, of course, struck fame as a sidekick to Jack Benny on his radio show before he came to Warners in 1937. Jones believes that Blanc was instrumental in making Daffy's zany and dogmatic career believable. Jones explains: "Daffy was insane. He never settled down. His personality was very self-serving, as if to say, 'I may be mean, but at least I'm alive.'"

Insane Daffy was. His pure slapstick antics on the screen put moviegoers in hysterics at a time when the United States was preparing for a second world war, and when everyone needed a good laugh. Daffy was not only good for the country's morale but also represented clean entertainment parents could take their children to watch. And as time marched forward, the stories and Daffy's character could do nothing but improve. His cartoons were in such great demand during the prewar years that Warner Brothers stepped up production of the Daffy series to accommodate requests by exhibitors.

One of Jones' more splendid Daffy cartoons during the 1940s is *To Duck or Not to Duck* (1942). The story of duck hunting, a tale often used in the Daffy series, is exaggerated beyond imagination in this cartoon. This time it is Elmer hunting the pestiferous Daffy rather than his other screen adversary, Bugs Bunny. Elmer has no problems shooting down Daffy (who proclaims that Elmer "couldn't hit the broadside of a duck!") and orders Laramore the dog to retrieve the duck. Elmer rejoices after catching Daffy by calling himself "a great sportsman." Daffy reacts vehemently saying, "What kind of protection does a duck have against a gun, or a dog, or a...." And so it continues in the fashion of Bud Abbott berating Lou Costello for not using mustard on a hot dog because it would throw the entire economic picture out of kilter. Daffy gets so upset that he starts ripping off Elmer's clothes, everything except his shorts, which at one point fall off briefly exposing his buttocks. He continues his glib, fast-talk with Elmer about him being "a poor defenseless duck" until he walks him right off the screen into the center of a boxing ring.

Suddenly a referee enters and announces the two challengers for the evening and the cartoon becomes a boxing match instead of a duck hunt. The arena is full of, what else, ducks. One gag that always gets solid laughs, be it live or animated, is when the referee shows the challenger that there will be "no rough stuff." Of course, the challenger gets brutalized as the referee demonstrates all the do's and don't on him—leaving doubt as to whether he has much of a chance in winning. By the time our fight begins, Elmer is broken down—he already has a black eye and he appears worn by the crushing punches the referee exploded on him. As soon as the bell rings, Elmer gets up and is knocked out by Daffy with lightning speed. The boxing arena faithful cheer wildly as Daffy is proclaimed the winner and new champion. Elmer, enraged that the match was fixed, corrals both the referee and Daffy and clobbers them before the cartoon fades out.

Violence was the primary ingredient for humor illustrated in this cartoon. Such violence was increased in numbers once directors molded and refined characters like Bugs and Daffy around their style of humor. It was an element that was as essential to the cartoon as the character itself, especially when producing slapstick comedy. Jones remembers the complaints that were voiced over the excessive amounts of violence—but disagrees that his cartoons were that violent. Remembers Jones: "Our basic goal in these films was to make people laugh—not for anyone we would identify with just ourselves. We never previewed and we certainly didn't have children in mind. The pictures went out with gentle little films like *I Was a Fugitive from a Chain Gang* or *Dr. Ehrlich's Magic Bullet*. The idea that they were to be on television was the remotest thing from our minds. It never occurred to us they'd be there. So when parents tell me I'm violent, I reply by saying that Chaplin was, so was Keaton in *The General*. The last ten minutes of *The General* was considered pretty violent because they were killing people. I never killed anybody in my cartoons. I loved splash—but I never killed them."

The same year *To Duck or Not to Duck* made its way to the screen, Jones directed another classic subject, one with less violence. Entitled *The Dover Boys*, the cartoon is written and timed in the style of a Jay Ward cartoon, creator of television's *Rocky and Bullwinkle*. The gags are mechanical, sophisticated, short, full of quick laughs, all of which are ingredients later realized in a Jay Ward cartoon. The story of this cartoon centers on the Dover Boys—Tom, Dick, and Larry—who are students at Pimento University (P.U. for short). In the background during the cartoon's opening can be heard the narrator singing the school's theme song: "Good ole P.U.—that fragrant scent in the air."

These three characters have something more important to undertake on weekends than study biology or take field trips. All are in hot pursuit of a young lady named Dora. She is a student at an all-girls college just down the road from P.U. But in a cartoon where love is a main focal point, there must be a villain lurking in the foreground. That villain is a Snidely Whiplash type who bears the name of Dan Backslide. Dan says if he can't woo Dora it may drive him to drink. Seconds after he delivers that line, the cartoon cuts to Dan suddenly up at a bar downing 20 rounds of scotch before he returns to finish his tear-jerking tale.

The cartoon has several great gags, one which involves the three Dovers and Dora. This occurs just minutes before Dan plans on snatching her away from the three Ivy Leaguers. They are seen playing a game of hide-and-go-seek. And as the rules dictate, Dora must keep counting until the Dovers tell her to come out after them. The problem is the Dovers aren't sure where to hide, as they scour the countryside from one hiding place to another, spouting, "No let's hide here!...No here!...No here!!...No here!!!" Jones continues in this fashion until they wind up hiding in Snooker Saloon, where Dan Backslide is seen drinking his sorrows away. His opportunity to capture Dora in sight, Backslide laughs villainously—noticing the Dovers had left his lovely—and takes off down the road in search of his loved one. He finds her still counting—now somewhere in the hundreds—and waiting for the Dovers to tell her to stop. Backslide picks her up and hot rods away in his automobile before Dora quits counting and starts screaming for "help." The Dovers can't hear her cry as they are about ten miles in town.

Imagination prevails in this cartoon, however, as a clearcut solution to saving Dora appears moments after her abduction. An alert Boy Scout, who discovers Backslide's hideout, waves flag signals to another Scout on top of a hill, informing the Dovers of Dora's whereabouts. The message is transposed into a telegram and delivered to the Dovers, who quickly act on finding Dora. All they picture is how this poor, defenseless girl must be screaming deliriously in the evil clutches of Backslide. Fortunately, it's not quite that way, since Dora is fending for herself nicely, as Backslide can't defend himself against her Popeye-like strength. By the time the Dovers arrive, Backslide has been pulverized by Dora and his cabin left in a shambles. The cartoon has its share of violent moments, but much less than those in *To Duck or Not to Duck* or Jones' later Roadrunner cartoons.

Between producing miscellaneous cartoon adventures, Jones continued to direct new one-reel films starring Daffy. Some of his other Daffy masterpieces included *My Favorite Duck* (1942), *You Were Never Duckier* (1948), *Duck! Rabbit! Duck!* (1953), and *Rocket Squad* (1956).

One Jones cartoon featuring Daffy that earns a lasting place on his mantel is *Duck Dodgers and the 24½ Century*. Jones may have been slightly ahead of his time when he directed this animated classic. Although the film deals with the prospects of space travel and exploration, only now with the new wave of science fiction films being produced can it truly be appreciated. Surely audiences in the 1950s appreciated this cartoon as America hadn't launched a space program yet, and the idea of travelling in outer space was bizarre. Of course, the idea of Daffy's commanding a spacecraft aided by his stammering space kidette Porky Pig is funny in itself.

The story of this eight-minute teaser is no more complex than zipping up a space suit. Daffy and Porky pilot a rocket ship in search of the unknown Planet X, which is clearly marked with a large "X" across its global front. Just as they land, it is being claimed by another pint-sized space traveler who claims to be a warrior from Mars. He is definitely small—shorter than Daffy anyway—and his face is hidden behind a Darth Vader-type helmet.

Our heroes become enbroiled in battle when Daffy insists that he's claimed the planet first in the name of Earth before the Martian. A heated argument between Daffy and the Martian ensues, eventually erupting into a full-scale war. Both parties fire atom cannons and disintegrating guns at each other, leading to the destruction of the planet with our heroes left falling through space.

The same year Jones picked up Daffy as an additional cartoon series in 1939, he also directed his first Bugs Bunny cartoon, *Presto-Changeo*. This early conception of Bugs is rather disappointing; he has no defined character and is drawn like a thin white rabbit. Bugs doesn't talk in this cartoon. Instead, he laughs occasionally when he pulls a joke on two dogs who become prey in a house of magic which belongs to "Shamfu the Magician." Bugs, in some ways, resembles a rabbit that one might expect to jump out of a magician's hat. He is lean, tall, and has long white ears. The cartoon has its moments, with Bugs performing magic tricks to the frustration of the two dogs, but it's not enough to rate among Jones' best.

The cartoon wasn't the right setting for Bugs. He had to be cast in a normal forest environment where he could use his dogmatic senses. Jones and other directors became aware of this and adapted Bugs to rabbit hunting pictures. This was a very successful format for some time until new possibilities were explored and challenged by directors like Jones.

Jones analyzes Bugs' personality as such: "Bugs stood with one leg straight and the other leg akimbo. Because he's not afraid, he engages in the matter. We always started Bugs out in a natural rabbit environment and somebody came along and tried to do him in. And then he fought back. So it was no more like Groucho Marx. Once the battle is joined you can't get him loose even with a pair of crowbars. Because it's a joy. As Groucho said, 'You know, of course, this means war!' And so it was with Bugs. He was something more personal and special to me, more than any other character I directed."

The man responsible for creating Bugs was also nicknamed Bugs. According to Jones, director Ben "Bugs" Hardaway had ordered cartoonist Charles Thorson to do a pencil sketching of a rabbit. Once Thorson had completed the drawing, he noted on the corner of the sheet, "Bugs' bunny." From there the

name just hung on and so did the character. By the time Tex Avery was directing Bugs, he had the bunny saying "What's Up, Doc?" and feuding with Elmer
Fudd.

But of all the Warner Brothers cartoon directors, Jones had directed the
most Bugs Bunny cartoons. He is credited with supervising more than 50 Bugs
Bunny films but realizes that he should thank Ben Hardaway for creating the
rabbit (or "wabbit"). Bugs proved instrumental in bolstering a staff of cartoon
regulars and gave Warners a key figure in cartoon animation who was as
popular as MGM's Tom and Jerry and Walter Lantz's Woody Woodpecker.

Whenever the Warner Brothers logo sprang onto the screen, audiences
everywhere recognized the studio name in direct association with Bugs. To them
Bugs was the studio. By far Bugs was the most productive cartoon character in
the history of Warners cartoon division, as he starred in more than 100 films and
didn't retire from the screen until 1963. Mel Blanc supplied the voice all those
wonderful years, and in the past while appearing at colleges and universities he
was always asked to do Bugs.

Under Jones's direction, Bugs' character became more amorous and
sophisticated than when supervised by either Friz Freleng or Bob Clampett.
Jones had a theory he adhered to. "We followed certain disciplines. Bugs always
first made his appearance in a natural rabbit situation. Unlike Woody Woodpecker, he was never mischievous without a particular reason. Only when he
was disturbed did he then decide the time had come to war. In a sense, he was a
counterrevolutionary."

Maybe so, but what made Bugs so memorable was his timing for the ab-
surd. In times of a crisis, the long-eared screwy rabbit would nonchalantly pull
out a carrot, take a few bites, turn to the audience and say in a Brooklynese
smart-aleck accent, "Eh, what's up, Doc?"

The world could be coming to an end, but Bugs opted to be the straight
man rather than the comic. Bugs was the straight man to a myriad of characters
in his cartoons: thugs, gremlins, aliens from outer space, and giants. By playing
it straight, Bugs delivered the necessary comic punch in putting the comedy
across. Bugs in the role of the straight man was as important to the success of
the comedy as Bud Abbott was to Lou Costello, or as George Burns was to
Gracie Allen.

Evidence of this is found in a 1945 Bugs Bunny cartoon, *Wackiki Wabbit.*
Bugs plays the straight man through the film to two moronic shipwrecked individuals. The real stars are these two stranded on a raft out at sea who act and
sound like Abbott and Costello. Salvation is near when they reach shore on an
uncharted island, where they meet Bugs Bunny. Immediately, these two starved
men chase after Bugs in preparation of a feast: roast rabbit. Bugs dresses up as a
Tahitian dancer and entertains the two. Cleverly, Bugs says in a native tongue
(a language no one can understand without subtitles), "What's up, Doc?" Under-
standing Bugs' question, the voyagers answer, "We want food!" This is trans-
lated into the native language on the screen, but comes out longer than it does to
say it. Puzzled by the subtitle's length the fatter explorer remarks to his thinner
partner, "You said that?"

Eventually they coax Bugs to remove his native garb and join them for dinner. What the main entree is Bugs isn't sure. But he gets a good indication when these two landlubbers, after capturing the screwy rabbit, sing in unison: "We're going to have roast rabbit! We're going to have roast rabbit!" The two adventurers place Bugs in a heated pot and begin to pour hot water over him. At first, Bugs believes he's receiving a warm bath. But when both men finish their jubilant song about having rabbit dinner, he makes a quick getaway. The only thing left on the platter is a turkey, which both men lunge at, but it comes to life and starts talking back—scaring both vagrants. Actually, Bugs has stringed it up like a marionette puppet and is controlling its every movement.

Bugs is saved, however, when a passenger steamer approaches the island. Both voyagers rejoice wildly upon spotting the large cruse ship by happily singing, "We're going on a boat! We're going on a boat!" The song doesn't become a hit, but Bugs does with the audience when he pulls off the gag of the century. As the boat drops its passenger ramp, Bugs bids farewell to our two islanders, who wave frantically back to Bugs as he hops on the ship before it quickly steams away. Both men realize they've been tricked and can only sit in disgust as the vessel sails farther in the distance.

Obviously filmgoers recognized the importance of Bugs playing the straight man in this picture. It was essential if the comedy was to mesh. And mesh it did. The same formula applied to whatever straight man versus comic combinations were developed for Bugs Bunny cartoons. Probably the largest example was Bugs and Elmer J. Fudd, the rabbit-killing hunter. He always tried to "kill that wascally wabbit" but was never successful.

This animated duo reminded moviegoers of the same chemistry seen in comedies starring Laurel and Hardy. Fudd was much like Laurel; he was a slow-thinker and even slower to react. He had a slow-burn quality about him that would have made Edgar Kennedy, the technician's originator, especially proud. In other ways, he was also like W.C. Fields since he kept his gestures close to his body. Bugs, in contrast, was like Hardy; he had quick reactions and was fast-footed when it was time to make chase. Like most slender comedians, Bugs gestured freely and was never afraid to go outside his own boundary; Fudd was.

Jones directed several cartoons costarring Elmer, many superb: *Elmer's Candid Camera* (1940), *Elmer's Pet Rabbit* (1940), *The Rabbit of Seville* (1950), *Rabbit Fire* (1951), *Hare Tonic* (1954), and *Beanstalk Bunny* (1955).

One of his most innovative Bugs Bunny cartoons without Elmer is *Lumberjack Rabbit*. The cartoon was produced and distributed in 3-D and proved that even in a field as complex as animation this effect can work remarkably well. The film was commissioned by Warner Brothers president Jack Warner, and was intended to be shown with such 3-D Warners' features as *Hondo* and *House of Wax*. *Lumberjack Rabbit* features a gruesome killer giant named Paul Bunyan and his dog Ralph, who have giant-sized plans for dinner: Bugs Bunny. In the tradition of most short subjects filmed in 3-D, the cartoon didn't generate much excitement, especially with film critics. The *Motion Picture Exhibitor* wrote, "This cartoon does not seem to take full advantage of the 3-D medium. The humor is not as sharp as in most Bugs Bunny cartoons, and gimmicks in 3-D are conspicuous by their absence." Even Jones had admitted that he was bored with the technique of 3-D. It obviously shows.

It was ten years after Jones's first Bugs Bunny cartoon that he entertained moviegoers with his most cherished creation, the Road Runner and Coyote. The series was shaped around the continuous adventures of the speedy Road Runner and the ever-scheming Wile E. Coyote in what has become the longest chase in movie history. Violent in nature, these cartoons showcased slapstick which not even the Three Stooges could master in live films. Jones first introduced the pair in the 1949 Technicolor release, *Fast and Furry-ous*.

Like all cartoons, the story depicted the sheer lunacy of the Coyote's setting traps to catch the lightning-quick Road Runner by using all sorts of Acme industrial devices as bait, only to suffer the consequences when each contraption backfires. Storyman Michael Maltese has been credited with cocreating the characters along with Jones.

Remembering how they conceived the "Beep! Beep!" voice for the Road Runner, Jones recalls: "Curiously enough, Mel Blanc didn't do the 'Beep! Beep!' That was done by a fellow named Paul Julian. He was walking down the hall carrying a load of backgrounds and couldn't see where he was going. He had about sixty drawings in front of him and he was going 'Beep! Beep! Beep! Beep!' That's when Mike and I were laying out the first picture and he went by our door going, 'Beep! Beep!' And so we looked at each other and thought that must have been the sound the Road Runner makes. So Mike looked up and said, 'O.K. God, we'll take it from here.'"

Jones imposed certain disciplines when animating the Road Runner series: The Road Runner always stayed on the road. He never injured himself; the Coyote injured himself instead. The same locale of the Arizona desert was used in each picture. Sympathy always fell in favor of the Coyote. No dialogue was furnished for either character in these films, with the exception of the Road Runner's traditional "Beep! Beep!" The Coyote almost always purchased mail-order machines and other weaponry from the Acme Corporation. In a good deal of their films, both characters were introduced by various bogus Latin names; the Road Runner was called *Accelerati Incredibus* and the Coyote was named *Carnivorous Vulgaris*. The splash technique of the Coyote falling off a cliff was largely incorporated in every film. And, lastly, the Coyote never catches the Road Runner.

Another interesting revelation is that the Road Runner cartoons had the same violent temper of MGM's "Tom and Jerry" series. Violence served as a means to humiliate the protagonist; the protagonist in this case is the Coyote. He is constantly embroiled in a battle of wits with the Road Runner, but gets foiled at every turn. It doesn't matter how he tries to catch the Road Runner — no device can thwart his speed — because he invariably winds up being smashed by a boulder or run over by a train as a result of his efforts. Such mental torment is similar to a technique director Bob Clampett often employed in his cartoons. If a character had been swindled by another, he used transformation images — changing the unlucky character into either a "jackass" or "sucker." The gag embellishes the utter frustration of the character by poking fun at it. Clobbering the Coyote with his own weaponry is similar to Clampett's technique, but results in greater hysterics on the part of the moviegoer.

Jones has said that he recognizes certain elements of himself in other characters but points out that his true alter ego is Wile E. Coyote. Jones explains: "The coyote is victimized by his own ineptitude. I never understood how to use tools, and that's really the coyote's problem. He's not at war with the gods, but with the minuscule things of every day life. It is out of this mounting frustration that the comedy develops."

Some other first-rate Road Runner cartoons were *Zipping Along* (1953), in which the Coyote sets up a trap on a telephone pole, believing it's a tree, causing a row of poles to pull down when the trap goes off. In *Ready, Set, Zoom* (1955), the Coyote spreads glue on the road this time, hoping the sticky substance can stop the fast-footed creature. The Road Runner splashes through the glue, throwing up the gook on the Coyote who becomes permanently attached to the roadway. The Coyote tries harpooning the Road Runner in *Zoom and Board* (1957) but gets his foot caught in the rope of the harpoon.

Basically, the Road Runner series used formula gags, but with each cartoon the material was fresh and innovative. It is because of such creativity and innovation that the series endured and never grew old. In all, Jones directed nearly 40 Road Runner cartoons between the years 1949 to 1968, the latter being produced at De Patie–Freleng Enterprises with Rudy Larriva sharing directing chores.

Though the Road Runner series made a long-standing impression in cartoon cinema, it never won an Academy Award. Instead Jones earned his first Oscar for a character that didn't have the same universal appeal of the Roadrunner or his other characters. His name was Pepe Le Pew. Again storyman Michael Maltese stepped in to refine the concept of the sophisticated French odiferous skunk. Pepe's mannerisms and voice distinctly resemble that of Maurice Chevalier and Charles Boyer combined.

The Pepe Le Pew cartoon that put Jones' name in the Academy Award record book was the 1951 Merrie Melodies film, *For Scent-Imental Reasons*. The cartoon, like those that followed, suffered from restrictions caused by using a formula premise. (Pepe was first introduced to the film world in *The Odor-Able Kitty*.) In every film, Pepe was the aggressive, amorous skunk falling madly in love with a cat who he mistakes for a female skunk. In Jones's Oscar-winning Pepe cartoon, the plot is similar: white paint is accidentally poured on the back of a female cat, giving her the appearance of a skunk. Pepe becomes attracted to the cat and tries his overripe remarks about his sexual prowess to win her over. The cat tries to repel him, but Pepe believes it's just a show of how much she wants him to chase her. Good as this cartoon was, some critics found it difficult to stomach more than one Pepe cartoon. So have historians, who have written off the series as a minor achievement in cartoon animation.

One year earlier, in 1950, Jones was also awarded an Oscar for his direction of best documentary. The film, *So Much for So Little*, was animated and commissioned by the Public Health Service. It became the first time in Academy Award history that a cartoon was awarded best documentary. Both Friz Freleng and Jones scripted the film and Freleng has said that he felt the cartoon was a way of reaching a lot of people with a message on the importance of health services and sanitation.

Another tremendous film Jones directed premiered five years later, in

1955. It was called *One Froggy Evening*. Jones has said that lead character, known as Michigan J. Frog, is his favorite because he doesn't "understand him." Film buffs love the film because of its bizarre story, in which a construction worker discovers a frog in the cornerstone of a demolished building. To the worker's astonishment, the frog produces a top hat and cane and begins singing loudly the popular melody, "Hello, My Baby." Fancying the thought of becoming a millionaire with a singing frog, the worker takes his prize possession to a theatrical agent. Before the worker enters the agency, the frog is merrily singing all sorts of famous Broadway songs. But once inside the agent's office, the frog becomes limp and acts like a normal every day pond frog—croaking for the agent instead of belting out songs.

Both are kicked out and this sorrowful tale continues with the same results until the worker gives up and buries the frog in the cornerstone of a new building. The cartoon segues to the year 2056. The locale is the Tregroweth Brown Building (obviously named after Warners' sound effects man Treg Brown) which is being demolished by a construction worker through the means of a disintegrator gun. When the construction worker explodes open the cornerstone of the building, out jumps the frog who starts to sing his top melody, "Hello, My Baby." The cartoon fades out as the construction worker casts money-making designs on the frog. Critic Jay Cocks says that "One Froggy Evening" is "a morality play in cameo that comes as close to any cartoon ever has to perfection." Whenever Jones appears at universities, his most requested film is *One Froggy Evening* as well as his other time-honored favorites.

Besides his regular cartoon productions, Jones directed cartoon training and education films for the armed services, including Private Snafu and Hook cartoons during World War II. These films have been difficult to document since not many prints remain in circulation.

Another good cartoon that Jones directed near the final months of 1955 was *Knight-Mare Hare* starring Bugs Bunny. Some Jones fans consider it to be his most enjoyable venture. The cartoon opens as Bugs is seen sitting beneath an apple tree and has his ears pinned back to dry after washing them. Suddenly in the midst of this tranquil scene, Bugs is clobbered on the head by a falling apple. The knock leaves him in a dream world and transports him into medieval times where he battles the Duke of Ellington and the sorcery of Merlin the Magician. The scenes between Bugs and Merlin are the prize winners in this cartoon.

In their first meeting, Merlin becomes insulted when Bugs pokes fun at his costume, saying it looks like something right out of a magic shop. Most magicians would take that remark as a compliment, but not Merlin. He shows his magical powers by changing Bugs into a pig, a horse, a donkey, and a cow. Each time Bugs foils his attempts by unzipping the costume of his new image and saying, "That's pretty good, Doc. Mind if I try?" Bugs casts the magical powder on Merlin and changes him into a horse. The only problem is that Merlin's image remains the same each time he tries to unzip out of costume. He frantically unzips his costume after costume, but no change results. He's still a horse. It is after this gag that Bugs awakes from his dream. Left a little weary, he remarks: "Boy, what a dream!" In the distance can be seen a farmer and his horse. Just at that precise moment, the farmer orders his horse, "Come along,

Merlin." Bugs does a profound stare at the camera just before the iris out of the cartoon.

Undoubtedly, Jones's years at Warners were the cornerstone of an illustrious animation career. As in most animator's careers, every film required a tremendous amount of work on the part of a large staff of talented individuals, many times resulting in enthusiastic reviews from critics. That's not to say Jones didn't have his share of misses. Jones had mostly misses when he left Warner Brothers in 1963 to produce and direct a new series of Tom and Jerry cartoons for MGM. When Warner Brothers closed down its cartoon division in 1963, Jones was one of the first directors to leave.

Jones and producer Les Goldman formed a cartoon production company named Sib-Tower 12 Productions (which was later renamed MGM Animation/ Visual Arts). They produced a lot of minor animation productions before approaching Metro about doing yet another Tom and Jerry series. Gene Deitch, a Czech cartoon director, had failed in his attempts to animate new Tom and Jerry cartoons. He wound up production in 1963, faulting MGM for the cartoon series' poor quality. Deitch has said that Metro wanted to produce the cartoons as cheaply as possible. He believed the studio was primarily interested in cashing in on the success of Tom and Jerry's television popularity and nothing else.

Jones convinced the stolid MGM brass that there was room for another Tom and Jerry series. One would think that after the Deitch disasters that Metro would have used better discretion before giving Jones the initial go-ahead. As it turned out, MGM learned another lesson, since all of these Jones cartoons were disasters. Even with a seasoned staff of old Warner Brothers associates on board the series failed. Jones contracted a reliable group of veterans to work on the series, including writer Michael Maltese, codirector and layout man Maurice Noble, background artist Philip De Guard, and animators Ben Washam, Richard Thompson, and Tom Ray. Each cartoon cost a whopping $42,000 to produce, which was $12,000 higher than budget. Metro was certainly robbed blind on this series.

The first in the series of klinkers was *Pent House Mouse*, which made its theatrical debut in 1964. Reactions to the cartoon were lukewarm as some critics said the film was "an extension of Jones's Road Runner and Coyote pictures," while others contended that the cartoon had some cinematic value. One anonymous MGM executive remarked after a board of directors screening: "These are god awful!" Even Jones later admitted he made a grave mistake in directing the series. As he once noted, "They were not my characters, and I didn't really understand them as well as, let's say, the Road Runner and the Coyote. The Tom and Jerrys I did look like Road Runner and Coyote in cat and mouse drag!" At least Jones admitted that the series and his supervision had its shortcomings. Jones didn't just attribute the series problems to his misunderstanding the characters. Another time he said the series failed from having a director with a different concept supervise someone else's creation, of course, meaning Hanna and Barbera.

The series had several encompassing problems, besides weak stories and poor animation. One was that Jones changed the external appearance of the characters. Tom had harrowing eyebrows that made him too similar to Jones's visage of the Grinch (a Dr. Seuss children's book character Jones animated for TV specials). It made him appear too vicious and eliminated the "helpless cat" image that was so common in earlier vintage cartoons.

Then there was Jerry. The mouse that once graced the screen with his impish grin and adorable face had been reduced to a nauseous Goody-Two Shoes. His ears were rounder, similar in shape to Disney's Dumbo, and his eyes and face underwent drastic changes. The friendly rivalry that existed in Hanna-Barbera Tom and Jerrys was virtually nonexistent in Jones's cartoons. Chase scenes took up most of the cartoon's footage, but comedy didn't. Even the violent humor that gave MGM's initial series such flavor had been sharply toned down.

Although Jones's stay at Metro proved somewhat frustrating, he did have some important successes that overshadowed his many disappointments. Around late 1964, Jones freed himself from directorial chores on the Tom and Jerry series to work on unusual shorts – *The Dot and the Line* and *The Bear That Wasn't.*

The Dot and the Line (A Romance in Lower Mathematics) is a marvelous, innovative film based on Norton Juster's book about a straight line and squiggle falling in love with a dot. British actor Robert Morley narrates the film, which closely follows Juster's book. The film was so intriguing it won an Academy Award in 1965 as Best Animated Short Subject. Besides marking Jones's third Oscar, it dated the first time a MGM cartoon had been so honored since Tom and Jerry's *Johann Mouse* took all honors in 1952.

The Bear That Wasn't (1967), Jones's second cartoon special, was based on Frank Tashlin's book of the same title. The film wasn't as successful as *The Dot and the Line*, nor was Jones's feature film that followed, *The Phantom Tollbooth* (1968). That same year, MGM decided to terminate the Tom and Jerry series. The decision came as no surprise since the cartoons weren't doing as well as Metro had expected.

Though his years at MGM had been disastrous, Jones came away from the studio partly satisfied. Several years later he conceded, however, that "I would never be satisfied if I had to work for another studio that had such stringent controls on animation." Thus, Jones formed his own company so he would have some control. The studio he evolved was named Chuck Jones Enterprises and its purpose was to produce commercials and television specials for CBS. Some of Jones's animated specials for CBS have included *The White Seal, Rikki Tikki Tavi* (both adaptations of Kipling) and *How the Grinch Stole Christmas.*

Jones continues to produce new cartoons for television and for theaters. *The Bugs Bunny/Road Runner Movie*, a new animated cartoon movie by Jones consisting of five complete Bugs Bunny shorts as well as scenes from 24 other cartoons, opened April 6, 1980, in Salt Lake City, Columbus and Houston and received disastrous reviews. *Los Angeles Times* critic Charles Champlin, one of the many disenchanted patrons, wrote: "The [previous] cartoon always left you wanting more, not less. It's the other way around here, the only disappointment of this nostalgic slapstick smorgasbord." The 92-minute feature contained only material created by Jones when he was member of Warner Brothers cartoon division. Originally titled *The Great American Cartoon Chase*, it was issued in celebration of Bugs Bunny's fortieth anniversary.

Jones and cowriter Michael Maltese both produced, directed, and conceived 20 minutes of new animation for the movie, including scenes set in Bugs Bunny's carrot palace in Beverly Hills. Bugs provides a tour of a gallery of his mansion which sports paintings of his creators, everybody from Robert McKimson to Friz Freleng, excluding Bob Clampett for some unknown reason. Spotted throughout the film, the new animation utilizes Bugs as a narrator introducing scenes. The five complete shorts starring Bugs were *Hareway to the Stars*, *Duck Amuck*, *Bully for Bugs*, *Rabbit Fire*, and *What's Opera, Doc?* In addition, excerpts from eight more of the rabbit's funniest cartoons were included. The movie also contained 31 comedy-action routines culled from 16 vintage Road Runner cartoons featuring the speedy desert bird and his persistent enemy Wile E. Coyote. Keeping with tradition, the unique voice of Bugs as well as those of many other cartoon characters seen in the film were voiced by Mel Blanc.

The new animation is sleeker, more linear and contemporary. Gags are often more violent than before, and talk between characters is sharper and more sophisticated. In short, the film was a valiant commemorative effort on Jones's part to honor Bugs. But, like most film compilations, it proves one theory to hold true: cartoons are enjoyed when watched sporadically, not in large bunches. Jones might have been better off animating a brand new eight-minute Bugs Bunny cartoon, if he honestly wanted to honor the award-winning rabbit.

He animated another theatrical venture for Warner Brothers called *Duck Dodgers and the Return of the 24½ Century*. The cartoon never reached the theaters but aired as part of *Daffy Duck's Thanks-for-Giving Special* on CBS in November, 1980. Original plans were for Steven Spielberg to work on the film in exchange for Jones working on *1941* as a comedy specialist. Fortunately for Jones, the deal was not consummated, though Spielberg did make a contribution to the new cartoon.

The idea of producing a 25-year-later sequel was brought about in part by *Star Wars* producer George Lucas, Jones says. The three-time Oscar winner recalls, "He [Lucas] refused to run *Star Wars* in San Francisco unless they ran *Duck Dodgers in the 24½ Century*. He did. I had dinner with Lucas and went and saw it. It was kind of startling after years of seeing it on a small 16 millimeter screen. He told me in order for them to show it they had to link it into 70 millimeter Dolby sound which they did. So, they were paying Warners $250 a week for a cartoon made twenty some years ago—which was very satisfying to me personally."

It was a short time after this that Jones proposed the idea to Warners and was contracted to animate the sequel. He continues to develop new and fresh ideas for his ageless Warner characters with the same amount of enthusiasm he showed as a young animator. As Jones says of his current projects, "I love working on the old characters again."

And moviegoers love Jones for bringing back cartoons they can laugh at for old times sake.

Chapter 4

Hanna and Barbera

No director of motion pictures, let alone of animation, can claim to have won seven Academy Awards — except for two men: William Hanna and Joseph Barbera.

Neither planned to be an animator. One might wonder what changed their minds. Certainly it wasn't the prestige or money. Maybe it was the opportunity to work steadily in a creative and exciting position. Whatever the case, the fact remains that these two gentle giants of animation have never been forgotten. Today hundreds of letters pour in to Hanna–Barbera Studios in Hollywood, addressed to both men from new fans who have habitually watched the misadventures of Tom and Jerry on television. In addition to the creations of their own studio, Bill and Joe will be remembered mostly for inventing and directing MGM's ever-popular dueling cat and mouse team.

The businessman of the two, William Hanna, was born in Melrose, New Mexico, in 1911. Hanna never intended to become an artist. Instead he had been fascinated with the principles of engineering. Hanna majored in engineering and minored in journalism at the University of Southern California. He later moved to Hollywood where he employed his talents as a structural engineer for the building of the Pantages Theatre.

When his interest in engineering began to wane, Hanna wondered if he had entered the wrong field. At the advice of a good friend, he went to art school where he studied intensely for several months. Upon graduation from the art institute, Hanna made rounds to all the major cartoon studios. One of them, Metro-Goldwyn-Mayer, offered him a contract to animate Hugh Harman and Rudolf Ising cartoons. Hanna started immediately.

One reason his job hunting proved to be successful was that animation had been expanding. New technology, such as sound and two-strip Technicolor, had pronounced impact on the job market, as it prompted the studios to bolster their animation staffs to maintain a high production output each year.

Hanna started like any newcomer at the bottom; he washed cels and wrote story ideas for Harman and Ising. In due time, however, Bill was promoted to the position of director. Shortly thereafter, Barbera joined the MGM staff and the partnership began.

Joseph Barbera, the salesman of the two, was born in New York in 1905. He continued his education at New York University and the American Institute of Banking, where he majored in accounting. Upon graduation, he went to work for New York's Irving Trust Company. An inveterate doodler and dreamer, Barbera began to peddle his "doodles" on lunch-hour rounds to publishing companies. As he once said in an interview, "Every day I left one pile of cartoons with a magazine while I dashed over to another to see if my previously submitted material had sold." Although editors turned down his sketchings, Barbera never gave up.

An optimistic go-getter, he continued his daily rounds to New York's magazine publishing firms. Finally, *Collier's* magazine bought one of his cartoons, and Barbera became a sketch artist. Spurred by his success, Joe stepped up his output and soon became a regular contributor to leading magazines.

With his accounting career over, Barbera believed he had made the right decision. He later recalled: "Animation was something I truly wanted to do. But it took me some time to figure out exactly if it would be worth it. Now I'm glad I did it." Contributing to various leading magazines gave him the experience a novice sketch artist needed. Barbera disciplined himself with set working hours and began to produce his cartoon ideas more rapidly as well. After much practice, Joe was able to sketch a drawing with just ten strokes of the pen. His determination helped him become a top-flight artist.

But a good sketch artist like Barbera would be wise if he took on a higher paying job to match his skills. One that not only offered better company benefits, but an opportunity for promotion. Animation offered these possibilities. With this in mind, Barbera decided to seek a career in cartooning as opposed to the world of finance. So he quit freelancing and landed a position as a sketch artist at Van Beuren Associates, a small independent cartoon studio in the Bronx. There he moved up the ladder from sketch artist to animator, before moving west in 1937 to tackle a job as an animator at MGM.

In June, 1937, Joe arrived at Metro and was put to work on the Harman and Ising series. Little did he realize that his lifelong business associate-to-be, William Hanna, had been employed in the animation department several weeks before him. According to Barbera, for nearly two years they never worked as partners. Their partnership didn't evolve until April, 1938, when MGM teamed them to produce a single, seven-minute animated short. The two animators rapidly developed a rapport and began a successful relationship. As Barbera stated in an interview: "We understood each other and had mutual respect for each other's work." Producer Fred Quimby, the head of Metro's Cartoon Division, believed that Hanna and Barbera had talent and thought that in time he'd witness both men using more of their untapped creativity.

Hanna's talent blossomed earlier than Quimby had anticipated. With Friz Freleng and Robert Allen, Bill shared the directorial chores on MGM's new cartoon series, "The Captain and the Kids" (also known as "The Katzenjammer Kids"). It was Hanna's first try at directing. Freleng was a veteran director who came over to Metro shortly after his long success at Warner Brothers directing Merrie Melodies and Looney Tunes. Allen, like Hanna, was new to cartoon directing; he had previously been an animator.

The Captain and the Kids were characters created by cartoonist Rudolph Dirk, who penned the strip for United Features Newspaper Syndicate. It depicted the misadventures of a family of German immigrants in the United

States. Starring in the series was the Captain, who spoke very little English; the Inspector, the Captain's bumbling friend; Mamma, the Captain's wife; and his mischievous sons, Hans and Fritz.

The series was originally intended to be filmed in Technicolor, but MGM decided to save money by filming the cartoons in black and white and releasing them in sepia tone. Friz Freleng has said that even though the series was animated in black and white, the budgets were much larger than Warner's budget for Merrie Melodies and Looney Tunes. But as Freleng remarked, "It didn't help the pictures because they had the wrong concept to begin with." To put it simply, the series ended up being something of a disaster.

The first cartoon Hanna directed and the second of the series was *Blue Monday*, which was released April 2, 1938. The story has the Captain grumpily arising on a Monday morning. He accuses Mamma (that's Mrs. Katzenjammer) of "poorly managing the household." With that remark, Mamma puts the Captain in charge of vacuuming the house, washing the clothes, and other chores. He finishes all these odd jobs with the incapable assistance of his addlebrained friend, the Inspector. It is after this scene that Mamma returns home only to find the house in shambles. Like many cartoons in the series, *Blue Monday* opened to mixed reviews. Despite lukewarm critical reception, the cartoon provided Hanna with a new challenge.

Eager to prove he was a capable director, Hanna went on to supervise a handful of Captain and the Kids cartoons that year, including *What a Lion*, the rollicking adventures of the Captain and a lion, and *Old Smokey*, in which the Captain is swindled into buying an old broken down fire horse.

The cartoons had weak stories and primitive animation. Some were mildly amusing at times, but usually "merely boring," said one MGM animator. The characters just didn't transfer from the comic strip to animated form. When MGM executives realized the cartoons were fizzling at the box office, they dropped the series at mid-season. Only three Captain and the Kids cartoons were produced in 1939: *Petunia National Park*, *Seal Skinner*, and *Mamma's New Hat*. Since the series had been languishing, some theater managers who normally carried the series withdrew from screening the final cartoons. Some exhibitors inserted Harman and Ising cartoons instead.

When the series ended, Hanna went back to animating Harman and Ising cartoons, but only temporarily. As Hanna remembers: "I still wanted to direct. Joe wanted to also. It was just a matter of getting that big break."

The "big break" both men had been hoping for came in early 1940. At that time the boys had been discussing possibilitites for characters and story-lines. The final product depicted the wild adventures of a cat and mouse. Hanna recalls: "We asked ourselves what would be a normal conflict between characters provoking comedy while retaining a basic situation from which we could continue to generate plots and stories. We almost decided on a dog and a fox before we hit on the idea of using a cat and mouse." Bill and Joe also thought these characters might form the basis for a series. The boys ended up calling the cat Tom and the mouse Jerry, based on names submitted by hundreds of studio employees in a contest staged by Hanna and Barbera.

After they completed drafting a story and a few quick sketches, they put the proposal before Quimby. He thought it was ridiculous. "What can you do with a cat and mouse that would be different?" Quimby asked. The boys told him to give them a chance to show him the idea could work. Show him they did.

Production was soon under way for the first Tom and Jerry cartoon, *Puss Gets the Boot*, which was released on February 10, 1940. In this pilot, directed by Hanna and Barbera, the Tom and Jerry characters had been clearly established. They were just a typical house cat and mischievous mouse trying to outwit one another. The cartoon opens with Mammy, a black woman who was a regular in the series, warning Jasper the cat (he wasn't named Tom in the film) that if he breaks one more thing he'll be banished from the household. That sets the stage for a mouse (unnamed in the cartoon) to get back at his feline adversary and threaten his relationship with Mammy. So the mouse naturally goes around threatening to break a glass or prevailing object in the house that would bring harm to Jasper. And as expected, there is a seesaw battle between the cat and mouse, before Jasper finally gets the boot.

The *Motion Picture Herald* saw in the cartoon "an especially clever portrayal of the smug superiority of the cat dictator." Already Jasper (or Tom, if you prefer) had established his character; he was the feline tormentor. Jerry was the tormented. But somehow, Jerry usually won the battles.

Puss Gets the Boot got good reviews from the trades, and from Fred Quimby as well. It took some time to sell Quimby on the idea, but once the film became an enormous hit and was nominated for an Academy Award, he saw the light. As a result, Quimby gave Hanna and Barbera the go-ahead to produce two more cartoons in 1941, followed by four more in 1942. And so the illustrious career of Tom and Jerry had begun.

As the first cartoon indicated, the fighting cat and mouse characters were already off to a fast and glorious start. But in *Puss Gets the Boot*, Tom and Jerry were much more restrained than in later cartoons. The characters looked homey; just your average cat and mouse. By the late 1940s, however, a gradual change in the characters' appearances was apparent. Tom had taken on a mean, raspy-looking appearance, complemented by lurching eyebrows that billowed on his forehead. Just by looking at Tom, moviegoers knew he was the troublemaker. Jerry, on the other hand, was sprightly, lovable, good-natured. Although he instigated most of the trouble, Jerry's cherubic face never made people suspect him of being involved in any evil-doings.

Even though Tom and Jerry's appearance changed in later cartoons, their brand of humor didn't. If a waffle iron was sitting open in the general vicinity of Tom's tail, the audience knew the iron was planted there for a reason. Despite the fact that Tom and Jerry cartoons had one formula — each character trying to do the most damage to the other — neither the formula nor the characters grew tiresome. It was just a matter of setting the formula in the proper situation first.

Without a doubt, Hanna and Barbera were the creative force behind the success of Tom and Jerry. They not only held bull sessions to throw back ideas for possible stories, but each carried responsibilities of their own. Joe wrote all the stories, drew all the sketches, made all the layouts, while Bill wrote the exposure sheets. Some animators have said that Barbera's ideas came off the end of his pencil as fast as he could move it!

Before handing out work to the animators, Hanna and Barbera held a meeting to discuss each film and act out the entire picture for the staff. Some animators have remarked that Bill and Joe acted these scenes "in a very hammy fashion," but that it was just right for animation. That especially holds true when animating such a delicate art form as slapstick comedy. Exaggeration is one of the necessary ingredients that make the comedy work.

But before Bill and Joe could plan out each scene, they had the animators work up pencil tests of the cartoon. Often animators had to redo specific scenes as many as four times. Usually such precision was necessary to catch the right expression or tighten up the timing of a gag.

These cartoons really grew to epic proportions when Hanna and Barbera gained the assistance of the studio's talented musical director, Scott Bradley. Since Tom and Jerry didn't talk, a swift brand of music was necessary to keep the action scenes moving. In some cases, it was Bradley's music that made the cartoons so successful. He had a marvelous knack for timing his music with the action in each scene, and seemed to have a good ear when it came to scoring comedy. It was his musical arrangements that often made these films so unique.

There were other people, besides film critics, who thought these cartoons had some special qualities worth recognizing. The board members of the Academy of Motion Picture Arts and Science believed Tom and Jerry's distinctive brand of comedy deserved more than an Oscar nomination. In 1943 a Tom and Jerry cartoon, *Yankee Doodle Mouse*, won an Academy Award for Best Short Subject of the Year. Even though the film has nothing to do with patriotism, it does have Fourth of July fireworks, the kind which only Tom and Jerry can provide. The cartoon brought the war between Tom and Jerry up to date. By using blitz tactics, Jerry severely punishes Tom by means of ingenious war machines: a banana-throwing catapult, light bulb bombs and a rocket which finally carries Tom up into the heavens.

By winning that year's coveted Oscar, Hanna and Barbera became the second directors in the history of MGM's cartoon department to win such an honor. Not since Rudolph Ising took the award in 1940 for his cartoon *The Milky Way* had the studio won in the Academy Awards contest.

Now that their work had received this honor, one would think that Hanna and Barbera would be remembered by their peers. Such was not the case in the inner sanctums of MGM, where president Louis B. Mayer presided. When someone suggested to Mayer that Bill and Joe animate a segment combining the talents of dancer Gene Kelly and Jerry Mouse for the studio's forthcoming movie, *Anchors Aweigh*, Mayer inquired, "Bill and Joe who?" Showing that Hanna and Barbera's talents were no better remembered by others than Mayer is a story involving Kelly: Even though *Anchors Aweigh* was being produced at Metro, Kelly approached Walt Disney with the idea of animating the dance scene of him with Jerry!

As it turned out, Bill and Joe animated the scene of Jerry and matched Kelley's live footage of him dancing step for step. It is one of the most remembered dance segments out of MGM musical history. The success of this film later spawned similar segments using Tom and Jerry in another MGM feature, *Dangerous When Wet*, starring Esther Williams.

Hanna and Barbera's importance to the studio was again recognized when they produced another Academy Award-winning cartoon in 1944, *Mouse Troubles*. Up to his usual tricks, Tom decides he must secure some outside help if he's going to ever succeed in catching Jerry. Therefore, he picks up a copy of a fabulous do-it-all book, *How to Catch a Mouse*, which offers some orthodox methods of attack and capture which Tom can put into practice. It appears, after a series of mishaps, that Jerry must have read the book's counterpart, *How to Stop a Cat*, since he manages to escape everytime and causes more harm to Tom than the book was worth.

By now, Tom and Jerry and their slapstick formula hit their stride. There were some changes in technique, in that the cartoons moved with much greater pace. Gags didn't take as long to build. They just zipped off the screen as fast as they were developed. The comedy style was becoming very similar to Tex Avery's, another MGM cartoon director known for his violent style of humor. Tom and Jerry were violent, of course, but after Hanna and Barbera hung around Avery, it became even more so. The wild double-takes that was often a characteristic of Avery's cartoon characters suddenly appeared as a new trait for Tom and Jerry. Eyes springing out of their sockets and jaws dropping to the ground were just some of the wild takes that Bill and Joe pawned off Avery.

Avery's influence on Hanna and Barbera's comedy style made Tom and Jerry cartoons that much better to watch. These new cartoons were produced at a much faster rate and pacing was accelerated as result of some of Avery's comedy influences. Some animators have said that it became sort of a race between cartoon units as to which could produce the fastest cartoon; Avery's or Hanna and Barbera's. But these alterations in style didn't break the routine comedy formula that intensified each cartoon, they just enhanced it. In fact, the formula worked so well that the series went on to win five Academy Awards.

The next Oscar winner was the 1945 cartoon, *Quiet Please!* in which Tom and Jerry's antics awaken the family bulldog. In order to resume the chase, Tom feeds the dog knockout drops and continues to battle Jerry until the canine recovers and puts a stop to it.

Though the series had attained great success, some industry officials believed the series was bound to experience an off year. Most felt that since the series had won two Academy Awards in two consecutive seasons, eventually Hanna and Barbera's empire would be challenged. Of course, exhibitors hoped that the series would retain its award-winning status since it was among the top moneymaking subjects in the field of animation.

The main reason some exhibitors were apprehensive about Tom and Jerry's future can be clearly defined. As 1946 approached studios grew uneasy about the future of cartoons and feature films. Waiting in the wings was a new threat to the box office called television. With the success of television, fewer people went to the movies.

As theatre attendance declined, so did the reign of Tom and Jerry, at least temporarily. The same year theatre owners faced a crisis at the box-office, in 1946, Tom and Jerry lost the Academy Award to Friz Freleng and his Warner Brothers cartoon, *Tweetie Pie*, starring the precocious Tweety and Sylvester. Long after the victory, some animators noted the obvious similarities between

Tom and Jerry and Tweety and Sylvester. Each had the same basis for comedy: one character trying to outwit another. Much like MGM's cat and mouse series, Tweety and Sylvester's success was based upon setting them in a proper situation first. Bob Clampett, who created these characters at Warners, has denied that he teamed the canary and cat to rival the success of MGM's Tom and Jerry series.

Like politicians running for a second term, Tom and Jerry rebounded in fine fashion the following year, recapturing the coveted Oscar for *The Cat's Concerto*. A reviewer for the *Motion Picture Herald*, a major Hollywood trade paper, said: "The one-reel subject is packed with amusing situations which will appeal to children and adults alike and it makes most of the skilled animation in unfolding the humorous story."

The humorous story has Tom as a concert pianist whose specialty is a rendition of Listz's *Second Hungarian Rhapsody*. His dazzling keyboard techniques thrill concert goers, but disturbs Jerry the mouse, who's fast asleep inside the piano. Unaware of Jerry's presence, Tom continues to play, awakening the mouse and jostling him around as the piano keys move. The cartoon has few traces of violence; the comedy is more subtle than in any previous Tom and Jerry cartoon. The cartoon, incidentally, beat out a similar cartoon produced at Warners called, *Rhapsody in Rivets*. The film was directed by Friz Freleng, who has implied that Hanna and Barbera took his idea.

With the return to the top, Hanna and Barbera likewise regained their thrones as kings of cartoon directors, and they had done so by casting the cat and mouse in atypical situations. Fortunately, changing the team's material from roughhouse slapstick to sophisticated comedy was successful, when it could have easily been disastrous. Extract all the violence and all that remains of Tom and Jerry are two normal cat and mouse characters. Yet, even though the violent spirit had been excised from the characters, the charming personality still remained. And that charm was what enabled Tom and Jerry to consistently provide quality entertainment in cartoons, with or without violence.

Another factor in the series' success was that only four or five cartoons were released to theaters each year. Because of this carefully planned release schedule, Hanna and Barbera were able to spend a sufficient amount of time on each cartoon to make stories and animation top-notch.

As their cartoons show, even in showings today, they were more than careful. Although they didn't have to worry about casting live acting talent, they had to be cautious whenever a change was made in animating a scene, as continuity was important. They also had to be extremely careful in preparing the script for each production, as it had to pass through the Hays Office, a movie censorship board. The board had clamped down on motion pictures and cartoons some years earlier for using excessive violence and sexual implications. Fortunately, they had a fine staff of writers who sometimes worked with them in creating enough new situations for Tom and Jerry. Likewise, the cartoons were well animated by animators like Irven Spence, Pete Burness, Kenneth Muse, George Gordon, Ray Patterson, and Ed Barge.

The end result was success and recognition, yet to be matched by anyone in animation. In 1949, Bill and Joe garnered their fourth Oscar for *Little Or-*

phan. The story of this Technicolor release centers on "the appetite of a baby mouse, that with Jerry's aid, helps itself to a bountiful Thanksgiving dinner. When Tom the Cat intervenes, the utensils on the table become deadly weapons which rout the enemy. It has everything a cartoon should have and a little more than some other 'greats' in the field," wrote a critic for *Box Office* magazine.

There were other cartoons produced that year that deserved similar recognition, including *Heavenly Puss*, *The Cat and Mermouse*, and *Tennis Chumps*.

As Hanna and Barbera pressed forward into the 1950s, they tried developing new supporting characters for the series. Up until then they used a couple of regulars—including Mammy and Spike the bulldog—in a large volume of cartoons. Now it was time to introduce some new faces to the screen, characters that had similar charm and personality. So Bill and Joe promptly invented with a stroke of the pen Little Nibbles (who sometimes was called Tuffy) as Jerry's infant counterpart. Nibbles made his first appearance in *The Milky Waif* (1946), and later figured prominently in cartoons like *The Two Mouseketeers* (1952), *Two Little Indians* (1953), and *Touché Pussy Cat* (1954). In *Southbound Duckling* (1956), they unveiled a squawky-voiced duck who bore a striking resemblance to a later Hanna and Barbera TV creation, Yakky Doodle. Two other characters introduced near the final productions of the series was a bulldog and son team named Spike and Tyke. They served as a basis for Hanna and Barbera's television characters, Augie Doggy and Doggy Daddy. These characters gave the series some new life that helped solidify its foundation as one of Hollywood's top moneymaking cartoon series.

By now, however, movie theaters were experiencing some financial problems that would affect the longevity of series like Tom and Jerry. Television had become a dominant medium; in order to keep patrons coming, theaters went to double features and eliminated the showing of cartoons in some cases. This meant less return on the dollar for cartoons and other short subjects that were affected by the change. As one industry official said, "There just wasn't any money left in cartoons."

Nonetheless, cartoons managed to endure, including Tom and Jerry. During this time of box-office blues, at least one cheerful note can be added. In 1952, Hanna and Barbera won another Oscar for *The Two Mouseketeers*. Set in 17th century France, Jerry the mouse and his screen companion, Tuffy, are the king's musketeers. When Jerry and his fellow musketeer arrive at the palace, they notice a huge table garnished with food, which is guarded by Tom. When the starving mice attack the table, Tom puts up a game fight to protect the food. As one movie critic wrote: "Only one fault could possibly be found with this cartoon. It's not long enough."

The film was the third cartoon to costar Jerry's impish companion, Tuffy. The cherubic mouse proved to be a perfect counterpart for Jerry, and served as an extra shot of comedy relief at times when the cartoon needed it. His moon-faced grin and naive appearance made him just right for the part. In fact, Tuffy was so popular that he returned in a 1954 Tom and Jerry cartoon, *Touché Pussy Cat*, which was a sequel to *The Two Mouseketeers*.

Many Hanna and Barbera fans consider *The Two Mouseketeers* Tom and Jerry's all-time best, while others prefer the Academy Award-winning

Johann Mouse (1954). Narrated by Hans Conried, the cartoon details the exploits of Tom, a would-be pianist whose master is Johann Strauss. A critic for *Box Office* magazine remarked: "The delightful and original idea and the slightly accented narration have rarely been equaled in the short field."

The cartoon was more of a showcase of classical music than comedy; it lacked the punch and zest of the usual Tom and Jerry cartoon. But it showed that Hanna and Barbera were able to emphasize aesthetic rather than physical comedy values. If anything, the cartoon won the Oscar because of its excellence in portraying something other than the typical slapstick comedy Tom and Jerry had done so often.

Later in 1954, Bill and Joe got permission from Fred Quimby to produce a serious cartoon, one that would "leave audiences thinking," Barbera said. *Good Will to Men* was a chilling story told by animals about the destruction of the human race by the H-bomb. "No pun intended," Hanna says, "It was a real bomb." The cartoon was actually a remake of Hugh Harman's award-winning MGM film, *Peace on Earth*, which won several honors, including a *Parents' Magazine* medal. Hanna and Barbera's effort was animated almost scene for scene like *Peace on Earth* but the actual story was much different than the original. Bill and Joe were hoping this Cinemascope cartoon would make a statement that would stick in everybody's minds. The film was effective, but not effective enough, says Hanna.

In 1955, the man who had been in charge of Metro's cartoon department since 1942, producer Fred Quimby, retired. Hanna and Barbera were inserted in his place. They became executive producers and directors, and produced all remaining MGM cartoons through 1957. Quimby's departure came at a time when the studio's cartoons had been failing at the box office. In trying to remedy this problem, Hanna and Barbera tried a myriad of gimmicks. CinemaScope was one of them; the creation offered a larger screening space.

Bill and Joe produced the last group of Tom and Jerry cartoons from 1955 to 1956 in CinemaScope. The newer cartoons — ones like *Busy Buddies, Tot Watchers,* and *Royal Cat Nap* — weren't as imaginative as their earlier films and animation was sleeker and linear. Characters looked like cardboard cutouts going through animated movements, with stories that gave them no new comic terrain to explore.

Besides their use of a much less expensive process of animation, the addition of new animators to the staff may have affected the quality of these cartoons. Many of these animators had never drawn Tom and Jerry before; people like Lewis Marshall and Ken Southworth. Unlike earlier animated favorites, there was a thicker ink line around the body of the characters as well. It made creatures like Jerry look fatter and distorted the overall appearance of other time-honored characters, including Tex Avery's "Droopy."

Bill and Joe had hoped that CinemaScope cartoons would bring the public back to the movies. It didn't. Besides a slumping box office, the two had to deal with a reduced production budget. Other major cartoon studios had already adopted the UPA (United Productions of America) style of animation, which used less cels per second and eliminated unnecessary costs. Simply stated, the basic drawings were there but without the detail of full animation. By incorporating this less costly style, Hanna and Barbera hoped to keep the MGM cartoon unit operating.

Despite these efforts, Metro's executives believed that CinemaScope cartoons were not drawing and that limited animation didn't save as much money as they had predicted. These financial drawbacks spelled the end for MGM's cartoon department. Barbera explains: "We got a phone call and were told to discontinue production and lay off the entire animation staff. Twenty years of work suddenly ended with a single phone call!"

Bill and Joe tried to persuade MGM to let them produce low-cost cartoons for television, but the studio turned them down. Metro production executive Eddie Mannix said the studio's decision stemmed from the fact it believed there was no future in cartoons made for television. Others accused Hanna and Barbera of just wanting to keep their jobs.

Whatever the case, the decision was final and Tom and Jerry's adventures came to a close as well. (Several attempts were made to revive the series in the early 1960s, with Gene Deitch and Chuck Jones producing.) Although MGM's decision was expected, Hanna and Barbera never thought it would mean shutting down its animation department permanently. After all, the department had produced nearly 300 cartoons and had won numerous Oscars. But by the time MGM's final cartoon, *Scat Cats* (1957), reached the theaters, Hanna and Barbera had left their offices at Metro and were anxiously looking for new positions.

Instead of joining another cartoon studio, Bill and Joe opened their own, named after themselves, at 3400 Cahuenga Boulevard in Hollywood. They intended to produce cartoons for television and theatrical release, but first they had to find a distributor. "We were turned down by MCA, ZIV, and 20th, none of whom would see cartoon stories for television," Barbera has said. "Then, we went to Screen Gems, put the storyboard on the floor, explained it and in fifteen minutes we had a deal."

Since then, Hanna and Barbera Productions has become the largest single producer of Saturday morning cartoons, with its own line of popular series: Yogi Bear, the Flintstones, the Jetsons, Huckleberry Hound (who was spawned from a MGM cartoon character named Billy Boy), Quick Draw McGraw, Pixie and Dixie (shaped after Tom and Jerry), and their most recent, Scooby Doo. Bill and Joe have been just as successful in turning out animated features, such as *A Man Called Flintstone*, and *Hey, There, It's Yogi Bear*, both of which received critical acclaim. Then, in 1975, Hanna and Barbera came full circle by producing a new series of nonviolent Tom and Jerry cartoons for television.

As far as the future is concerned, Hanna and Barbera plan to produce full-length animated features, television specials, and a special blend of cartoons for Saturday morning. Explains Hanna: "We plan to put out the kind of entertainment that both adults and children can watch. It's something that is so desperately needed in today's circle of entertainment."

One just doesn't argue with a success story like that of Messrs. Hanna and Barbera — two supreme cartoon directors.

Chapter 5

Bob Clampett

Generations have grown up loving the cartoon and puppet characters that he entertained audiences with for over four decades: Porky Pig, Daffy Duck, Bugs Bunny, Tweety Pie, Beany, Cecil the Sea Sick Sea Serpent, Capt. Huffenpuff, the Dishonest John. Yet for some ineffable reason Bob Clampett hasn't received the recognition given several of his Warner Brothers contemporaries.

What makes this difficult to explain is the fact that Clampett's cartoons, especially those from the 1940s, are consistently wilder and funnier than those produced by his contemporaries. His anything-for-a-laugh style carried him to borders of sick and black humor. Many Clampett cartoons deal with such subjects as insanity, suicide and senility, but through exaggeration he makes them appropriate and hilarious comic terrain.

Bob Clampett was born a hundred miles south of the movie capital, in San Diego, California, but moved to Hollywood while still a toddler and lived next door to Charlie Chaplin (and his brother Syd). Clampett recalls seeing the filming of movies on the street and in the studios over the years—from Valentino, Mack Sennett and Hal Roach's Our Gang to Bogart, Cagney, Bette Davis, Errol Flynn, Busby Berkley's Gold Diggers, Spencer Tracy and Katherine Hepburn. His high school yearbook bears the autographs of not only chums but Stan Laurel, Oliver Hardy, Charlie Chase and other notables.

Clampett had always been fascinated with movies, cartoons, magic and puppetry. With his mother's help he made original hand puppets and put on shows for the neighborhood kids. Some of his classmates and even his uncles kidded him mercilessly for what they called "playing with dolls." After all, that was something that only girls were supposed to do. In spite of these comments, his interest in puppetry never waned, even during all the years he was making animated cartoons.

Bob drew cartoons from the time he was very young, sketching all sorts of ideas including his own comic strips. When he was 12 he had some cartoons published in the *Los Angeles Times*, particularly an entire page in color which William Randolph Hearst, then considered the king of comics, saw. Hearst offered him a contract to take effect when he finished school. This contract was signed by Bob's father, and he spent off hours in the art department of Hearst's local newspaper the *Los Angeles Examiner*, where he worked under a fine array of cartoonists such as Robert Day, later of the *New Yorker* magazine, also

Webb Smith and Charles Philippi, who became key Disney artists on *Snow White and the Seven Dwarfs* and other classic films.

George Parmenter, head of the *Examiner* art department, told Bob they could hire many people who could draw well, but only a few had original ideas for stories and characters. And that was why he was chosen. But Parmenter advised him that it was important to learn realistic figure sketching, anatomy and perspective, and sent Clampett to the Otis Art Institute for additional training. Here, Clampett learned to draw with pastels, charcoal and water colors, and also picked up how to sculpt and paint with oils. Clampett's years at the *Examiner* and Otis Art Institute proved of great value to him in his future work.

Young Bob's knack for cartooning was even appreciated by those that went to school with him, and even as early as grade school he was known as "the cartoonist." At Theodore Roosevelt Junior High School he invented a character called "Teddy the Roosevelt Bear," which appeared in the school newspaper. Teddy became so popular that, even after Bob graduated, other cartoonists carried it on for years.

Clampett moved on to Glendale's Harvard High School, where several years earlier, at age 10, he had watched the varsity football team practice (coached by James Pierce who later played Tarzan in movies and on radio and married Edgar Rice Burroughs' daughter, Joan). A guard on the team was Marion Morrison, later famous in films as John Wayne. A good friend of Bob's was Betty Scribner, pretty sister of an aspiring artist who later became a key animator in Clampett's Warner Brothers cartoon unit — Rod Scribner.

Bob drew cartoons for the yearbook. He was given an unprecedented number of full pages to fill with a comical history of the year's events. Then at Hoover High School he studied art under Gladys D. Merrick (still a close personal friend of Clampett's). Again he drew the year's history, and was sports editor and humor writer on the school's paper as well as doing advertising art for local merchants.

While still in high school, Clampett and his enterprising aunt Charlotte Clark teamed up to design and make a Mickey Mouse stuffed doll. Charlotte made her living selling cookies and novelties to department stores. She thought that there was a ready-made market for a new novelty doll. Mickey Mouse had just made his debut on the screen, and the design of the doll came from sketches Clampett had drawn as he watched a Mickey Mouse cartoon at the Fox Alexander Theatre in Glendale. From his sketches Charlotte and he made the first Mickey Mouse stuffed doll. Charlotte was about to try selling the doll, not realizing she needed to secure permission from its creator and copyright owner. The name Walt Disney was not yet a household word.

Clampett's father — after some difficulty — located the small Disney Studio on Hyperion Avenue, and drove his son over to show the doll to Walt. Walt and Roy Disney, who at that time hadn't one single Mickey Mouse toy or doll or game on the market, were delighted with the doll, so much that a house was rented near the studio (which Bob nicknamed "The Doll House") where additional Mickey Mouse stuffed dolls were manufactured by the gross. Heading up the working crew was Clampett, his father as head salesman, and six young seamstresses working under Aunt Charlotte. During this period, Clampett had an opportunity to peek over the animators' shoulders and see how the Disney movie cartoons were made.

Upon leaving high school, in early 1931, his one ambition was to become a film cartoonist. Clampett was already familiar with the backer of the new Harman-Ising *Looney Tunes* cartoons being released through Warner Brothers. His name was Leon Schlesinger. When Bob was 12 he filmed a silent comedy with a home movie camera which he wrote and directed as well as playing the comedy lead. Not truly satisfied with his hand-printed title cards, young Bob went to the Pacific Title and Art Studio in Hollywood to inquire how much they would charge him to print up his titles. Bob was ushered into the proprietor's office and met Leon Schlesinger for the first time. Pacific Title during the twenties was the same company which supplied film titles for Warner Brothers and other studios' silent features. Possibly amused to meet such a young writer and director, Schlesinger did the job for Clampett at no charge.

So, several years later upon leaving high school, Clampett dropped in to see Schlesinger at the same office at Pacific Title. He showed him samples of his cartooning. Schlesinger then sent Clampett over to the Harman-Ising Studio in the Cecil B. DeMille building on Hollywood Boulevard. Hugh Harman, Rudolf Ising and business manager Ray Katz, who was Schlesinger's brother-in-law, reviewed Clampett's drawings with interest.

Clampett soon went to work animating on the studio's very first Merrie Melodie cartoon, *Lady Play Your Mandolin* (1931), which premiered on the same bill with Jimmy Cagney's *Public Enemy* at the Warner Brothers Hollywood Theatre. Bob started out animating crowd scenes and incidental characters. The fact that he was given animation immediately was surprising. "I was there at the studio less than one week and already Hugh and Rudy were giving me scenes to animate," Clampett recalls. "Today, if you go to, say, Disney's, they will give you years of training before allowing you to animate."

During his first week at the studio, Clampett attended several evening story sessions and submitted an idea for a sequence which was accepted and used in the second Merrie Melodie. Creating stories and comedy bits was always one of his specialties. Even as a director, Clampett usually came up with a majority of his story and gag ideas himself.

In the first several years, Warner Brothers cartoons relied on two primary cartoon stars, Bosko, a blackfaced character, and his girlfriend, Honey. Competing studios, like Disney's, had a handful of stars reclining on the animator's sketch boards—characters like Mickey and Minnie Mouse, Pluto and Goofy, with Donald Duck soon to appear. It made it that much more difficult for other cartoon producers to win an audience—especially for animators at Warners, since its two creative heads, Harman and Ising, quit in 1933 to produce a new series of cartoons for MGM. To add insult to injury, they took along the studio's only cartoon star, Bosko. This initially left Schlesinger with only the titles of Looney Tunes and Merrie Melodies and one of the original staff members, which was Clampett. Harman and Ising later produced a new supply of Bosko cartoons at Metro but without the same success of the earlier series.

In the meantime, Schlesinger introduced a new lead character in Looney Tunes named "Buddy," which had been created by gag man Earl Duvall. Buddy was proving to be a "nothing," and a new character was desperately needed. Schlesinger was encouraging his entire staff to come up with new characters, story ideas and gags. He offered a money prize to the staff member who turned in the best story, a contest which Clampett won. Bob was good at originating story and gag ideas and was enthusiastic about the opportunity to turn in ideas.

Schlesinger suggested to his staff that if they couldn't think of one good character, they could perhaps come up with a group of characters, an animal version of Hal Roach's Our Gang series. The Our Gang comedies always had an appealing little fat boy and a cute black youngster named after something to eat—"Farina" (a breakfast cereal) and later "Buckwheat." One of the staff thought of twin dogs named "Ham and Ex" and this led Bob Clampett to think of the names "Porky and Beans" (after a can of Campbell's Pork & Beans). He submitted a sketch of Porky, a little fat boy pig, and Beans, a black cat, to Schlesinger who liked the ideas and okayed their use.

With the addition of the stuttering voice of Joe Dougherty, a contract actor on the Warner lot, who actually stuttered, Schlesinger's "Gang" made their screen debut in a color Merrie Melodie directed by Friz Freleng titled *I Haven't Got a Hat*, the first of a number of cartoons in which Dougherty voiced Porky.

This first "Gang" cartoon had a schoolroom setting, which became a frequent locale in Hal Roach's Our Gang comedies. The teacher has her students recite nursery rhymes in front of their classmates and parents. Her first couple of students have a bright, gay time reciting, one doing "Mary Had a Little Lamb." Then up struts Porky who tries relentlessly to orate "The Midnight Ride of Paul Revere," but is overcome by his constant stammering.

The immediate success of the new characters prompted Schlesinger to have the Looney Tunes main title redesigned replacing the likeness of Buddy with that of "gang" members Porky, Beans, Kitty and Oliver Owl.

Many of Clampett's ideas, he has said, stem from films he saw as a youngster. His major comedy influences were Charlie Chaplin, Stan Laurel and Oliver Hardy, Harry Langdon, Buster Keaton, and the bespectacled comedian Harold Lloyd. Lloyd, who was a friend of Clampett's father, is best remembered for his comedy stunts, such as hanging from the hands of a clock in *Safety Last* (1923). What Clampett means, in essence, is that certain bits and pieces, attitudes, actions, timing, posing, facial expressions and gags that top comedians executed in their movies became a source for animators to draw from and refine.

Bob continued turning in story as well as character ideas to Schlesinger, and in 1935, when Schlesinger hired Tex Avery as director of a new unit, he put Clampett with Tex to help him gag his stories and then animate. Taking over their own little wooden building on the Warner lot which they named "Termite Terrace," Tex, with Bob's assistance, made some very funny cartoons including the one that introduced Daffy Duck to the screen, *Porky's Duck Hunt*.

In 1935 and 1936 while working on the Porky cartoons, Clampett approached famous author Edgar Rice Burroughs, the creator of Tarzan, with the idea of creating an animated cartoon series based on his imaginative *John Carter of Mars* stories. The project appealed to Burroughs; he was making money from newspaper strips and movies of Tarzan, so why not try an animated version of his Mars books?

This was the opportunity Burroughs had waited for, the chance to see his John Carter stories on the screen. His son, John Coleman Burroughs, better known as Jack, had just graduated from college and also became interested in the project. Bob and the Burroughs filmed a test reel and took it to MGM, where Burroughs' Tarzan feature films starring Johnny Weismuller were tremendously successful. The studio executives liked the test film very much and told Burroughs and Clampett that they wanted to proceed immediately with the series.

Clampett relates: "I had already given notice to Warners and was preparing to start on the John Carter series when MGM's change in decision came down. The studio said, 'No, we do not want the John Carter thing, we want Tarzan.' Aesthetically, Jack Burroughs and I were very inspired by the Mars project. And the idea, as much as I like Tarzan, to do the alternate series was simply not the same. Somehow I just lost my enthusiasm for the new project."

Film historian Carl Macek, after viewing footage of Clampett's Mars test reel, stated: "There were scenes of John Carter leaping over the Martian surface, swinging in beautiful described arcs, and short sequences of vivid color and surreal appearance. The imagery was lush and yet simple, captivating and whetting one's appetite for more. The technique of animation was bold and striking even after a period of forty years. This small segment of film is something that must be seen in order to fully appreciate the pioneering spirit necessitated by Bob Clampett and Edgar Rice Burroughs' unfinished project. Had the John Carter series been filmed, the entire focus of animation might have been altered significantly."

Although Metro wanted Clampett to proceed with the production of a Tarzan series, Leon Schlesinger invited Bob to meet him, and asked what it would take to keep him at Warners. Clampett replied that above all he wanted to head his own unit, write and direct his own cartoons. Leon promised Bob the next directorial post and offered him a new seven-year contract, with raises included. Clampett returned to Warners and was given two color cartoon sequences to direct, a prologue and an epilogue in a new Joe E. Brown comedy feature, *When's Your Birthday?* (1937).

Everyone seemed pleased with the results and Clampett anticipated that, per Schlesinger's promise, he would be given some Warners cartoons to direct. But rumors began circulating that Schlesinger was considering hiring veteran animator Ub Iwerks to direct some of the Looney Tunes. One of the advantages in hiring Iwerks was that Ub already had an animation studio and equipment set up to produce cartoons. Nevertheless, Clampett thought he had been betrayed. "I went to see Leon," Clampett recalls, "and he told me what he had in mind was to put me with Ub, and then when Ub left, the job would be mine."

After directing two Porky Pig cartoons, Iwerks did leave. Clampett, a great admirer of Iwerks, believes Ub quit because "his heart just wasn't in it." Ub sold his cartoon camera and equipment to Schlesinger and then moved on to make *Color Rhapsody* cartoons for Columbia. He later returned to Disney where he won many honors, including an Oscar for his brilliant work on *Mary Poppins* (1964).

In May 1937 Clampett replaced Iwerks as director. His first cartoon was

Top: Friz Freleng. **Bottom:** cartoon brainstorming session with (left to right) Chuck Jones, Les Goldman, Bo Cannon, Friz Freleng, T. Hee, Ted Pierce, and Pete Burness. Courtesy Warner Bros.

"JUNGLE JITTERS"
A MERRIE MELODIE CARTOON
in Technicolor

A LEON SCHLESINGER
Production

"THE WABBIT WHO CAME TO SUPPER"
A MERRIE MELODIE CARTOON

IN TECHNICOLOR

FEATURING: BUGS BUNNY

A LEON SCHLESINGER PRODUCTION

"SPEEDY GONZALES"

The GOOFY GOPHERS in "PESTS for GUESTS"

A Merrie Melodie
CARTOON
COLOR BY TECHNICOLOR

© WARNER BROS. CARTOONS INC.

A WARNER BROS. CARTOON

Opposite: lobby cards for two of Freleng's cartoons (1939 and 1942). **This page, top:** Freleng's personal creation; **bottom:** Freleng also directed these pesky cartoon aristocrats (lobby card). Courtesy Warner Bros.

Ub Iwerks sketching the immortal Mickey Mouse. Courtesy Walt Disney Productions.

Iwerks during his final years at Walt Disney Studios. Courtesy Walt Disney Productions.

Opposite: scenes from three of Iwerks' "Flip the Frog" cartoons (top to bottom), *Spooks, Techno-Cracked,* and *Soda Squirts* (in which Laurel and Hardy make a rare animated appearance). **This page, top:** Iwerks' "Flip the Frog" *Funny Face* (in which Dr. Skinnum's wall of satisfied customers come to life); **bottom:** an Iwerks Comicolor cartoon, *Aladdin and the Wonderful Lamp.* Courtesy Blackhawk Films.

Top: Chuck Jones helps his cartoon contemporary, Bugs Bunny, blow out the candles on his 40th birthday cake; Daffy Duck is not impressed. **Bottom:** Wile E. Coyote after the Road Runner. 1979. Courtesy Warner Bros.

Top: Jones' most famous creation, the Road Runner. **Bottom:** Jones' Tom and Jerry. Courtesy Warner Bros.

A scene from the Chuck Jones–directed CBS-TV "Tom and Jerry" series of the 1960s. Courtesy M-G-M.

Top: John Burton (left), Chuck Jones and Friz Freleng. **Bottom:** a 1951 cartoon story-board session; leader unidentified; front row, from left: Chuck Jones, Friz Freleng, un-identified, Ed Selzer's secretary; back row: Ted Pierce, Bob McKimson, Warren Foster, and John Burton. Courtesy Warner Bros.

Top: codirectors William Hanna (left) and Joseph Barbera (right) flank producer Fred Quimby while discussing a new M-G-M Technicolor cartoon. Bottom: Hanna–Barbera's most popular cartoon characters.

Top: the Termite Terrace Crew, 1935. From left: Virgil Ross, Sid Sutherland, Tex Avery, Chuck Jones, and Bob Clampett. **Bottom:** lobby card from the 1938 Clampett cartoon. Courtesy Warner Bros.

Opposite: two Bob Clampett creations as drawn by him. Courtesy Warner Bros. **This page:** Clampett as he looks today. Courtesy Bob Clampett Productions.

Top: lobby card for Bob Clampett's 1943 *Tortoise Wins by a Hare*. Courtesy Warner Bros. **Bottom:** scene from Clampett's Edgar Rice Burroughs cartoon, *John Carter, Warlord of Mars.*

Porky's Badtime Story. Carl Stallings composed the cartoon's musical score.

Schlesinger was pleased with the result and put Clampett in charge of the Porky series. So, for the next four years, Bob wrote and directed some of Porky's most memorable cartoons including *The Lone Stranger and Porky* (1938), which won the Grand Shorts Award. This was the first cartoon to burlesque *The Lone Ranger*. In *Chicken Jitters* (1939), Porky is the proprietor of "a cheerful chicken farm." Officer Porky is dispatched to investigate a deserted house in *Jeepers Creepers* (1939). Another Clampett creation, *Porky in Wackyland* (1938), one of the first surrealistic cartoons, won critical acclaim. Clampett teamed Daffy with Porky in some of these cartoons, and first introduced the final Daffy Duck voice, the now familiar slurred sibilant way of speaking which, unsped, also became Sylvester's "Sufferin' succotash!" voice.

In addition to writing and directing Porky and Daffy cartoons, Clampett also branched out into other mediums. In 1938, he and one of his Porky aides, Al Kendig, opened a puppet studio in an old garage across the street from Warner Brothers. Schlesinger modified Clampett's exclusive contract allowing him to create new properties of his own so long as Warners had the right of first refusal to release the films.

At his own studio, Clampett with Kendig launched the development of a new, more sophisticated process for making stop-motion films using puppets, which they acquired patents on. Since prospective buyers wanted already famous characters, Clampett proposed the filming of a series starring Edgar Bergen's wise-cracking dummy Charlie McCarthy (who was already famous on network radio). Bob also experimented with ways of filming Clifford McBride's nationally syndicated comic strip characters Napoleon and Uncle Elby. It was for the very human-acting dog character Napoleon that Clampett first invented his unique method for achieving controlled human-like facial expressions (which he later transferred to his early Cecil hand puppet).

McBride discovered that an option he'd given on Napoleon several years earlier hadn't yet expired. But, with Bergen's blessing, Clampett and Kendig began production, and with their patented stop-motion process were able to make Charlie walk and run free of Bergen's lap for the first time. Along with the McCarthy reel, Clampett also shot test footage of his own hand puppets, and then arranged a screening for Schlesinger. The cartoon producer reacted very well to the McCarthy footage, but seemed to enjoy the spontaneity of Clampett's hand puppets even more. But, after consideration, Schlesinger decided that since his plant was tooled up for animated cartoon production that he'd best take a rain check on the puppet series.

At the time that Clampett was making his John Carter animation for MGM, he wrote a letter to a musician friend on a sheet of MGM letterhead paper, which bore the familiar Leo the Lion logo. Beside it, for no particular reason, he doodled in a baby bird looking out and saying, "I tink I taw a titty-tat!" Bob's friend sent word back that all the members of the band got a kick out of his "Titty bird.

So, several years later when Bob was starting to write a story for a Merrie Melodies cartoon, *A Tale of Two Kitties* (1942), the idea of this defenseless baby bird came back to him. Mindful of possible censorship, he altered his original phrase from "Titty-tat" to "I tawt I taw a Putty-tat!" Tweety's innocent stare at the camera, and basic design is based in part on Bob Clampett's own nude baby picture.

"Sometimes a character comes to you in just one night," Clampett explains, "and other times it comes in little tiny individual pieces like a jigsaw puzzle that finally all come together in one magical moment. In school I remembered seeing nature films which showed newborn birds in a nest. They always looked so funny to me. This stuck in my mind; the helpless bird in the nest. One time I kicked around the idea of a twin pair of baby birds called 'Twick 'n' Tweet', who were precursors of Tweety."

To complement Tweety in this first cartoon, Bob developed two "putty-tats" who visually resembled the film comedy team Abbott and Costello, calling them Babbit and Catstello. The classic theme of Abbott conning Costello runs throughout this light cartoon adventure. Babbit tries all sorts of gimmicks on his pal Catstello in a vain attempt to snatch Tweety from his telephone pole-high nest. Babbit puts Catstello on stilts, has him climb telephone poles, and propels him by "pin power" to reach his nest. Yet Tweety proves victorious in the end. *Box Office* magazine, a major Hollywood trade publication, said the cartoon's "imaginativeness and gags are as good as they come."

This was not the only time Clampett lampooned prominent movie and radio stars in his cartoons. Bogart and Bacall starred in *Bacall to Arms* (1946), and countless luminaries such as Frank Sinatra, Jimmy Durante, W.C. Fields, Danny Kaye and Jack Benny are seen throughout the films.

Tweety shot to instant stardom. After the success of his first Tweety short, Clampett asked for and was granted sole rights to make the Tweety series. It was in the second Tweety, *Birdy and the Beast* (1944), that Clampett first introduced the name "Tweety" to the audience.

In 1943, Clampett had another hit cartoon which starred Bugs Bunny: *Falling Hare*. The cartoon has a solid formula for laughs and first-rate direction, and was selected by Warner Bros. as their choice for Academy Award consideration.

The cartoon opens on a patriotic note as the camera zooms in on the site of a U.S. Army Air Field. Before introducing Bugs, Clampett provides a well-planned patriotic build-up at the beginning by panning the air field and showing a squadron of bombers flying overhead.

The camera stops on a sign which says:

U.S. Army Airfield

Location	Censored
No. of planes	Censored
No. of men	Censored
What men think of Top Sergeant	CENSORED!!!

Then Carl Stalling's patriotic score winds down as the camera zooms in on Bugs. He is shown reading a book, *Victory Thru Hare Power*, in front of a B-52 bomber. As he continues to read he laughs loudly as he comes to a passage concerning gremlins. Gremlins are described as a constant menace to pilots, as they wreck planes with diabolical sabotage. Bugs finds the thought of these little green men as a threat to the United States' air power hilarious. "Little green men," Bugs remarks, choking back the laughter. "Oh, brudder!" On cue, a gremlin scoots by Bugs.

The gremlin shows Bugs what kind of menace he can be. He begins to pound viciously on a blockbuster bomb with a large mallet. Bugs watches innocently, munching nonchalantly on his carrot (and managing a few "What's up, Doc?"'s). The gremlin states that he's out to sabotage the plane by exploding the blockbuster bomb. It looks like fun, so Bugs decides he'll take a whack at it himself. As the mallet comes within millimeters of hitting the warhead, Bugs suddenly stops and screams: *"What am I doing??* Could that be...no it can't be...say — could that have been a *gremlin?"* "It ain't Wendell Willkie," the gremlin cracks.

With his identity uncovered, the gremlin steps up his sabotage plan by abducting Bugs and piloting the B-52 bomber on a wild rampage in the sky. Bugs tries to take over command of the plane but in his attempts, he is single-handedly beaten by the gremlin. During a wild chase, the gremlin politely opens the side door of the plane to allow Bugs to run out. Stranded in mid-air, Bugs changes into the image of a "jackass" before finding his way back to the plane. ("Transformation" gags such as this were common in Clampett cartoons.)

When Bugs turns pilot, the plane goes haywire and rapidly loses altitude while gaining speed. The speedometer goes crazy and stops momentarily to read: "Incredible, ain't it!" As the plane plummets, it looks as if a fatal crash is about to take place. Luckily, the plane suddenly sputters to a stop in mid-air about six inches from the ground. "Sorry folks, we ran out of gas," spouts the gremlin. "Yeah, you know how it is with these A cards," Bugs remarks. The A card which Bugs refers to was used during World War II as part of a gas rationing plan by President Roosevelt.

During Bugs' first years on the screen, Clampett and other directors at Warners began to explore the outer boundaries of his possibilities. As Clampett later said: "We originated and developed a number of divergent formats, each of which was tremendously successful. For one of the strengths of Bugs Bunny is that, like all we humans, he has varying moods. At one time he is at peace with the world and slow to react to an invasion of privacy. At another time, he is in a playful and mischievous mood, full of practical jokes. At other times, he is irritable, bugged by the claim that a tortoise can beat a hare, or whatever. So as you can see we made every effort to keep Bugs in character — to retain his true personality — but this never meant keeping him at all times exactly the same."

Clampett remarked: "Leon never held us back from experimenting. He thought it was healthy and was the only way to find out if you were right."

By the mid-1940s, Clampett was doing such masterpieces as *Corny Concerto*, a takeoff on Disney's *Fantasia*. In Clampett's version, Elmer is the conductor of an orchestra playing "a waltz by Stwauss." Clampett made a wise choice in picking Elmer to spoof the sophisticated appearance of a symphony conductor. Elmer is dressed in a tuxedo coat that drapes over his hands; a stiff cardboard dickey constantly flips up in his face as he introduces another waltz. His unshaven face and awkward laugh of "heh-heh-heh-heh!!" are far from the normal conception of a symphony conductor. The only thing missing in this motheaten wardrobe is a worn-out pair of tennis shoes.

The cartoon's first segment, "Tales of the Vienna Woods," features Porky and a hunting dog tracking down Bugs Bunny through a woodland setting. Bugs does a good job of exasperating the dog while Porky continues his hunt. Eventually Porky and the dog meet up with Bugs and a fight ensues over Porky's hunting rifle. Bugs flings it into a squirrel's nest located in a hole in a tree. The squirrel is so angry after being hit on the head with the butt end of the rifle that he picks it up and fires a round of buck shot at Porky, the dog and Bugs. The three do a death scene that would have made Alfred Hitchcock proud. Porky and the dog survive, but Bugs remains flat on the ground — clutching his chest — and rapidly turns a shade of green. It's presumed he's dead. Not for long it isn't. Porky pries Bugs' hands away from the expected wound, only to reveal that the "wascally wabbit" is wearing a brassiere. Where the bra comes from no one really knows. The result is a hilarious finish and Bugs grabs the bra and pulls it down over the heads of Porky and the dog like a set of baby bonnets. In the meantime, Bugs, wearing a ballet dancer's tutu, toe-dances off to the music as the other two characters stare at the audience in shock.

The second segment, "Blue Danube," is not as strange as the first but it's just as funny. It features a white swan and her three babies quack-quack-quacking away upstream to the orchestra's waltz. Everyone quacks on key, except for an uninvited black duck trailing the pack — the ugly duckling (played by a baby Daffy). Rapidly losing patience with the black duck, the mother swan tries in vain to rid herself of him. She does everything from drowning the duck to swatting him upstream. (Her swat leaves a red bruise mark on the duck's backside in the shape of her hand.) Everything she tries is to no avail.

Into this scene enters the villain, a vulture by trade. Sporting a black feather tux, he's evidently dressed for dinner. A duckling dinner. Hiding behind a tree, he waits for the baby swans to go by, and plucks them one-by-one from the pond. When the ugly duckling swims by, he likewise plucks him but returns him to the water stamped with a "4-F rejected" sign stuck to his tail.

In the meantime, the mother swan becomes delirious when she finds her three babies missing. All is not lost, as the ugly duckling goes to the rescue. He takes the shape of a Flying Tiger aircraft and goes after the vulture, recovering the baby swans, and sending the villain to vulture heaven in the process. The cartoon comes to a close as the ugly duckling is accepted as a member of the family, and they all swim along together happily quacking in perfect harmony to the 40-piece Warner Brothers' Orchestra.

Other great Clampett's include *What's Cooking, Doc?* (1944), which combines live action footage of an Oscar ceremony with cartoon footage of Bugs Bunny who is convinced he'll win the best actor award. And in *Bacall to Arms* (1946) a Tex Avery-type wolf howls lasciviously while watching Lauren Bacall and her husband-to-be Humphrey Bogart in a cartooned parody of the

"If you want anything, just whistle" scene from *To Have and Have Not*. Critics and fans unanimously rave about such other Clampett cartoons as Porky Pig and Sylvester in *Kitty Kornered*, Daffy as Duck Twacy in *The Great Piggy Bank Robbery*, Tweety in *Birdy and the Beast*, Bugs Bunny and Elmer Fudd in *The Old Gray Hare* (which was the original Bugs and Elmer Fudd as babies cartoon), the Gremlin from the Kremlin musical *Russian Rhapsody; Bugs Bunny Gets the Boid*, which first introduced Beaky Buzzard to the screen; follow-up film *The Bashful Buzzard*, and *Book Revue*, which featured the great Daffy Duck double-talk song. "In this cartoon" stated one critic, "the Harman-Ising Magazine Rack genre is turned inside out, upside down, and sideways."

Other favorites are Bugs Bunny in *Tortoise Wins by a Hare*, Tweety in *Gruesome Twosome*, *The Wise Quacking Duck* in which Daffy does a cleverly animated strip tease, *An Itch in Time* with Elmer Fudd, a dog and a flea who sings the unforgettable *For There's Food Around the Corner*; the first color cartoon based on a Dr. Seuss book, *Horton Hatches the Egg*; and the brilliant Clampett musical *Tin Pan Alley Cats* with its "Rubber Band."

In addition to these masterpieces, Clampett directed a handful of cartoons starring Private Snafu and Hook, which were wartime training or bond selling films, as well as a theatrical three-minute patriotic trailer starring Bugs, Elmer, and Porky singing *Any Bonds Today* (1942) with music by Irving Berlin.

Clampett cartoons are distinguished by the lifelike personality he brings to each character. The characters in a Clampett cartoon are not only agile, full of vitality, insane and slapsticky, but also imbued with very appealing and believable personalitites. This spark of life his characters have is due in part to his own role-playing of each character. When making a cartoon, he visualizes and then acts out each character's complete performance—each movement, facial expression, voice inflection, nuance, each gesture of the hand.

As he explains: "If I'm doing Porky Pig I don't stand off removed from Porky directing him; I get inside of Porky and I think like Porky. I talk like Porky. I have a s-s-s-s-speech ppp-problem. I walk like Porky, and I feel like Porky. I, too, was short and chubby as a child, and I know exactly how Porky feels. I'm helpful, trusting, concerned, kindly and sometimes a trifle pu-pu-pu-put out. S-s-s-s-shucks, I am Porky."

He says the same applies to Bugs Bunny: "Bugs' personality is quite opposite of Porky's. And much more fun to do. When I do Bugs Bunny I get inside of him, and I not only think like, feel like, and walk and talk like Bugs [whispers] but confidentially, Doc, [yells] *I am the wabbit!*"

Besides introducing innovations in his cartoon characters, Clampett likewise experimented with the titling of his films. He was the first to use the word "wabbit" in Bugs Bunny cartoon titles. In *Wabbit Twouble* he went so far as to bill himself in the same cartoon as "Wobert Cwampett." Soon it became a common practice to title Bugs' cartoons by using a "w" in place of the "r" in rabbit. His cartoons also had one other discernible factor. He contributed a unique sound effect to his cartoons, which he did vocally, the sound "BeeEEwooOOop!" heard at the iris-out just before the "That's all, folks!" end title as the final punctuation.

During the thirties and forties all the cartoon studios used drawn parodies of the various dialect comedians or ethnic types popular on the stage, screen and radio. These would range from Italian dialects such as Marx Brother Chico, through Swedish, Greek, Irish, Scotch, Chinese, Hispanic and black. These figures, so well loved at the time, would today for the most part be considered stereotypes and rarely be shown on television.

Cartoon directors throughout the industry made their share of shorts featuring black characters, such as Walter Lantz's *Boogie Woogie Bugle Boy of Company B*, Friz Freleng's *Clean Pastures* and *Going to Heaven on a Mule*, Tex Avery's *Uncle Tom's Bungalow*, and Chuck Jones' *Angel Puss* and *Flop Goes the Weasel*. The best remembered of these films, noted for its originality, artistry and considered a classic by many, is Bob Clampett's *So White and the Seven Dwarfs*. The studio, concerned that the *So White* title might cause confusion with the Walt Disney *Snow White* feature, changed the title of the cartoon to *Coal Black and de Sebben Dwarfs*.

The *Motion Picture Herald* originally reviewed it January 13, 1943:

COAL BLACK AND DE SEBBEN DWARFS. Vitaphone–Merrie Melodies. 7m. A satire on Snow White done to black face, set in modern swing, is the best in a long time. It is very funny. EXCELLENT. (8707)

Unlike Disney's version, these dwarfs are "in the army now" and, even though there are seven dwarfs to protect So White, the Wicked Queen is able to sneak by them on a Good Humor vehicle and sell So White a poisonous apple on a stick. So White takes a bite of the apple and falls into a deep sleep. The dwarfs summon Prince Chawmin' to bring her back to life by giving her one of his powerful kisses. To the syncopation of a trumpet and drums the Prince tries to revive her, but his kisses just don't work. Prince Chawmin' finally turns various colors in the face and ages about 50 years as he tries desperately to revive her with his kisses. While Prince Chawmin' gasps for air, Little Dopey goes over and gives So White a kiss so powerful that her pigtails stand up unfurling into small American flags. Prince Chawmin' is dumbfounded and asks Dopey "What've you got that makes So White think you're so hot?" To which Dopey replies with a knowing smile "Well, that is a military secret."

Top layout artist Michael Sasanoff worked closely with Bob Clampett on *Coal Black* and most all of the other Clampett color cartoons. Sasanoff, as well as Bob McKimson, recalled that Clampett used to talk in the baby talk voice later used on "Tweety" while just kidding around at the studio.

Tweety was an almost immediate hit, with fan mail coming in after his very first appearance. And by his fourth year he was a very well established cartoon star with many fans speaking of him in the same breath as Bugs Bunny. And then a strange thing happened.

The censors suddenly exclaimed "Why, that bird looks naked!" Rather than put a little pair of Mickey Mouse-like pants on him, Clampett decided to cover Tweety with yellow feathers making him into a canary.

Sasanoff further recalls watching Clampett draw the first designs of Tweety as a canary, adding slight improvements in his appearance that they had discussed such as "a cuter head and face, smaller feet and yellow feathers."

Tom McKimson, who was art director of the Clampett unit, remembers the first drawing ever made of Tweety and Sylvester together. "It was at the time that we were starting work on the TWEETIE PIE story board. Clampett had already made sketches of Tweety as a canary. When we decided to team Sylvester with the canary I made the first drawing of the two characters together standing side by side as a size comparison model."

Sasanoff and McKimson were Clampett's closest aides on the making of many of his greatest Warner Bros. cartoons.

The last set of continuing characters created by Clampett for Warner Bros. were those polite gophers "Mac 'n' Tosh." And his last Bugs Bunny and Elmer Fudd cartoon, which featured an imaginative dream sequence, was titled *The Big Snooze*; in it Elmer symbolically tears up his contract with Mr. Warner.

After Clampett left Warners to start his own studio, his characters were carried on by other directors. Art Davis finished filming the *Goofy Gopher* story that Clampett had completed, and Friz Freleng inherited the Tweety series and later took over the gophers as well. The "Charlie Dog" character and story idea that Clampett introduced in *Porky's Pooch* was developed into a popular series by Jones.

Clampett was just a youngster when he first joined Warner Bros. and was still a young man when he left. His career of over a decade and a half at the "Wabbit factory" had proven to be highly productive. He left the security of Warners for only one reason: he wanted to try and start his own studio where he could try out ideas and techniques he had that went beyond the usual format of the Warner cartoon. And also so he could retain ownership of any characters that he created.

Long before Clampett asked to be let out of his Warner contract he had already established his own cartoon studio on Sunset Boulevard across the street from CBS. Warnerites like Michael Maltese, Tedd Pierce, Rod Scribner, Tom McKimson and Manny Gould were moonlighting with him up there.

He was also working with Leon Schlesinger, who was head of merchandise licensing of Warner Bros. cartoon characters, on possible television tie-ins. And Leon's brother-in-law, Ray Katz, who had taken over the Columbia Cartoon Studio, asked Bob to be his creative head over the story department and all unit directors. Bob did this just long enough to help Ray get the studio off the ground. Stories which began production under him were *Cockatoos for Two*, *Swiss Tease*, *Up 'n' Atom* and *Boston Beanie*.

At the same time he was discussing ideas of his own with buyers at movie studios, television stations and ad agencies. One of these was a cartoon short for Republic pictures in 1947 titled *It's a Grand Old Nag* starring Charlie Horse and Hay-dy LaMare. Republic pictures was, of course, best known for its Gene Autry, Roy Rogers, and Red Ryder horse-operas, serials and B musicals. When Clampett met with Republic Studio president Herbert Yates to propose a novel idea for combination live action-animation sequences in the studio's musical features, he was told they had just acquired a color process Tru Color and were anxious to test it out. Remembering how Disney's first color *Silly Symphony* short had helped make Technicolor a success, Yates hoped a color cartoon could likewise help prove his new process. The cartoon was well liked but, not owning their own chain of theatres, Republic had to try to sell the cartoon to theatre chains owned by the major studios. The major studios, of course, owned their own cartoon series and weren't interested. But Clampett wasn't discouraged. He was already working on ideas for other things including television.

"When I gave up a top post at Warner Cartoons to try to start my own studio, friends thought I had flipped" stated Clampett. "I've always done what I thought challenging and exciting even though it wasn't always necessarily lucrative at the beginning. I have never done something *just* to make money."

That was Clampett, always having fun with his creations. He truly enjoyed entertaining audiences. And his years of experimenting and entertaining with hand puppets was about to pay off.

Bob Clampett's entry into television was an auspicious one with his unique three-time TV Academy Award winning series *Time for Beany* featuring one of his most endearing creations "Cecil the Sea Sick Sea Serpent."

According to Clampett, the film version of *The Lost World* (1925) was tremendously influential in his evolution of the Cecil character. This was the first feature film ever to combine human actors with prehistoric creatures, and it was a sensation in its day. It was not just the exciting adventure story and overall effect that held young Clampett spellbound, but he was especially taken with the believable dinosaur character brought to life on the screen by special effects animator Willis O'Brien, who later also did the original *King Kong*. The long necked dinosaur who swam out to sea at the film's conclusion gave Bob the initial idea for his sea-going Cecil character.

Clampett has described Cecil as "all heart." He doesn't know his own power. He is lonely. He was raised as the world's only sea serpent. He did the bit about being green – a different color – long before Kermit the Frog ever did it on the *Muppets*. He is very trusting and he believes in people. If somebody gives him a wooden nickel it takes him a long time to catch on, but once he does he really gets his "dandruff" up. He works it up slowly, saying, "Now just a darned minute. What the heck! *Makes a guy sore!!!*"

In short, Cecil is a character full of all sorts of shifts in moods, attitudes and colorations of personality. What people like most about Cecil is his lovable personality.

The same can be said of his friend and shipmate on the good ship *Leakin' Lena*, Beany Boy. Children identified with Beany, who saw the world through a child's eyes.

Clampett gave Beany a touch of precociousness so that he wouldn't be just a "goody-goody." Another thing that Beany had going for him was that he wasn't just a comedy character. He could tug on your heart strings as well. Most everyone remembers Beany's famous cry "Help, Cecil, Help!" with Cecil dashing to the rescue as he called out "I'm Comin', Beany, I'm Comin'!"

Beany's uncle, Captain Huffenpuff, was also one of the most important characters on the show. Clampett says he based Huffenpuff on the bearded explorer in the *Lost World* portrayed by Wallace Beery.

"I based Captain Huffenpuff's personality on the idea of a Baron Munchausen type tall-tale-teller. He feels that he is smarter than anybody else," says Clampett. "He's the adult telling everybody else what to do. He's got the plan, he's got the map and he's going to take you on this adventure to find some fabulous thing. Maybe he will take you to find the World's Largest Diamond, which turns out to be a baseball field. The fun of it is for the child to see the adult figure prove to be not as smart as the little boy."

One cannot imagine a high seas adventure show without a villain. Someone has to spoil all the fun. That's where "Dishonest John" comes in. As he might say, "Nya, Ha Ha!" That was his code signal to the audience that trouble was on the way. Trouble spelled with a capital D.J.. Dishonest John was your typical villain. He wore a cloak and wide brimmed hat and reminded people of a villain straight out of a gay nineties melodrama.

During his first year at Warner Cartoons Bob Clampett almost daily used to make caricatures of his immediate boss as a villain with hook nose, mustache, toothy grin and a dirty laugh. Years later, Bob used this likeness as his inspiration when drawing the original sketches of Dishonest John.

Clampett transported his cast of characters and his audience on an unending series of quests to find and bring back such rare creatures as "The Terrible Two-Headed Freep" or "Ping Pong the Giant Ape." They would travel through the Jingle Jangle Jungle or to the Ruined Ruins in search of the Inca Dinka Doo bird, or rocket into space to visit the Moon's moon the Schmoon.

Time for Beany was not your run of the mill puppet show. Its conception and execution was brilliant. It had the sweep, the scope and the believability of a top-notch animated feature film. Some say better. Clampett wove all the elements together, the grand adventures, the danger, the excitement, the thrill of overcoming disasters, the subtle humor, the belly laughs, the warm human relations, the ever changing scenics and the musical sequences into a never ending tapestry so rich that adults raved about it.

Groucho Marx sent Clampett a letter saying that "Beany" was the only children's show adult enough for his young daughter Melinda to watch.

Professor Albert Einstein was an avid fan, never missing a show. The famous scientist reputedly was in a meeting with colleagues at the Cal Tech laboratories discussing a very important theory, when he suddenly exclaimed "Gentlemen! It's time!" His startled colleagues anxiously asked, "It's time for what, Professor?" "Why, it's *Time for Beany!*" exclaimed Professor Einstein as he headed for the TV set.

Time for Beany originally made its television debut over the Paramount owned station Channel 5 in Hollywood on Monday evening February 28, 1949, at 6:30 pm. In a relatively short time it went national, and as the number of television sets and stations increased the number of Beany fans multiplied rapidly. The *Saturday Evening Post* magazine called *Time for Beany* "the first successful Hollywood television show."

Beany and the other top national puppet shows have been called the "animated cartoons" of the first decade of television. But, then the heads of the networks decided that actual drawn cartoons were in, and puppets were out.

Elliot Hyman, head of Associated Artists Productions who bought up all the pre-1948 Warner Bros. cartoons and features, and all the original Fleischer Popeye shorts for sale to television, found a gold mine. He made over $3 million in the first nine months of sales for the old black and white Popeyes alone.

They asked Bob to develop a new cartoon series that would have a comparable amount of action to Popeye, and gags to a Warner Bros. cartoon. And on a budget much less than the cost of these theatricals.

Bob, with the aid of his wife Sody, produced a sample color cartoon titled *Beany & Cecil Meet Billy the Squid* in 1959. The Hyman sales group called it "very inventive" and to make a long story short, Hyman interested United Artists with which he had merged, to sign *Beany*.

United Artists asked Bob to come to New York to discuss the creative aspects of the contract. After Bob had returned home to Hollywood, United Artists phoned saying before the contract could be signed they had to have a complete list of the titles, story outlines and names of all new characters in the 104 cartoon shorts contemplated. U.A. called on a Thursday and said they had to have the list early the following week. Sody Clampett vividly recalls how Bob originated and wrote and she typed all 104 story ideas in that one weekend and got them to New York in time. The Beany & Cecil series you saw hewed closely to what Bob wrote that one weekend. He always felt that they could have been (even) better if he had had more time.

The first batch of Beany & Cecil cartoons were released theatrically by United Artists in Canada, Australia and various other foreign markets. Then in 1960 the Mattel Toy Company entered the picture and took over the series from United Artists. Mattel was interested in sponsoring the cartoons for television in a half-hour time slot. A short time later, negotiations began with the American Broadcasting Company to insure a spot for the Beany and Cecil cartoons on the network's fall kids'-show lineup. The contract called for Bob Clampett and staff initially to film 26 half-hours containing 78 color Beany & Cecil cartoons and a great amount of additional bridging material.

Matty's Funnies with Beany & Cecil made its debut over the ABC National Network in early 1962, opening out of New York City Saturday evening January 6, in prime time. The sponsor chose to open the show on the West Coast on Monday evening January 8 in the original Los Angeles Beany time slot of 6:30 pm.

Its popularity grew until it even outrated the very popular *Bugs Bunny* network show. The Beany series played on the ABC Network continuously for six years, and then went into syndication nationally through ABC Films, again topping such favorites as Popeye, Yogi Bear and Tom & Jerry.

Fans and critics alike have praised the series as being one of the two most literate, witty and clever cartoon shows ever made for television. "This animated version entitled *Beany & Cecil*," writes television historian Donald F. Glut, "had all characters, situations, puns and much of the adult satire that had gone into the original puppet series."

Brand new character creations such as Go Man Van Gogh, Lil' Ace from Outer Space, Swordfish Jack the Knife, Mama robot Venus the Meanest and son Venice the Menace, Davey Crickett and his Leading Lady-bug, Ol' Spot the Spotted Leopard, Beepin' Tom and the Guided Muscle missile, the Dreaded Three Headed Threep, So What the the Seven Whatnots (with Cecil as Prince Chowmein), duck Graham Quacker and his girlfriend Sody Quacker, Rin-Tin-Can, Peking Tom Cat, Ben Hare and son Hare-cules Hare, Snorky, Beany's girlfriend Baby Ruthy named after the Clampett's daughter, baseball-playing octopus Li'l Homer (one of the 20,000 little leaguers under the sea) which was voiced by the Clampett's son Rob and youngest daughter Cheri who was featured in the coloring books shared the spotlight with already established Clampett favorites Tearalong the Dotted Lion, Thunderbolt the Wonder Colt, Wm. Shakespeare Wolf, Buffalo Billy, Pop Gunn, Clowny, Dirty Birdy and Crowy the Crow's-nest Crow.

A few of the fans' favorite moments are the *Disneyland* amusement park spoof *Beanyland* (with its Darn old Duck pond), Cecil singing "Ragmop," the revelation that the Dreaded Three Headed Threep is a Three Stooges look-alike, the original Snorky lyrics and music that Bob wrote, and the viewers' first peek at the map showing the bathing beauty shaped island "No Bikini Atoll."

Many young people across the country could sing the words to the title song "And now here's Beany & Cecil in a Bob Clampett CartoooOOOn," but few knew Bob had anything to do with the popular Warner Bros. cartoons. This was due in part to the fact that many of his best Warner Cartoons were reissued as "Blue Ribbons" without the original title card crediting him and his key staff members.

But then, around ten years ago, avid young animators and film historians discovered his earlier work and he was invited to speak and show his films at various gatherings. The reaction was electrifying. And the word quickly spread.

In early 1975 Bob was invited for the first time to lecture at various universities, museums and film festivals throughout the country. From the University of Arizona to the University of Illinois and the University of Wisconsin, the Museum of Modern Art in New York, the Kennedy Center for the Performing Arts in Washington, D.C., and the University of Hawaii.

During the same year, through Tex Avery, Bob was invited to appear on the CBS Network show "Camera Three" telling about the early days of "Termite Terrace." And Tex, Friz and Bob appeared the same year in the feature film *Bugs Bunny Super Star.*

Mediascene magazine came out with an all-animation issue in which they pay tribute to what they called the Great Animators (the men who put the move in movies), saying: "The animated film grew up rapidly alongside its big brother, the live action film, since the dawning of the twentieth century. Thousands of artists, writers, producers, inventors and visionaries contributed to that growth and to the art of the animated film. Some have been eulogized, most have been forgotten — while a small handful of names persistently emerge to take their special places in the Animation Hall of Fame. Their contributions to the film form are immediately apparent, and their legacy will continue to endure as long as this most lively of the arts fills our movie screens — and our hearts." The eight chosen were Winsor McCay, Walt Disney, Ub Iwerks, Max Fleischer, Willis O'Brien, Tex Avery, Bob Clampett and Chuck Jones.

This was followed by a tribute to Bob by the *Cinemathèque Française* in Paris. Special guests were Guy Pierauld, the French voice of Bugs Bunny and Arlette Thomas, the French voice of Tweety. And he was also an honored guest at the National Film Board in Montreal, Canada.

At these personal appearances Bob usually shows a visual history of American animation, rare film clips and backstage shots of the making of the films, early Beany footage and a number of the classic Warner Bros. cartoons which he directed. Throughout the program, which is like a huge audience participation ad-lib jam session, Bob answers questions, tells humorous anecdotes and usually ends by introducing Cecil the Sea Sick Sea Serpent in person. He brings out the famous television hand puppet which he animates and voices and it always gets a tremendous reaction.

Time doesn't allow Bob and Sody to attend all the events that they are invited to. Along with their tours, they own and run their own studio in Hollywood. They have made a number of commercials for such sponsors as Maybelline, Ford, Farmers Insurance, Underwood Deviled Ham and the Magic Mountain amusement park. And working closely with their sales head Tom Einstein they have in the past few years sold the Beany & Cecil cartoon series throughout the world. From London to Hong Kong, across Canada both in English and on the French Canadian Network, to the Mexican National Network and throughout Central and South America. Recent sales have included ten Middle Eastern countries, New Zealand and Italy.

With Spanish, Portuguese and Japanese versions already in hand, they have recently recorded the series in French with new orchestra, voice and singing chorus tracks and freshly animated titles and subtitles. They are now preparing to make a completely new dub in the Italian language.

Bob, as he has done for years, continues to experiment with new ideas, characters and techniques. He is as high as ever on the medium of animation. Not as to how it is *now* being done, but how it *could* be done. Bob says, "The joy of animation is that we can forever do new, fresh, unpredictable and even as yet unheard of things. An artist can take pencil and brush in hand an on pieces of paper create any setting, be it an ancient city or a strange planet, and then animate figures doing anything at all that comes to his or her imagination, which can then be shown on giant theatre screens and television tubes worldwide. There is no other medium that allows the creator to control every little detail on every frame so completely. It's a marvelous medium. Too marvelous to end its existence at the Saturday morning television level."

"I have great hopes for the young animators that I know and confer with," he continues. "They have the same youthful enthusiasm and determination to break through existing limitations that Tex, Chuck and I had back at 'Termite Terrace'."

Clampett could certainly give lessons on how to successfully conceive, direct and animate cartoons. His achievements and credits will go unmatched. No one will ever come close to topping the looniness that permeates a Bob Clampett cartoon. When asked how he would like to be remembered, he answered he would be pleased if he was "just remembered. Period."

No doubt he will be. Either for the characters he created or helped make famous, or for the body of his work. His classic Warner Bros. cartoons and Beany & Cecil the Sea Sick Sea Serpent films will live forever.

Chapter 6

Tex Avery

Described as a loner, a perfectionist, a wildman, Fred "Tex" Avery revolutionized the theory of movie cartoon-making from 1936 to 1956. Originally a director at Warner Brothers, he invented Daffy Duck and by 1940 introduced Bugs Bunny and Elmer Fudd to the screen. His humor was shaped around adult concerns: sex, status, and survival.

As producer-director Walter Lantz explains: "The thing about Avery is that he can write a cartoon, lay it out, do the whole thing himself. And when he's finished, it's great. He just *knows* comedy."

Avery's comedy ingredients were simple: take a few tawdry gags, mix in a couple of sexual innuendos, and blend carefully with a generous topping of exaggeration. His cartoon characters are as strange as his ingredients for humor. A typical character in an Avery cartoon does enormous double-takes: his eye balls pop out, his jaw springs to the floor, and his tongue rattles as he gives a frightening high-pitched scream. And once all these ingredients have been successfully compacted into an eight-minute film, it's time to enter the comedy world of Tex Avery.

A lineal descendant of both the hanging judge Roy Bean and Daniel Boone, Frederick Bean "Tex" Avery was born on February 26, 1908, in Taylor, Texas. He adopted the nickname "Tex" when he moved to MGM in 1942; he was billed as Fred Avery in Warner cartoons until that time.

Dabbling in art at the tender age of 13, Avery became a cartoonist on the North Dallas High School yearbook and penned a freelance cartoon strip. Later he enrolled in a three-month summer course at the Chicago Art Institute, where he learned life drawing, still, color, and composition. These courses were instrumental towards the development of his cartooning talent.

The main reason he found the Institute's curriculum rewarding, though, was because of the professional staff of cartoonists it employed to teach the course. Professional comic strip artists came over from metropolitan newspapers like the *Chicago Tribune*. They included such notable newspaper cartoonists as McKutcheon and Schumaker.

Graduating from high school one year later, Avery drove west to California in search of a job as a comic strip artist. Once he had improved his rough artwork and weak storylines, he sent a sample of the strip to magazine and newspaper editors. But his efforts proved fruitless.

Avery permanently shelved the cartoon strip and channeled his energies towards a career in cartoon animation. Avery had realized that "animation was the coming thing." Newspaper simply had too many popular comic strips, making it difficult for just about any young artist to break in.

Avery discovered that finding a job in animation proved to be a lot less frustrating than selling a potential daily cartoon strip. One of his friends told him to put in an application at the inking and painting department at Walter Lantz Studios. According to Avery's confidant, the Lantz studio, which had recently been producing Oswald the Rabbit cartoons, was looking for young artists to bolster its depleted corps.

Confident in his abilities as an animator, Avery followed his friend's advice and within a couple of days he was hired into the department. His duties included painting backgrounds for Oswald cartoons. Eventually he became an inbetweener, providing drawings that went between those that animators had produced. Avery once recalled how he landed his first venture as animator: "I wanted to be a newspaper cartoonist. I kept sending in drawings and drawings but none were ever accepted. A guy across the street had a girlfriend who was in inking and painting and she got me a job at Universal Pictures working for Walter Lantz. I became an inbetweener and slowly learned the art of animation. Then, I drew a couple of storyboards and they worked out pretty well."

But even though Avery had found his proper niche in life, he still wasn't content with his situation. Avery had no ill feelings about his job or boss. Instead, he was upset at himself for not putting out "good enough drawings." Avery was a perfectionist and it concerned him that he couldn't finish a cleaned drawing; he had to have an animator come over and smooth out the rough edges for him. In order to rectify the situation, Avery spent long hours at the studio and remained up late at home to work on his drawings.

As months dragged on, they began to improve and even impress his contemporaries. But even though Avery's improved drawings had met with encouraging words from fellow animators, he was one to remain humble. As former Warner Brothers story man Michael Maltese has said: "He'd rather back off then step forward and take justifiable bows." That was normal for Tex, remembers author Joe Adamson, who has said that Avery never acknowledged himself in times of glory and credit. Tex always used "we" during the course of his conversation, passing credit onto others.

No matter how well one of Avery's cartoons did, he never lost his incentive to make a better cartoon. That is something truly rare in Hollywood's present film factory, or cartoon factory, for that matter.

Examine, for instance, the cartoons that are currently produced for Saturday morning television: the animation is rushed and never properly supervised. Stories are milky and the overall quality is considerably lacking. Yet, despite these glaring weaknesses, the producers of these shows can face the media straightfaced and boast about the exceptional line-up of new cartoons they've produced.

Blah!

Now examine a Tex Avery cartoon and compare it to one of the new made-for-television subjects. Needless to say, anyone can notice that Avery's control — in both animation and story — wins out. Stories are balanced and gags are well executed. There's just no comparison to today's grind-them-out animated television fare.

With his career on the upswing, Avery continued to ink cartoons for Walter Lantz through the early 1930s and eventually was promoted to inbetweener. The inbetweener served as fill-in artist, in that he sketched essential drawings that were important to the smooth, continuous movement of each character movement. In addition, Avery wrote gags and stories for a few Lantz cartoons, two of which he directed without receiving screen credit.

But his tenure at Lantz didn't last long. Tex left the studio because Universal Pictures, Lantz's cartoon distributor, refused to offer him an additional $10 to $15 a week. He was fortunate to get a job at Warner Brothers as a director, replacing Tom Palmer, who had directed Looney Tunes.

The word was out that Leon Schlesinger, Warner Brothers Cartoon Division boss, had been particularly dissatisfied with Palmer's work, so he brought in Avery. When Schlesinger first met Avery, he told him he'd try him out on one picture first. His stay at Warners was contingent upon how well his first cartoon did and how he got along with his crew of animators. Schlesinger warned Avery about his staff of animators, saying that they were "not satisfied with the people they were working with." He wished Avery good luck.

Actually, the animators Schlesinger had warned Avery about need no introduction. All of them have carved an impressive niche in the Warner Brothers Cartoon History Book, and later went on to direct Warner cartoons themselves. Heading Avery's "hard to get along with" animation staff was Chuck Jones, followed by Bob Clampett and Bob Cannon (later a director at UPA).

Avery couldn't have been assigned a more astute animation crew. Clampett and Jones provided him with one of the most creative tandems ever. Bob Cannon was a highly rated draftsman.

Full of enthusiasm, Avery plotted the animation of his first Warner Brothers cartoon, *Golddiggers of '49*, featuring Porky Pig (a character created by Bob Clampett). Released in January 1936, the movie came at a time when theatre exhibitors were looking for cartoon stars. The star system, which had long been in vogue for feature-length movies, was becoming more prevalent in animated cartoons as well. Until then, there had been a few prominent cartoon stars—Popeye, Mickey Mouse, Betty Boop—but aside from them there were none with substantial box office drawing power. Therefore, theatre exhibitors were clamoring for innovative series that showcased a regular lead character.

Porky seemed to be that star. After his impressive cartoon debut, he returned to entertain moviegoers again in more cartoons directed by Avery: *Plane Dippy* (1936); in which Porky learns to fly but becomes the victim of a robot plane; *Milk and Money* (1936), a cartoon which has Porky out to save his father from losing his farm to a mortgage-broker; *Porky and the Wrestler* (1936), in which Porky stars as a boxing challenger; and *Picador Porky* (1937), in which he is a bull-ring master. Each cartoon fared well at the boxoffice and lived up to the Avery ingredients for humor: never let the audience down; always keep them laughing.

Funny as these are, one of Avery's wackiest cartoon ventures at Warners was *Porky's Duck Hunt*. This 1937 Looney Tunes production introduced one of the studio's greatest cartoon luminaries, Daffy Duck. Shaped around a simple idea — Porky the duck hunter out to snatch Daffy for his dinner — it is the amount of hilarious sight gags which makes the cartoon so zany.

In his cartoon debut, Daffy's character was just plain silly. He was a screwball duck who reminded audiences of a glib, fast-talking used car salesman laughing at his own jokes. In many of the earlier cartoons, that's exactly what Daffy did; he reacted wildly to the practical jokes he pulled. Whenever he foiled Porky's efforts to capture him, he turned handsprings and danced on the lake crying "Hoo-Hoo, Hoo-Hoo, Hoo-Hoo!!" In later years Daffy's crazy character was toned down and instead he played the foil whose devilish schemes constantly backfired.

Another Daffy cartoon of major significance, Avery's second in the series, was "Daffy Duck and Egghead." The plot has Egghead hunting for Daffy, yet unlike other hunting pictures starring the unruly duck this one has a gay, brightly executed comic twist in the end. Egghead, having already shown his temper by shooting a member of the audience, is exasperated from the long chase. Suddenly he is dragged offscreen by a group of little ducks in white suits.

Egghead was Avery's latest addition to Warner's well-stocked stable of cartoon characters. Legend has it that the character was adapted from a popular radio comedian of that time, Joe Penner of "Wanna buy a duck?" fame. Penner, incidentally, was under contract with Warner Brothers in 1937 to star in two-reel comedies and feature-length movies.

In the beginning, Egghead was just as silly as Daffy. Rather than complement one another, they played against each other. There was no straight man to set up the comedy interaction. Instead, the laughs resulted from two characters bungling and mugging constantly. In time, though, Egghead developed into a primary character, one that has yet to be matched.

Three years after his birth, Egghead turned up again in a Bugs Bunny cartoon, but not as Egghead. This time he was billed as a character named Elmer J. Fudd, rabbit hunter, "Heheheheheheh!" His first cartoon as Elmer, which was Bugs' first as a star, was *A Wild Hare*. Avery's fifth cartoon in the 1940 season, it was nominated for an Academy Award, but lost to MGM's Hugh Harman one-reeler *The Milky Way*. The cartoon did not mark Bugs' film debut, as he had costarred in two previous efforts; *Porky's Hare Hunt* (1938) and *Hare-um Scare-um* (1939), both which were directed by Ben Hardaway and Cal Dalton. As Joe Adamson writes in his book, *Tex Avery: King of Cartoons*, the directors had "managed to misdirect the character so thoroughly that he was more annoying to the audience than he was to his antagonist."

Adamson has made a very valid point. Bugs' original screen character was obnoxious; he was more high-strung than Daffy Duck. The silliness that permeated Daffy's character seemed appropriate; one expected a duck to act looney. But the audience could never swallow the same behavior in Bugs' original character. After all, a rabbit is passive and afraid, not obnoxious and annoying. It seemed that Bugs had no real screen character. Instead he just delivered a bunch of comedy lines that had no purpose.

In some ways, Bugs visually resembles one of Walt Disney's cartoon luminaries, Max Hare. (Hare made his cartoon debut in a Disney Silly

Symphony, *The Tortoise and the Hare* (1935), which won an Academy Award.) But when Avery took over the series, Bugs' character soon changed. His new personality was in the same vein as Groucho Marx. He had a Brooklyn accent and the subtleness of Groucho. The short pause, bite of the carrot, and "Eh, What's up, Doc?" was far more accepted by moviegoers than the hopping lunatic he portrayed in earlier cartoons.

Avery has said he believes Bugs was successful for one special reason: "He was a smart-aleck, but he was casual about it. The opening line in the first one [*A Wild Hare*] was 'Eh, What's up, Doc?' And, gee, it floored 'em! They expected the rabbit to scream, or anything but make a casual remark — here's a guy with a gun in his face! It got such a laugh that we said, 'Boy, we'll do that every chance we get.'"

Avery created the "What's up, Doc? catchphrase. Being a native Texan, he often remembered how people hailed him on the street with, "Hey, Doc! Whaddya know!" or "How ya been today, Doc?" When he came west to work at Warners, Tex used those same slang phrases in the daily course of his conversation. Finally, one day, another cartoonist asked him where he "got all that doc stuff." Then it clicked. It was then that Avery decided to develop a similar phrase for Bugs.

Despite Avery's early accomplishments — his creation of Daffy Duck and the spawning of Bugs Bunny and Elmer J. Fudd — it seems that he was at his best when he produced documentary or travelogue parodies. One of his comedy travelogues, *Detouring America*, was nominated for an Academy Award in 1939. Spoofing the MGM-produced James Fitzpatrick Traveltalks series, Avery ended his cartoon with a similar message often provided by the narrator in the Fitzpatrick films: "As we fly off into the sunset we bid you a good night." Avery, of course, used a myriad of gimmicks to poke fun at this. In one, the sun suddenly plunges from the sky before the narrator finishes his usual pitch. A more sadistic gag features a "human fly" climbing up the side of one of New York's tallest buildings, only to plummet to his death, screaming and all. The *Motion Picture Herald*, a Hollywood trade journal, reviewed the film as "one of the better and more amusing in the Merrie Melodies series."

In a way, Avery's travelogue shorts reminded audiences of the MGM Pete Smith Specialties: the comedy was bizarre and so was the subject matter. The narration was done straight, which contrasted with the animated vignettes.

The Looney Tunes series provided Avery with greater opportunities to develop gags than Merrie Melodies did. The Melodies were constructed around swing music, and never allowed Avery the luxury of creating an ensemble of gags. In general, the majority of Avery's cartoons at Warners were too tame. He really didn't open up until after he left Warners to produce cartoons at MGM in 1942. The Warner cartoons just didn't express his radical style of humor.

In 1941, Avery had came up with a revolutionary live action cartoon series, using animals as the main characters. In the films, animals would speak — thanks to animation. Animated mouths were double exposed over the live footage of the animals, creating a believable illusion that animals could talk.

Believing he could sell Warners on the idea, Avery showed boss

Schlesinger the script for the cartoon pilot. Leon thought it was hilarious and told Avery to show the idea to Gordon Hollingshead, who was head of Warners' live-action short subject department. Hollingshead loved the idea and told Avery to make a pilot. Avery then returned to Schlesinger to tell him the news, but Leon had a change of heart. He wanted Avery to concentrate on his animated cartoons, and let Hollingshead's department produce the series. For collaboration on the series, Schlesinger told him he would be paid just for his scripts and gags. But Avery wanted to produce the series, so he advised Schlesinger he couldn't agree to such terms. He would either have total control, or nothing.

Avery got nothing. He tried to convince Schlesinger to change his mind, so much that he lost his temper and got in a heated debate with the short-subject boss, who laid Avery off for eight weeks. Prior to his dismissal, Schlesinger told him he could do anything he wanted with the idea, as long as Warners had nothing to do with it.

Abiding by Schlesinger's agreement, Avery went elsewhere with the proposal. Remembering his good friends Bob Carlysle and Jerry Fairbanks, producers of "Odd Occupations" shorts for Paramount, he submitted the pilot to them. Both producers thought it was a fantastic premise for a series. So fantastic that in no time, Avery's cartoon presentation had become a large-scale, short-subject production, *Speaking of Animals*.

The series lasted seven years, winning one Academy Award. Avery, however, lasted but three cartoons, selling out to Fairbanks. His reason for leaving was a falling out he had with Fairbanks over money.

Fortunately, Avery was soon back to work in animation. Shortly after he left Paramount, he joined MGM's cartoon department as a unit director, replacing veteran directors Hugh Harman and Rudolf Ising, producers of independent cartoons released through Metro. Although Avery has said he made the decision on his own, in recent years it was learned that Avery's old Warner Brothers friend, Friz Freleng, was also partly responsible for his new job.

Freleng remembers: "I told Tex that I thought they [MGM] would be more happy if he desired to direct there, never dreaming that he would consider applying. He told me later that he certainly regretted his decision to leave Leon and go to MGM. But once on the job, he stuck it out, until the demise of the cartoon studio."

The head of MGM's cartoon division was Fred Quimby, who, unlike Schlesinger, "wasn't as easy to get along with. There you had to fight for what you thought was right," says Avery. "He was strictly a businessman and knew nothing about cartoon stories or gags. You had to explain the cartoon storyboard to him in order for him to understand. But he didn't. As he said he 'couldn't understand what was so funny.'"

Needless to say, Quimby's unfortunate shortcomings in the field of animation never stood in Avery's way. Tex went on to produce practically every major non-Hanna–Barbera MGM cartoon from 1942 to 1955, starting with *Blitz Wolf*.

Nominated for an Academy Award, the cartoon deals with a subject as unfunny as World War II. It features the Three Little Pigs as American soldiers who put up a game fight when the Wolf, who has a remarkable resemblance to Hitler, struts into the picture. *Box Office* magazine said: "They don't come any better. Audiences, recovering from their laughter, will stand up and cheer for this one. Tex Avery, who directed, is a man to watch." The cartoon, unfortunately, lost the award that year to a similar war-themed effort, Walt Disney's *Der Fuerher's Face* starring Donald Duck.

Although Avery's cartoon lost, it did bring to surface one important fact: Tex became more aggressive with injecting crazy humor into the formerly "cute" MGM cartoons, although he had less creative freedom than he did at Warners. Once Avery moved to Metro, it seems that everyone started to appreciate his humor more than before, including movie critics. Critics not only guffawed at his cartoons, but at his new cartoon characters as well.

While studio mates William Hanna and Joseph Barbera were producing Academy Award-winning Tom and Jerry cartoons, Avery was busy developing a new cartoon character, one that had similarities to the deadpan silent film comedian Buster Keaton. And yet, Droopy the Dog could have adventures that not even Buster himself could since he was animated. Droopy was also based on Wallace Wimple, a supporting character in radio's "The Fibber McGee and Molly Show," played by Bill Thompson who voiced Droopy.

Introduced in the 1943 cartoon *Dumb Hounded*, Droopy stars as a police dog who foils the Wolf's attempted prison break, popping up every place the Wolf finds shelter. The plot becomes the basis for a great running gag, one that only Droopy can play for laughs. Even though the gag was originally used in his 1941 Bugs Bunny cartoon, *Tortoise Beats Hare*, Avery reworked it to the point where it is better than the original. Every time Droopy catches up with the Wolf, he tells him, "Now promise me you won't move." Of course, the Wolf never keeps his promises; he trots off to find a new hiding place. There waiting for the Wolf is, of course, Droopy, who manages to say: "You moved!" The gag repeats itself until it builds to a hilarious climax. Later Avery expanded the gag in a similar Droopy cartoon, *Northwest Hounded Police* (1946).

In his first cartoon and those that followed, Droopy made the impression that he was a weak, sickly canine, with not much muscle. His dwarfed size, compounded by the deadpan, gave Droopy an innocent, humble appearance. But in reality Droopy could be aggressive when the situation called for it. In many cartoons Droopy thwarts the meanest characters by showing off his hidden brute strength. In others, it was purely the "survival of the fittest" theory that resulted in Droopy's emerging victorious.

Yet the series has one basic formula: it was the big guy versus the little guy premise exaggerated to epic proportions. Who would ever believe that a pint-sized bloodhound would be capable of causing so much destruction? Nobody, except the audience. Basically, the same premise was used in every Droopy cartoon. Though the premise grew old at times, the humor didn't.

Some of the finest Droopy cartoons were: *The Shooting of Dan McGoo*, a spoof of MGM's feature *Dan McGrew*; *Northwest Hounded Police* (1946) with Droopy as a Canadian mountie on the chase after the Wolf again; *Senor Droopy* (1949), in which the winner of a bullfight gets "anything he wants in all Mexico"; *Daredevil Droopy* (1951), which matches Droopy and Spike in track and field competition; and *Homesteader Droopy* (1954), a story by Heck Allen that has Droopy out West to stake his claim, but not without interference from the Wolf.

Besides these masterpieces, there were two Droopy cartoons Avery directed in the 1950s that deserve more than a passing reference: *Droopy's Double Trouble* (1951) and *Dixieland Droopy* (1954). Of the two, *Double Trouble* was the most inventive Avery cartoon animated during this period. In this Technicolor cartoon, Droopy is cast as a footman who is advised by the butler, Mr. Eeves, to "locate a reliable person" to replace him while he goes on vacation. The only person Droopy can think of is his twin brother Drippy, a musclebound brute who nevertheless looks exactly like Droopy. The audience soon distinguishes the difference in characters, though, when Drippy makes his entrance by crashing through the door. "That's my brother, he's strong!" Droopy remarks.

When Eeves learns who Droopy has hired, he does a tremendous double-take. One of them is bad enough, but two! Nonetheless, Eeves advices Drippy that above all he is to protect the property and allow *no* strangers on the premises.

Just minutes after Drippy's indoctrination, Spike (now sporting an Irish brogue) enters the cartoon as a hobo trying to mooch a meal off Droopy. He succeeds in winning an invitation to dinner, but Droopy tells him to wait outside while he fetches him something to eat. Spike prepares himself by tucking in his napkin and holding out his plate. He then remarks, "Okay Droopy, let me have it." In comes Drippy who delivers by popping him one in the chops and sending Spike on a free trip south. Droopy returns to the back door and finds Spike standing and waiting. There is a noticeable difference in Spike's appearance since Droopy last talked to him, as he has black rings around his eyes and appears to be in a state of shock.

Droopy pulls Spike through the door and sits him down at the table. He tells the Irish bulldog to rest easy while he prepares a meal. Droopy leaves the kitchen and Drippy returns through the opposite swinging door. Without batting an eyelash, he picks up the dining table and smashes Spike on the chin with it. It sends Spike sailing out towards the tennis court, bouncing off the net, and landing in a seat behind a table on the patio. Droopy returns and remarks, "So you'd rather eat on the patio." Droopy leaves Spike with a ham to chomp on while he goes back to retrieve some mustard. Just then Drippy enters with a bottle in his hand and Spike says, "Okay, let me have it." He gets it all right, as Drippy grabs him and swings him back and forth before throwing him into the swimming pool. Droopy enters and quips: "Now, Spike, you shouldn't swim so soon after you eat." He removes Spike from the swimming pool and brings him indoors to dry off.

The cartoon continues in the same fashion: each time Droopy runs to do something for Spike, Drippy enters to crush him. The cartoon closes with Spike believing that Droopy is cracking up. He calls an ambulance to come to the house and take Droopy away. When the ambulance arrives, Spike calls for Droopy. Two attendants stand by Spike as they wait for Droopy to answer. He does and so does Drippy, as they both call out "Yes, Spike!" in unison. At that precise moment, Spike's jaw drops, his eyes bulge out, he gasps, and slaps his face with his feet. Although neither of the two diminutive footmen is a basket case, the ambulance attendants' trip is not wasted. They haul the hysterical bulldog away in the ambulance as the cartoon fades out.

Avery's humor became even more offbeat when he produced *Dixieland Droopy*. Set to Dixieland jazz, the cartoon features Droopy as John Pettybone, an inspired musician who lives in a city dump. His single ambition is to lead a Dixieland Band in the Hollywood Bowl.

Droopy finds out that not everyone appreciates Dixieland, especially the manager of the dump who throws him out. There are some good gags that have Droopy trying to get people to appreciate Dixieland, hoping it will lead to his eventual start as a conductor. In one scene, he invades an Italian organ grinder's territory by putting a record of Dixieland music in the grinder's box. The organ grinder doesn't appreciate it and throws out the record. Adding insult to injury, the monkey comes up to Droopy and holds his tin cup out for a tip. Another clever idea has Droopy bothering a Good Humor salesman. Instead of the truck playing its traditional melody, Droopy changes the record to the sounds of "When the Saints Come Marching In." But the ice cream salesman tosses out the record. It rolls down the street and into a circus, leading Droopy into a sideshow featuring a flea circus starring Pee Wee Runt, the only existing flea Dixieland bandleader. Droopy abducts the flea band in hopes that they'll make beautiful music together and eventually make it to the Hollywood Bowl as an act. The owner of the flea band chases Droopy right into a theatrical agent's office.

Droopy runs inside even though the sign outside the door says "No dog acts." The agent spots Droopy and tells him to get lost. As the agent counts "1-2-3," the flea band takes this as the downbeat and blasts out some Dixieland for the agent. The flea musicians, of course, have housed themselves in Droopy's fur so the agent can't see them. He does see money to be made, though, and signs Droopy up to play the Hollywood Bowl. The cartoon ends on a positive note at least, with Droopy a success as a Dixieland conductor. But like others of Avery's later Droopys, the ending is weak.

One thing Avery maintained throughout the Droopy series was a stable foundation to base the comedy situations around. His survival of the fittest theory not only worked in this series but even in miscellaneous cartoons he produced in the 1940s and 1950s, some of which are classics.

The first one was produced in 1943, the same year Droopy made his screen debut. Only his fifth cartoon at Metro, *Who Killed Who?* has enough good material and gags to rank as a classic. In this murder mystery spoof, one novel idea is Avery's use of a live actor at the beginning of the film. He is the host of this eight-minute dilly, and explains that the purpose of this cartoon is "to prove that crime doesn't pay."

The cartoon switches to the first animated scene, a dark stormy evening with bolts of lightning cracking over an ominous mansion. Inside is a middle-aged dog rocking in his chair and reading a book entitled *Who Killed Who?* The sage old dog's ears prick up when he comes to a spine-tingling passage in the book. He tells the audience that "if this is anything like the book, I get bumped off." Just as he delivers this line a knife goes screaming by and secures itself on the nearest wall with a note attached. The note says: "You will die at 11:30." Unnerved, the dog remarks, "But I can't die at 11:30!" Right on cue, another knife whizzes by and hits the wall. The note attached this time reads: "P.S. Okay, we'll make it 12:00."

Punctual as most killers are in murder mysteries, our unseen villain shoots the dog at exactly 12 midnight, seconds after the cuckoo clock goes off — with the cuckoo himself getting shot. In comes a canine private investigator (one patterned after Fred Kelsey, the perennial hotel detective of thirties and forties films). Arriving at the scene of the crime, the lawman yells to everyone in the household, "Don't anybody move!" Suddenly we see the silhouette of a moviegoer leaving his seat. The detective notices the man and shoots him. "I said *nobody* move," he remarks.

Remembering his reason for being there, he rings for the mansion's servants. A chauffeur, a maid and a butler pop up from nowhere. All are standing suspiciously as most crooks do: beady eyes staring, body crouched over, hands curled defensively in front of them. The inspector wants to get to the bottom of this murder mystery fast. So he doesn't waste any time in asking them "Who did it?" In unison, they respond like a bunch of brattish children, "Now wouldn't you like to know!" then return to their sinister pose. Upset, the inspector growls, "One of you bums killed him. When I turn out the lights, I expect one of you guys to put the gun on the table." He lowers the lights, but when he puts them back up a few seconds later, he discovers a huge arsenal of guns piled on the table.

"Cut out the funny stuff, we'll try again," he orders. Again he turns down the lights, but when he turns them on this time he finds the room empty of guns, table — and suspects.

A good array of sight gags keeps the cartoon moving. One has the inspector peering behind a curtain with a flashlight. His flashlight unveils a wall of paintings secluded in a backroom. As he continues his search for the suspect with the flashlight on the wall, he stops on a painting of a partially nude woman. Immediately the inspector swings the flashlight back, only to find the woman fully clothed. Another gag has two eyes suspiciously peering out a slot in a closet door. When the door closes on them, the eyes are separated from their owners and have to knock on the door to get in.

Avery even spoofs the murder mystery cliché of finding a bound and gagged body in the closet. But the inspector finds not just one body, but 17. They fall out like dominoes. During a pause in his drop, one of the cadavers says, "Ah, yes. Quite a bunch of us, isn't it!" And down go 13 additional bodies.

Finally a suspect reveals himself. He emerges from a closet, dressed in a black hood. He tells the detective to reach for the ceiling, and holds a gun to his back. The detective obligingly stretches his arms three stories to the ceiling. But just as the suspect tries to pull the trigger on his gun, a guage on it reads: empty. The suspect chases the detective but stops when he sees a pair of shapely legs standing behind a curtain. He rips the curtain open to find out what luscious female awaits him. It's none other than the inspector on stilts like a woman's legs. He clobbers the suspect with a mallet and rips off the culprit's hood. And who is the killer? The host from the live-action prologue.

One cartoon that equals *Who Killed Who?* is the 1947 Metro release, *King-Size Canary*. This one is based on an often-used theme in Avery's one-reel subjects: the survival of the fittest.

Survival in this case concerns a cat, a mouse, a dog, and a canary. First the story centers on the starving cat. Fish scales don't measure up to his expectations of a well-balanced diet, but they're all the poor cat can rummage up. While he plucks bones out of a row of trash cans, his feast is stolen when three cats spring out of the last trash can and grab the bones from his plate.

The frustrated cat is famished, but salvation is near when he spots a refrigerator in a nearby house. He imagines a lot of food can be found in that trusty old refrigerator so he takes off for the house. As he races towards the house, he passes Atom the bulldog who is sleeping in his doghouse. Atom, sensing a trespasser, opens his left eye to survey the premises. His eye becomes a built-in flashlight, which enables him to peruse the entire ground with one large sweep. Once he spots the cat attempting to break into the house, Atom charges after the frisky feline, but the cat thwarts his efforts by dumping a handful of sleeping pills in his mouth. That takes care of the dog; now back to raiding the refrigerator. The cat eagerly swings open the refrigerator door to find it absolutely empty. Well, almost absolutely. The cat does find a can of sardines. He peels it open only to be greeted with a sign which reads, "Kilroy Was Here." Frantically searching through the cupboards, he comes at last to a can of cat food. Opening the can, he finds a mouse who quips, "What are you trying to eat me for? Before this picture is over I save your life!" The mouse tells the cat instead to sink his teeth into a big fat canary bird caged in the living room.

The cat likes the idea, zooms into the living room, and grabs the covered cage from its stand. He uncovers the cage and pulls out the canary bird. By no means is the bird as fat as the mouse remembered. Rather it is the size of a thimble. As it clatters on the plate, somehow it musters up the strength to remark, "Well...I've been sick." The cat pushes the plate away in disgust.

He continues his search for food and stumbles across a bottle of Jumbo-Gro, a chemical plant food. On the label it shows how this stuff will turn tiny, frail, withered plants into large, sturdy plants. The cat suddenly gets the idea that the same may apply to his little canary bird, so he drowns the bird in the elixir. Suddenly the canary becomes bigger and bigger, growing to epic proportions. Once he tries to eat the bird, he realizes that one problem exists: the bird is mightier than he is. In order to rectify the situation, he too takes a small swig of the solution and outgrows the bird. Finished with the bottle, the cat tosses it out the window. It lands in the mouth of Atom, the bulldog. He too gets a dose of the plant growth food. The cartoon abruptly cuts back to the cat and canary chasing each other around the house. But the canary comes to a sudden stop for reasons unknown. The cat likewise comes to a halt, trying to anticipate the canary's next big move. The cat steps aside as the canary smugly displays his huge new ally: Atom, who lurches over the house. Glaring at the cat, Atom takes the bottle of Jumbo-Gro and tosses it down the chimney.

The bottle rolls directly to the mouse, who is seen reading, *The Lost*

Squeekend. Like all the others, he takes a small swig of the mighty stuff before the cartoon cuts back to the dog chasing the cat. As the cat cuts around one corner of the skyscraper-filled city, he stops dead in his tracks. The gag is inevitable as the mouse enters the picture as tall as a skyscraper and thumps the dog. "Just as I told you, I save you in the end," the mouse remarks. The cat never shows the mouse his gratitude — he is "still hungry." All he can do is cast hungry eyes on the mouse as he walks away, thinking how juicy the mouse would be for dinner. He goes after the mouse and corners him in parts unknown. They fight over the bottle of Jumbo-Gro, each sipping out one last remaining drop. Finally it gets so silly that the mouse says: "Sorry folks, we ran out of stuff. Good night." The camera pulls back to show the cat and mouse waving as they stand erect on the planet Earth.

Of all the survival cartoons, Avery's best is *Bad Luck Blackie*. This 1949 Technicolor release is a switch from *King Size Canary*, in that instead of commercialism as the topic it pokes fun at superstition. Avery makes fun of those ancient notions that black cats bring bad luck. The myth comes true, at least in this cartoon, when a maltreated kitten hires a black cat to defend him from a sadistic bulldog.

The bulldog doesn't know when to quit picking on the innocent, defenseless kitten. He causes harm to the kitten in ways unseen before, like planting a mousetrap in the cat's milk dish and other cruel acts of violence.

Rescuing the kitten from the ferocious bulldog is a black cat. His occupation is casting spells of bad luck on targets of his clients' choice. The fast-talking cat guarantees his feline counterpart that he can do the same for him. All he has to do is blow an ordinary household whistle and he'll come to the rescue. On cue, the black cat will scamper in front of the bulldog and prompt unexpected harm to the dog. The kitten agrees, so the battle between him and the bulldog resumes. Only this time, the kitten has the upperhand. Every time the dog attacks, he just blows the whistle and out of nowhere appears the black cat.

The cat's presence results in a string of misfortunes for the bulldog. One time a flower pot smashes the bulldog, saving the kitten, followed by another pot and another. Other times the dog becomes a target of such weaponry as a heavy trunk, a cash register, a fire hydrant, four horseshoes, a safe, and an anvil. Feeling weary, the bulldog doesn't know whether it is safe to go out on the streets!

Ever scheming, the bulldog gets his revenge. He plants a mopful of white paint to fall on the cat and cancel out his black color and power forever. Even short playbacks of *Comin' Through the Rye* heralds no response. With the cat powerless, the bulldog takes advantage of the situation and begins to pulverize him. In the meantime, the kitten wisely paints himself black in hopes that he can now assist the white cat with the same kind of black magic.

The whistle, which before had prompted the shower of merchandise, is accidentally swallowed by the bulldog and sounds everytime he hiccups. As he hiccups uncontrollably, objects of all size and nature fall from the heavens. The dog tries to escape and everything from a steamroller to the *U.S.S. Arizona* hit the ground as the bulldog runs off into the sunset. The cartoon fades out with the white cat and black kitten shaking hands. But not without a close-up of the black kitten chuckling as menacingly as the bulldog did. That gives the film a remarkable comic twist, coming full circle to the kitten-turned tormentor.

Avery remembers having problems in developing an ending. "One picture we didn't know how to end was *Bad Luck Blackie*. We built that picture so that it went from the bulldog getting hit by a flowerpot to the kitchen sink to a battleship. To sort of get a little humor into the thing we had Blackie run across the dog's path differently each time—once on tip-toe, once like a Russian dancer. This was a gag within a gag. Finally we couldn't think of anything else to drop on him. How do you end it? Well, you're obliged to come back to the hero at the end of a cartoon. So you pull a switch—the kitten turns nasty and laughs like the bulldog did all through the picture."

Another one of Avery's survival cartoons that made a respectable impression was *Ventriloquist Cat* in 1950. This Technicolor cartoon features a cat who discovers a mouthpiece which allows him to throw his voice like a ventriloquist. With the device, he is able to play all sorts of unkindly tricks on Spike the bulldog.

One of the tricks he pulls has the dog believing the cat is inside a church bell. The dog hears the cat's voice coming from the bell and decides to investigate. When he does, the cat rings the bell leaving the dog in the shape of the bell. Another gag has Spike riding on top of a kite. Holding the kite's string is the cat, who is busily preparing to launch a stick of dynamite through the means of a sail. Once airborne, the dynamite explodes, leaving a gigantic hole through the kite—and the dog. The gag's aftermath has a lone duckling flying through Spike's open-air abdomen. One of the funniest tricks the cat pulls involves a string of clothing store mannequins. By throwing his voice, the cat makes the dog think he's hidden inside one of the mannequins. So, he starts to rip the clothes from each dummy, hoping to find the cat. After tearing apart two mannequins, he still hasn't found his feline tormentor. He starts on a third mannequin, which is dressed like a policeman. Problem is, it is a policeman. The defrocked cop gets even by ripping off Spike's fur.

Finally the dog smartens up and hopes he can catch the cat by playing a game of his own. He dresses like a beautiful female feline and walks up to the cat swinging his hips and puckering his lips. The cat begins to pant lasciviously. But the cat finds out it's none other than the dog and the chase begins. The cat runs safely past a quartet of dogs, but Spike doesn't get by so easily. As the cat throws his voice, the dogs start to gang up on him, believing he's a cat. The dog is chased up a telephone pole and later the same happens to the cat. Come the finish, both characters find themselves atop a telephone pole as dusk nears. This is a good, lively animated subject by Avery and is complemented by a nice string of funny gags.

When Avery's cartoons didn't center on survival, they did poke fun at another taboo: sex. Prime examples of his sexually-themed cartoons were his updated versions of nursery tales: *Red Hot Riding Hood* (1943), *Swing Shift Cinderella* (1945), and *Uncle Tom's Cabana* (1947). All of them feature a lustful Wolf who at the sight of a curvacious female costar turns into a pretzel of delirious sexual desire. His eyes pop out. His tongue pants lasciviously. Meanwhile, the buxom female has her dress turned up to show off her stuff. One wonders how Avery was able to get his cartoons out of Metro and past the Hays Office, the movie censorship board then in operation. Yet, somehow they were all done tastefully, which may have been the reason no formal complaints ever came to pass.

Even though the bulk of Avery's cartoon releases in the late 1940s starred Droopy, he did manage to create two more cartoon series. His second, in 1944, starred a squirrely-looking character who was absolutely insane, more so than Daffy Duck or Harpo Marx. He starred in just five cartoons and had all the credentials to be a full-fledged maniac; his name was Screwy Squirrel. Unfortunately, Avery was unable to properly exhibit Screwy's wild and brash humor.

Originally, when Avery created Screwy, he couldn't think of a name. So before he tabbed the character "Screwy," animators at Metro just referred to him as "the squirrel."

The year Screwy made his Technicolor movie debut, MGM made quite an effort to sell the new character by releasing three cartoons: *Screwball Squirrel*, his first, in which the pestiferous squirrel encounters a mean-looking but peace loving canine named Meathead. In *Happy-Go-Nutty*, Screwy escapes from a sanitarium and is chased by a dog who has been dispatched after him, and in *Big Heel-Watha*, Big Chief Rain-in-the-Face wants to catch Screwy and prove that he's one of the Braves.

Despite intriguing stories and good characterizations, film exhibitors' interest in Screwy waned fast. Two years later, in 1946, the series died with the cartoon release, *Lonesome Lenny*, a takeoff on Steinbeck's *Of Mice and Men*. That same year, a new Avery tandem would splash onto the screen to replace Screwy; George and Junior, a cartoon parody of the characters George and Lenny also from the novel and film *Of Mice and Men*.

George the Bear was the overbearing straight man, half the size of Junior, with exceptional intelligence. Junior — well — he didn't know what the word intelligence meant! Cast as the numbskulled, brontosauric fall guy, he always managed to spoil George's plans.

Premiered for audiences in *Henpecked Hoboes* on October 26, 1946, MGM's latest cartoon stars try to make a dinner out of a barnyard chicken but fail repeatedly. Even though the cartoon received only fair reviews, George and Junior returned to star in two more one-reel subjects; *Red Hot Rangers* and *Hound Hunters* in 1947, and finally, *Half-Pint Pygmy* in 1948, which received the series' worst reviews.

The final cartoon's critical reception resulted in the termination of the series. Unfortunately, Avery's fine idea of a destructive and often hilarious cartoon comedy team just didn't muster up enough box-office interest.

With Screwy Squirrel and George and Junior permanently retired, Avery went on to finish the remaining years left on his Metro contract. He directed about a dozen more Droopys and two dozen more assorted specialties, which included looks into the future, with cartoons like *Cars of Tomorrow* (1951), *TV of Tomorrow* (1953), and *Farm of Tomorrow* (1954). His last cartoon for the studio was *Cellbound*, codirected by Michael Lah and released in 1955, one year after Avery left MGM. Two additional cartoons by Avery were remade with new animation by Hanna and Barbera; *Millionaire Droopy* (1956), a remake of

Wags to Riches (1949), and *Cat's Meow* (1957), another CinemaScope remake, this time of *Ventriloquist Cat* (1949).

Avery believes he succeeded in some ways at Metro but not as fully in developing a really successful character. "I never did develop a character as good as Bugs Bunny," says Tex. "I think I came close with Droopy but never really succeeded like Bugs did in my opinion."

In 1954, Avery departed from the lion's lair because Walter Lantz had offered him a lucrative contract to come to work for his studio. Signed to a 20-year pact to produce and direct, Avery was put in charge of the Chilly Willy animated series. There was one Chilly Willy in 1953, but Avery in effect has as much to do with creating Chilly as he did with Bugs Bunny. Chilly was a silent penguin who in his quiet way was just as devious as Screwy Squirrel.

Avery's first Chilly Willy cartoon for the new studio, *I'm Cold*, was released on November 29, 1954. Not one of Avery's stronger Lantz cartoons, it has Chilly seeking shelter from the frigid plains of the North Pole. He eventually secures himself in a fur warehouse, but not before he meets a watchdog whose delinquency is matched only by Chilly's ingenuity. That's when the chase begins. Overall, critics thought the cartoon "had its moments but not enough" to rank among Avery's better.

With the cartoon's success, Avery produced two more light-hearted cartoon subjects that year: Chilly Willy in *The Legend of Rock-a-Bye Point*, and a non-Chilly Willy film, *Sh-h-h-hl!!*

The latter is by far his funniest film endeavor under the Walter Lantz banner and stars a piano player, Mr. Twiddle, in desperate need of peace and quiet. Twiddle is told by his psychiatrist to visit Hush Hush Lodge for the long rest he deserves. This is thwarted by a couple in the next room who are playing the trombone and yakking it up. Mr. Twiddle bursts into their room, only to find that the cackling couple are — you guessed it — his psychiatrist and his nurse. The story bears similar resemblance to Abbott and Costello's famed *Crazy House* sketch.

In short, Avery was pleased by the results of his work at Lantz. But he wasn't overly pleased. His main complaint was with his contract, which was primarily a percentage deal. Under the agreement, Tex would earn a regular salary plus a percentage of each cartoon's box-office gross. What Avery didn't realize was that his profit came off the bottom instead of the top. So once everything was deducted, including production costs and publicity, there wasn't much of anything left. Avery has said if he continued to work under this agreement, it would have taken him two to three years before he turned a profit.

Walter Lantz offers a different perspective of the situation. "I made Tex a wonderful offer. I even went so far as to offer him a share in the pictures, which I've never done with anyone. Tex was always interested in getting that paycheck every week. He wouldn't gamble. If Tex had gambled, he would have been a millionaire if he had stayed with me. I think it was one of the biggest mistakes Tex ever made."

Despite Lantz's offer, Avery felt it was no longer for him, so he quit. Lantz chose Alex Lovy, long a director at Walt Disney, to head up Avery's cartoon unit.

After retiring from theatrical cartoon-making in 1955, Avery joined forces with Cascade Studios and produced television commercials, including the Raid insect spray spots and ads with the Frito Bandito (which was yanked off after protests from Chicano groups). Some of his other work included Cricket Lighter and Bryan Paint commercials.

Though Tex never made another cartoon, his old films were being rebroadcast on more than 200 television markets worldwide. As a result, he received thousands of fan letters from around the world. Joe Adamson, who wrote *Tex Avery: King of Cartoons*, has said he doesn't believe Tex answered "a fan letter in his life. His fan mail was delivered to a specific office building which he used as a mailing address. Nobody was ever there to receive the mail. Tex would come by and pick it up, but I can't ever remember him answering a fan letter. Tex just wasn't that kind of person."

Around 1978, Avery shut down the cartoon division of Cascade Studios and tried producing commercials with Bern Wolf, a veteran Disney animator. Nothing resulted from his efforts. In the meantime, Tex received job offers from old cartoon associates like Friz Freleng, who wanted Avery to help write Saturday morning cartoons. But Tex wasn't interested. He did have a change of heart about a year later, in 1979, when Hanna–Barbera Productions offered him a part-time job as a story man and gag man. To make him feel at home, the other animators hung a sign on the door to his office which read, "Welcome to Sun City."

Avery worked on two series at Hanna–Barbera Productions, both of which saw network distribution. His first was Quickie Koala, a koala bear who talks and acts like Droopy the Dog. The series was originally to be produced by special arrangement with a Canadian company and then be syndicated in the United States, to avoid some network restrictions. The pilot never sold.

His second series was a cartoon segment called Dino and Cave Mouse, which aired as part of "The Flintstone Comedy Show." Tex did the original model sheets for most of the cartoons and was responsible for editing stories and adding new gags.

Avery remained active at the studio until his death, of cancer, on August 26, 1980. A short time later, Walter Lantz remarked: "Tex was a one-man deal. He was just great. He had some problems working with writers, because they couldn't savvy his style of humor. But if Tex wanted, he could do it all himself. He was just one of the greats in our industry. I can't praise Tex too much."

Though Avery missed hearing the laughter his cartoons received in the theaters, he once said the laughs didn't always come easy. "I tried to do something I thought I would laugh at if I were to see it on the screen, rather than worry about 'will a 10-year-old laugh at this?'"

As Avery's career bears out, getting laughs were obviously the least of his worries. Like his predecessors, Tex has left behind a legacy of laughter that will entertain new generations of cartoon enthusiasts and filmmakers. His comedy tradition will endure forever.

Chapter 7

Walter Lantz

Walter Lantz, creator of Woody Woodpecker, knows like his wood-boring friend what the word *survival* means. Much like Hollywood's rags-to-riches stories, Walter's life was a struggle from the start. He had to support his family before he reached his teens since his mother died giving birth to his younger brother Michael, and his father was physically incapacitated.

Years before his start in animation, Lantz ran the family grocery store in Middletown, Connecticut, and raised his two brothers, Alfredo (who died in 1966) and Michael. Born in New Rochelle, New York, on April 27, 1900, Lantz never let his boyhood responsibilities prevent him from taking a mail order cartoon course. It later proved vital to his success as an animator.

When he was 15, Lantz had a burning desire to get started in cartooning. Comic strips and cartoons both caught his attention; he'd be content working in either field. Friends had told him that most cartoon artists got their start in New York, so Lantz trekked off to Manhattan to find a job, while brother Michael managed the grocery store. There he got a job as office boy at $7 a week on the *New York American* and was soon jack-of-all-trades in the department. The staff included such noted artists as George Kerr and Willy Pogany. As Lantz remembers: "They let me do an occasional lettering job and gradually let me draw some of the characters in their comic strips."

New York was the stamping ground for most great animators in the business: people like John Randolph Bray, Earl Hurd, and Raoul Barre founded many of the first real cartoon studios. Lantz had similar dreams of becoming a profound animator. So he enrolled in night classes at the Art Students League and took two drawing courses by mail that cost $25 each. Although he earned just $7 a week, he managed to afford these classes since he lived at the YMCA.

His thirst to become a full-fledged animator did not go unnoticed. In 1916, when newspaper magnate William Randolph Hearst started producing cartoons based on Hearst comic strips, Lantz was hired to animate them. He remembers how he landed the job: "Morrell Goddard, the editor of the *American*, called me to his office and told me about the studio that was to be set up by Hearst. He said I'd be paid $10 a week and that it would be a long time before I'd make that much on the *American*. He also told me a close friend of his, Gregory LaCava, would be in charge of the studio." Incidentally, Goddard was the same man responsible for inventing the Sunday color funnies supplement, which is still a vital part of newspapers today.

Once Lantz got his release from the American, he went to work at the Cosmopolitan Studios, where he joined LaCava and others in animating the adventures of such well-known strips as "Bringing Up Father," "Happy Hooligan," "Jerry on the Job," and "The Katzenjammer Kids." LaCava, incidentally, later found his niche in life as a feature film director, turning out classics like *My Man Godfrey* (1936). Before Lantz got to animate cartoons, he worked his way up from camera assistant to animator. Lantz wasn't the only staff member who didn't know how to animate. His associates — including George Stallings, Bill Nolan, Jack King, Frank Moser, and John Foster — all learned how to animate cartoons with Lantz. In an interview, Lantz remarked, "All they knew how to do was walk a character from left to right. If they were going to make them talk, they'd animate their mouth with four drawings and hold a balloon over their head to give the audience enough time to read what the character was saying. That was the extent of their training."

Just two years later, in 1918, the staff was thinned out when most of the animators were drafted for World War I, leaving but two — LaCava and Lantz. Young Lantz wasn't drafted because he was underage. So with practically the entire staff depleted, Lantz went on to animate by himself a series of Jerry on the Job cartoons, which George Stallings originally animated. "I animated one 250-foot 'Jerry on the Job' every two weeks," Lantz recalls. "The drawings in those days were black and white on paper. We'd pencil the drawings, then ink them in, and photograph each sheet."

The series did so well that LaCava gave him another to animate, Tad's Daffodils, a series of short silhouettes which played at the end of newsreels. The series didn't endure because regular cartoon stars were in greater demand. It became one of Hearst's last cartoon series as the animation studio was shut down in 1918 because of financial problems. Film cartoons weren't as profitable as Hearst first believed, so he pulled out before producing them could put him greater in debt. Initially left jobless, Lantz found work as an animator at the Barre/Bowers Studio, where he animated Mutt and Jeff cartoons.

Lantz stayed there until he worked up a solid enough reputation that enabled him to land a job elsewhere. Many of his peers marveled at his natural talent and reputed him to be "a young genius." The genius of his work soon attracted the attention of rival cartoon studios who were interested in winning over the young cartoonist.

The studio that won him was headed by pioneer animator J.R. Bray. Bray saw unlimited potential in Lantz and decided to give him a chance. The two got together in 1921 when Walter left the Barre/Bowers Studios and became George Stallings' assistant director. The cartoons Lantz directed were similar to those animated by Max and Dave Fleischer and a young Walt Disney. His series utilized the technique of combining live footage of actors with animated drawings of characters. Bray studios produced much more than just animated cartoons. It turned out annually a large volume of educational films and two-reel comedies as well.

At the time of Lantz's indoctrination, Bray had been animating a series that he created and considered that studio's most famous, "Col. Heeza Liar." It featured the adventures of a fibbing army colonel; hence the origin of his name.

Lantz served in three roles on the series: animator, writer, and later director. He avoided topical ideas, believing if that rule was observed a cartoon would play for years. As a result, the colonel was normally cast in classic romps that spoofed everyday situations.

In 1923, Lantz was named director of the series when former director George Stallings, who was also the studio's production manager, became ill. Just 23 years old, Lantz had reached a status unachieved by most his age. He had climbed the ladder of success and was now the boss of his own cartoons. Yet, Walter remembers it was Stallings' illness that got him there. Lantz recalls that Stallings did more than just direct cartoons. "Stallings often acted in two-reel comedies Bray produced and I soon found I had to do the same. The first time I tried I didn't know how to put make-up on."

Lantz, like Stallings, got his opportunity to clown in front of the camera. In 1924, with Heeza Liar gaining momentum, Lantz switched his energies towards developing new ideas for cartoon animation. His newest creation was a meek, young boy named Dinky Doodle and his dog Weakheart. Both were cast in a series of Dinky Doodle cartoons, which Lantz started writing, animating, and directing in 1924. Lantz became the live actor in the films and got himself entangled in all kinds of mishaps with Dinky and Weakheart.

Discussing his role, Lantz has said, "I was short and not especially funny looking, so I imitated Harold Lloyd's prop-eye glasses. All the comedians of those days used something—Chaplin had his tramp outfit; Conklin a walrus moustache; Langdon that ill-fitting peaked cap. The glasses weren't too good a trademark for me, but then I wasn't aiming to be a full-time comedian."

The cartoons were structured much like Max Fleischer's Out of the Ink-well series, where the animator appeared live first before he introduced the film's animated characters. In the Inkwell cartoons, however, Fleischer always sat behind an animator's table and conceived that picture's story on sketching paper. Seconds after the initial sketchings were drawn, the characters and animated story came to life. That was a stock opening that Fleischer used for several years. Lantz's concept was unlike his competitor's in that he didn't work just out of his office. "We never opened a cartoon with the same setting. We went out to a field, and didn't just work at a desk like Fleischer did. Fleischer never left his office," Lantz remembers. "We went outside to do our stories. We went to a beach or Buckhill Falls in upstate New York. We went all over."

The incredible part was the cost of these productions: they were produced for a meager $1800 per one-reel short. That included the cost to produce the live action and animation for a 700-foot cartoon! Lantz made sure he squeezed as much imagination out of every foot of film. The shame in remembering these films is knowing that most of them were tragically destroyed in a warehouse fire some years back. The films that remain, however, give credence to the belief that silent cartoons represent some of Lantz's finest work.

The Dinky cartoons were shaped around classic fairytales or standard everyday romps. The fairytale cartoons were a wonderful blend of live action with animation and are considered Lantz's favorites. The best of his fairytale films were *Cinderella* and *Little Red Riding Hood*. Some others that Lantz fondly remembers include *Lunch Hounds*, with Lantz as a cook in a cafeteria that

Dinky and Weakheart leave in shambles, and *Cleopatra* with Lantz as the famed Egyptian queen in drag! Walter found producing Dinky cartoons a memorable experience—more than he did Heeza Liar. His reason: "I enjoyed the series, naturally because I created it and felt closer to the characters. Not only that, but Colonel Heeza Liar was one of these Baron Munchausen types where he does nothing but tell a big fib. After a while that grew old." (Baron Munchausen was a character Jack Pearl played on his NBC radio show in the 1930s. He coined the popular catchphrase, "Vas you dere, Sharlie?")

These films were so popular with filmgoers and exhibitors that practically every cartoon first opened at the Capitol Theatre in New York. The fairytale versions, of course, drew big laughs, as did the classic romps. They also provided a good intermixing of live action and animation and were as entertaining as the fairytale stories. One such romp that used this formula in razor-sharp fashion was *Bone Dry*. It is a fish tale in which Weakheart fishes and catches a fish in a "live" pond, while Lantz fishes in a cartoon lake and winds up with a cartoon fish. Lantz baits his hook, using animated worms, and in the background can be seen live footage of real animals in the forest. The cartoon makes good use of combining live and animated footage. A similar standout is *The Hunt*, which has Lantz in live footage being chased by a cartoon bear. When the bear closes in, Lantz springs forward quickly to elude the grizzly.

Another series Lantz created and directed was Pete the Pup in 1926. The series, which was also known as Hot Dog Cartoons, featured the lovable but pesky pup and jocular tramp sidekick in screamingly funny misadventures. *For the Love o' Pete* was the first, released on October 2, 1926.

Lantz can't explain what prompted him to spawn Pete, but he offered: "You create them. You really don't know why you create these characters. No one had ever done a dog and a boy. The same went for Woody Woodpecker. No one had animated a woodpecker, or a panda, or a walrus, or a buzzard. I always tried to pick something that hadn't been done."

That same year, in 1926, another series Lantz invented was shown to the public. Unnatural History, a series of outlandish history fables, became Lantz's fourth cartoon series for Bray. David Hand and Clyde Geronimi (who was his assistant on his two previous Bray cartoon series) supervised and animated the series. Child actors played opposite animated characters in stories that told some deep moral. People like actress Anita Louise, later a contract player at 20th Century-Fox, starred in Unnatural History cartoons.

Like earlier productions, Lantz's staff was limited to about seven people. Walter performed the writing, directing, and animating of most every cartoon. He even starred in all of them! His assistant was Clyde Geronimi, and other staff members in positions of inker, painter, background artists, and cameraman. That was it!

That doesn't sound like many people by today's standards of cartoon-making. But Lantz overcame adversity and as a result turned out some really magnificent work.

Both cartoon series—Pete the Pup and Unnatural History—remained in production until the Bray Studios was shut down in 1927. There wasn't much money left in silent cartoons anymore. Sound was in the offing, and competition

Tex Avery in 1979.

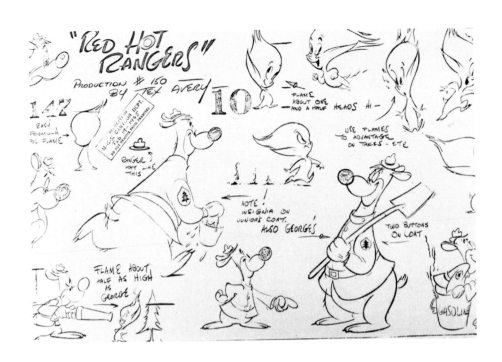

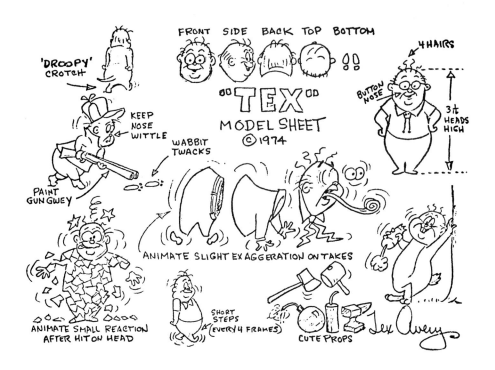

Opposite, top: model sheet for Tex Avery's George and Junior, from *Red Hot Rangers*. Bottom: model sheet for Avery's cartoon star, Droopy. Courtesy M-G-M. This page: a tongue-in-cheek "model sheet" Avery did for himself in 1974.

Top: poster from Tex Avery's *Dumb-Hounded,* with Droopy on the phone. **Bottom:** a scene from Avery's classic *Who Killed Who?* Courtesy M-G-M.

Walter Lantz with his stable of cartoon stars. Courtesy Walter Lantz Productions.

Opposite: Walter Lantz with his famous silent cartoon character, *Col. Heeza Liar*. Courtesy Walter Lantz. **This page:** Lantz accepts honorary Academy Award from Robin Williams in 1979.

1941   1945

WOODY WOODPECKER®

1950   © Walter Lantz   1960

The metamorphoses over the years of Walter Lantz's most famous character, Woody Woodpecker. Courtesy Walter Lantz Productions.

Poster from Dave Fleischer's Betty Boop in *A Hunting We Will Go*.

Opposite: the Fleischer brothers' cartoon star, Koko the Clown. Courtesy Museum of Modern Art. **This page, top:** model sheet from Dave Fleischer's Popeye series. **Bottom:** detail from Fleischer's *Popeye Meets Sinbad the Sailor.*

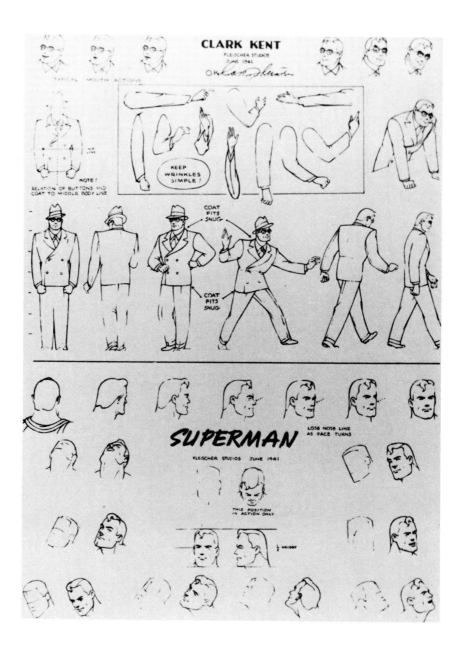

Model sheet for Fleischer's Superman cartoon character, 1941.

Hugh Harman and Rudolf Ising, circa 1920s. Courtesy Walt Disney Productions.

Model sheet from Harman and Ising's *The Three Bears*.

"The HONEY-MOUSERS"

TECHNICOLOR®

A LOONEY TUNE CARTOON

© 1956 WARNER BROS. PICTURES INC.

A WARNER BROS. CARTOON

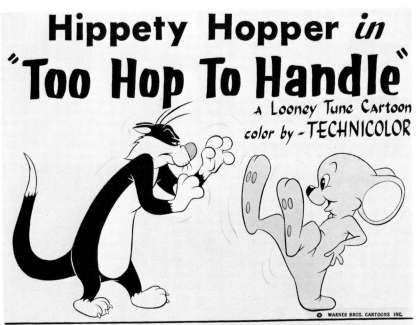

Hippety Hopper *in*

"Too Hop To Handle"

A Looney Tune Cartoon
color by -TECHNICOLOR

© WARNER BROS. CARTOONS INC.

A WARNER BROS. CARTOON

This page, top: Robert McKimson's best Warners' cartoon, *The Honey-Mousers*. **Bottom:** McKimson directed the Hippety Hopper cartoons. **Next page:** McKimson directed the irrepressible Bugs Bunny in *Half-Fare Hare*. Courtesy Warner Bros.

BUGS BUNNY *in* "HALF-FARE HARE"

A Merrie Melodie
~CARTOON~
COLOR BY TECHNICOLOR

was becoming stiff. Bray just couldn't challenge his larger, more powerful opponents much longer. So he decided to close down the studio's cartoon department completely. That put his entire staff — numbering around seven — out of work, including Lantz.

Lantz saw opportunities over the horizon that didn't exist in New York. Much like the sage old prospector Horace Greeley, Lantz heard the call to move west — and go west he did. During his years at Bray, Walter was fortunate enough to have saved $10,000. With that money, he bought a Locomobile and drove to California. Once there, he found a room at the Hollywood Athletic Club, which just happened to be next to one occupied by Frank Capra (who was working for Mack Sennett). Lantz discussed at length the possibilities of working for Sennett.

Walter vividly remembers his conversation with Capra. "Mr. Sennett had a problem. He was doing a feature film and wanted to show a cootie. A cootie was a bug that got into the uniforms of soldiers during the first World War. In this picture, Sennett had a scene where all these soldiers are in the trenches and all of a sudden there comes along a cootie. A tremendous cootie — just gigantic — who scares all the soldiers so much that they jump out of the trenches and head for the horizon. Sennett had had several animators try to animate the cootie, but nobody could do it. He heard about me and asked if I could do it. I said it wouldn't be any problem. I did it in about two days and showed it to Capra. He told me to hold off showing it to him for about two weeks or else Sennett wouldn't appreciate it as much. All I had to do was silhouette a cootie, which required about forty-five drawings. When I finally gave my work to Mr. Sennett, he was just delighted."

Lantz worked for Sennett as a gag man, writer, and animator for some six months. Walter was fortunate to secure the job by "being at the right place, at the right time." He was not so fortunate, however, when Christmas 1927 rolled around. On that date, Lantz and his colleagues were fired by Sennett. No reason was given, other than that their services were no longer necessary. Lantz hung around Hollywood, hoping to find employment elsewhere. With his talent, he just couldn't miss.

Walter soon found a job on the Andy Gump comedy two-reel series for Universal Pictures as a storyman and animation gag man. As he once explained, "I came out to Universal and made a few animated shots on the 'Andy Gump' series. One, for instance, had Andy dreaming that he was going to the moon. I showed him asleep. While he was asleep, I made his mattress take off with him out the window off to the moon. That's how I became known at Universal."

Such innovation eventually turned up an eyebrow of studio president and founder Carl Laemmle. Young Lantz impressed Laemmle so much that he asked him to set up a cartoon studio on the Universal lot. Lantz was, of course, enthusiastic over the opportunity to run his own studio and told Laemmle his needs to form one. Founding a new cartoon studio was a remarkable achievement for anyone in cartoon animation, but even more so for Lantz. He was just 27. As he recalls, "It was in the latter part of 1927 that Mr. Laemmle asked me to set up a cartoon department. In order to do so, I had to build one. They gave me a big sound stage and we converted it into a cartoon department, later adding desks, drawing boards, cameras, and a good staff of animators. I got a lot of animators I knew from New York to come out here and work for me."

Up until that time, Universal had purchased distributing rights to a series of cartoon featuring Oswald the Rabbit that Charles Mintz was producing. Walt Disney originated Oswald and supplied the cartoons to Mintz, who served as middleman between the producing studio and distributor. But when Disney held out for more money in 1927, his partnership between Mintz came to an abrupt end. Mintz told Disney that Universal Pictures controlled rights to the character and that he would get someone else to animate the series, rather than pay more money.

As it turned out, Mintz wound up losing out on the deal. He contracted his brother-in-law, George Winkler, to set up a cartoon studio—complete with staff—to animate new Oswalds. But since Universal owned the rights to Oswald, Laemmle saw fit to have his own studio animate the cartoons instead. Thus he had Lantz create the studio's first cartoon department. The move put Mintz and Winkler out of business, and Universal back in the saddle again. They now tried to compete with other more established cartoon studios, including Disney. Lantz went so far as to staff his animation corps with former Disney animators—people like Hugh Harman, Rudolf Ising, and Friz Freleng, long at Warners. But nobody could match Disney, not even Lantz.

In the meantime, Disney and his long-time associate, Ub Iwerks, invented a new screen character that would, in the words of Lantz, "save Columbia Pictures" (Disney's distributing company). That star was none other than Mickey Mouse. Lantz respected Disney as one of the top cartoon producers in the industry. Oftentimes Walter has praised the late Disney for his wonderful cartoon achievements, which Lantz believes have gone unmatched over the years.

Although Lantz respected Disney's work, when he took over the Oswald series, he felt that many drastic changes were necessary in the rabbit's appearance. As Lantz says, "The Disney stories were great, mind you...very funny. But I didn't like the rabbit. He was just black-and-white. He wouldn't have any appeal for commercial items like comic books, or that sort of thing. So I took it on because if I could change the rabbit I would do it." Change Oswald he did. Lantz made Oswald more "cute" in nature, a natural white rabbit that people often found in children's books. That metamorphosis gave Oswald a certain ray of charm that not even the Disney character provided. Animating cute cartoons stars was something that one of Lantz's animators, Hugh Harman, later became known for at MGM.

Lantz's first job was to add sound to six unreleased cartoons that Winkler had animated, the first being *Ozzie of the Circus*. The process of striking sound to these films was as unorthodox as the cartoon stories themselves. "It was funny how we did it," Lantz recalls. "We had a bench with all the props on it—the bells, and so on. And we'd project a cartoon on the screen and all of us would stand there in front of the cartoon. As the action progressed, we'd take it and make the sound effects, dialogue, and all. We never prescored these films. We did everything as we watched the picture. It was the only way we knew how to add sound."

Lantz has admitted that after the first series of Oswalds there was definite room for improvement. He believed that stories were inhibited and animation wasn't up to par. But as time moved on, Lantz worked closely with his staff to smooth out the rough edges to present a solid cartoon. After refining his work, Laemmle asked him to contribute an animated segment for the studio's all-talking extravaganza, *The King of Jazz Revue*, starring Paul Whiteman. The film lost an enormous amount of money and was filmed entirely in two-strip Technicolor. Lantz's job was to animate a sequence showing how Whiteman was crowned king of jazz. That scene showed Whiteman as a bandleader and as a big-game hunter stalking wild animals. Whiteman's singing voice was provided by a member of his Rhythm Boys Trio, a young talented man named Bing Crosby. It is believed to have been the first time Crosby recorded a song for a motion picture. To make the segment more buoyant, Lantz even put Oswald the Rabbit into the act. Oswald was a fine addition to the film, menacing other characters in the scene and taking part in some hilarious antics. The finale, however, has as much going for it as the entire sequence. It's just as clever and shows much innovation on the part of Lantz. In the end, a cartoon lion conks Whiteman on the head, thus creating a bump that mushrooms into a crown — officially designating him the king of jazz.

Believing Lantz's animated segment stole the show, a critic for the *Motion Picture Herald* wrote: "'The King of Jazz Revue' is a symphony of color and music with a blending of comedy, sensational settings, and intimate numbers to make the production commanding entertainment.... From the animated color cartoon at the start, showing a comedy conception of how Whiteman was crowned King of Jazz through the stupendous 'Melting Pot' finale, the all Technicolor production is packed with genuine entertainment."

That Lantz animated the sequence in two-strip Technicolor was a distinction that no other animator could claim. Ub Iwerks animated a few Flip the Frog cartoons in two-strip Cinecolor, but that was some time after *The King of Jazz Revue* was released. Being *first* was something that Walter proudly remembers, notably the audience reaction. "They had never seen anything like that before. It was the first two-strip color cartoon, and Bill Nolan and quite a few others did the animation, along with myself. It was just a terrific vehicle!"

As amazing as the cartoon segment was, its animation wasn't a winsome undertaking. First, Lantz was dealing with a limited range of colors, mainly red and green. Most damaging of all was that artists found the paints they used didn't adhere to the cels. Often the paint chipped off before the camera could film the scene. Despite these setbacks, Lantz prevailed and delivered precisely what Laemmle had ordered: a cartoon that was bright, funny, and well animated.

Upon completion of the film, Lantz concentrated his energies towards animating and directing 26 Oswalds a year. That demanded much of Lantz's time and prevented him from creating and producing new ventures in animation. To relieve unwanted pressures, Lantz assigned Bill Nolan as co-director of the series. The two men blended well together and produced a consistent series of sharply animated cartoons that entertained moviegoers for years.

One particularly well received film was the 1931 Oswald cartoon, *Mars.* The *Motion Picture Herald* praised it thusly: "When Oswald and Peg Leg flirt with a girl in the park, Oswald receives a kick that perches him on Mars. Oswald sings the 'Lucky Rabbit' number, while some particularly unique and unusual effects are achieved in cartoon work. The theme song idea for the shorts is one of the most striking ideas yet introduced into animated cartoons."

Lantz has said that the average budget for an Oswald cartoon was $4,000 a film. That wasn't as much as other producers had been spending to produce six and a half minutes of black-and-white sound vignettes. The reason for these low budgets can account for Lantz being a budget-conscious director. He knew how to run a tight budget for each cartoon — squeezing as much quality as possible from each dollar — without letting it become too expensive a medium.

The charm that permeated the Oswald cartoons can be attributed to good cartoon personas and nicely written stories. That charm wouldn't have been as realized if it hadn't been for the voice artists who brought Oswald to life. They included Mickey Rooney and Bernice Hansen.

Rooney was the first person to voice Oswald. He was just nine years old at the time, and as Lantz says, "He was just a wild kid then. Because of his age, he had the right squealing voice for Oswald. We'd sit down and do some dialogue with him, then take a rest, and then we wouldn't find him because he was probably in the rafters or somewhere. Mickey was cute — he did a terrific job!"

Rooney had just come off starring in a series of Mickey McGuire comedy two-reelers for the R-C Pictures Corporation. When Mickey's career suddenly took off, Lantz brought in the indomitable Bernice Hansen as his replacement. She, of course, did a solid job for the duration of the series' years in production. Hansen had been voicing cartoon characters for other cartoon studios, including Warner Brothers' Sniffles the Mouse, who sounded much like Oswald.

Production of Oswalds continued at a rapid pace, while Lantz studied other prospective ventures to produce for the cartoon arena. The main stronghold of each cartoon was the stories and gag situations. Much like Ub Iwerks' Flip the Frog, Oswald was always caught in the middle of precarious situations his supporting characters created. These story ingredients were just as important to the success of the film as was consistency in animation.

Such qualities pale in significance when compared to a landmark Oswald film, *Confidence.* This 1933 cartoon release is an excellent production that depicts the rueful period of the Depression. The film includes everything that crippled the American citizenry so sharply in 1929 — a bank scare, a stock market crash, and general lethargy on the part of everyone, including Oswald. Oswald searches for a cure that will bring the country back on its feet again. So he visits Dr. Pill for a cure. The doctor says he can't advise a cure but knows of a cure-maker, saying, "There's your doctor!" as he swiftly points to a frame picture of President Franklin D. Roosevelt in his office. Oswald immediately flies to Washington, D.C., to ask FDR for the cure. After hearing Oswald's plea, the President sings "Confidence," thus restoring that rabbit's faith in our country and a cure. Oswald returns home to inject the local citizens and farm animals with a shot of confidence from a hypodermic needle. The serum does the trick and re-establishes the U.S. economic stature at home and abroad. Unlike some Oswalds, the story rates as one of the strongest in the series. Lantz considers the film one of his favorites, saying, "I thought it was very timely then and believe it still applies even today."

Lantz found the formula for using caricatures of famous global personalities so intriguing that he produced a series of similar cartoons. One of them, *Merry Old Soul* (1933), is a charming effort that situates Oswald in a tooth-pulling episode with his dentist. After the dentist gives him the gas, Oswald dreams that Old King Cole, deep in the blues, needs some cheering. He manages to bring the king out of his doldrums with the aid of caricatured comedians representing Laurel and Hardy, the Marx Brothers, Chaplin, and Durante. The cartoon was so entertaining and brilliantly animated that it was nominated for an Academy Award; it lost to Walt Disney's *Three Little Pigs*.

One year earlier, in 1932, Lantz introduced to the screen his second cartoon star, Pooch the Pup. Lantz describes the series' genesis: "The situations were like this: there was a little tramp with a small bundle on his back walking down the railroad track with his dog, Pooch. The stories were like the ones I made for Bray—like Dinky Doodles. I got the idea from those, using similar situations." Some familiar stories that Lantz exclusively relied on were children's fairytales. He found them to be most rewarding vehicles in terms of good stories and first-rate characterizations. Fairytales had a cult following of their own and Lantz was just popularizing the art by producing them for the screen. Enhancing the beauty of each production was very stylish animation that added to the film's authenticity.

Pooch appears at his best in *Hot and Cold* (1933). The film is shaped around an old film tune, "Turn on the Heat," which was originally scored for the 1929 Fox feature *Sunny Side Up*. The story is rather clever, in that a weather king who lives at the North Pole tries controlling the climate. Pooch tries convincing the weather king to return the climate back to normal.

Two other entries—not with Pooch but Oswald—that splashed onto the screen in 1934 deserve honorable mentions. One of the most effective of the two is *Kings Up*. The film is every bit as explosive as the dialogue sung in this light opera. Oswald, hoping to gain knighthood from the Queen, battles the villainous Black Knight. He puts away the dastardly knight and wins the Queen's hand in marriage.

Another good entry, *The Toy Shoppe*, makes use of a Disney/Harman and Ising story where the toy shop comes to life after dark. It is one of the series' brightest ventures, with a remarkable combination of splashy backgrounds and character movements. As was the case in Oswald cartoons around this time, the prize-winning rabbit appeared less in each film. He was given about a third less time on screen than moviegoers saw of him in earlier productions. With Lantz running fresh out of ideas, some immediate changes were necessary if the series was to survive. One was to put Oswald on the screen for a shorter period of time. Another was to replace his absence with lesser-known characters until his return.

Such manipulation paid off and kept Oswald afloat for four more years, which was longer than Lantz had expected. Keeping his mind active in creating new ideas, Lantz presented theatre exhibitors with his third cartoon series in 1934. Cartune Classics, a series of two-strip color fairytales, used a formula similar to Disney's Silly Symphonies series. The film was basically musicals, with less dialogue and more music and sound effects incorporated into the films. The first six cartoons, the first being *Jolly Little Elves*, were produced in color with all remaining films shot in black-and-white. Incidentally, *Jolly Little Elves* snatched up an Academy Award nomination in 1934 but lost to Disney's *The Tortoise and the Hare*. Other classic Lantz fairytale spectacles included *Toyland Premiere*, in which loads of Hollywood film stars join the fun, and *Candy Land*.

With as many as three cartoon series being produced at once, Lantz saw it necessary to expand his animation staff. Some of the 1934 staffers included George Nichols, Sid Sutherland, Ray Abrams, Steve Bosustow, George Moreno, Tex Avery, Ed Benedict, LaVerne Harding, Virgil Ross, Fred Kopietz, Cecil Surry, Cal Howard, Victor McLeod, George Grandpre, and Manuel Moreno. Some of them remained on Lantz's payroll for years, while others defected to other cartoon studio rivals like MGM and Warner Brothers.

Lantz has said that shouldering the responsibility of producing and directing all three cartoon series would have been impossible. Therefore, he was grateful to have had Bill Nolan as his codirector on many of these films. Nolan was a very competent director and was as budget-conscious as Lantz. He never went over budget, and as Lantz says, "He was always right on the mark." In 1935, the long association between both men came to a sudden close when Nolan bid farewell. Lantz, of course, didn't want to see as talented a person as Nolan head for greener pastures, especially since they had been business associates for some ten years.

That became the first of a series of executive and corporate moves that jeopardized the future of Lantz's cartoon studio. The largest number of promotions came later that year when Universal decided to clean house after president Carl Laemmle retired. One unpleasant management decision was to shut down the animation department. To some this would have spelled disaster; to Lantz it spelled a new opportunity. The opportunity was to form a studio of his own.

In order to construct a large enough facility, Lantz had to have an outstanding downpayment of $28,000. "I borrowed on my house, my car, my furniture, everything I had, but I could only raise $14,000. So I went to everyone I knew in Hollywood. Finally, Universal agreed to guarantee a bank loan and I was able to remain the sole owner of my company," Lantz recalls. In addition, Lantz seized distributing rights to all his cartoon series and contracted Universal as just a distributor. Thus he became an independent producer and a power separate from the studio itself.

In celebration of his new acquisition, Lantz produced and directed a new cartoon series in 1936 — his fourth series for Universal — called Meany, Miny, and Moe. These films starred three circus-dressed monkeys who acted in pantomime and incorporated broad comedy gags that made the Three Stooges so famous. Thirteen cartoons were produced between 1936 and 1937, with the first being *Turkey Dinner*. Originally 26 Oswalds were to be produced that season, but Lantz cut that number in half so he could start production of his new series.

Lantz has fond memories of his cartoon monkeys. "They were just three lively monkeys who got tangled in all sorts of situations. I recall one in particular where they were going to play golf. One was a caddy, one drove a cart, and the other was a kibitzer—and they just had one terrific time on the golf course. They had trouble with the cart, wrecked the golf course, and got in all sorts of trouble." The cartoon Lantz remembers is *The Golfers*, the first 1937 production and undoubtedly one of the series' best. A critic for *Motion Picture Herald*, however, wrote, "The finale of the monks' score with a robot golf machine provides some rapid fire and occasionally humorous situations. The youngsters, of course, and perhaps the golf minded of the audience will find something in the gags to chuckle about."

Lantz cites the use of pantomime as one reason for the series' success. He says, "They were more like the Three Stooges, where the actions were very physical gags and broad action. We didn't need any dialogue because they were doing the kind of pantomime like Charlie Chaplin and Harry Langdon. They didn't need to talk to be funny. Neither did these characters."

Some other great additions to the series included *House of Magic* (1937), which has the monkeys take refuge in a house of magic during a storm. In *The Big Race* (1937), the three chimpanzees win top prize in a big auto race; they have similar fun as riveters on a construction site in *Steel Workers* (1937).

Lantz discontinued production of the series in late 1937. As he said, "There just wasn't much else we could do with the characters." One year later, in 1938, Lantz pulled Oswald from the screen for a different reason. He remembers, "We just ran out of ideas. We had done just about everything imaginable." Lantz produced a couple of short-lived series in its place, one of them starring Baby Face Mouse (who resembled Warners' Sniffles character) and another featuring Li'l Eightball, a small black youngster. Neither of them caught on, but one Lantz creation that was introduced in 1939 did, that being Andy Panda.

The first cartoon, *Life Begins for Andy Panda*, was directed by Alex Lovy (who later became a director at Disney and Hanna–Barbera Productions). The cartoon was an acceptable first venture, so much so that Lantz had Lovy direct two more Panda cartoons, *Andy Panda Goes Fishing* (1939) and *100 Pygmies and Andy Panda* (1940). It was after these films that Lantz directed his first cartoon in the series, *Crazy House*, which was the series fourth cartoon and third entry in the 1940 season.

Lantz recalls some changes he made when he took over the series: "In the first cartoon, Andy wasn't wearing any clothes. He was just a cute little panda bear. As we went along, we gradually dressed Andy. We gave him a pair of pants, little hat, shoes, and like Woody Woodpecker, we modified him and made him into a very cute character. After we tried many voices we settled on Walter Tetley. He did a very fine job. Then we got into a series where we brought his father into it. As a result, Andy was always correcting his father because in various incidents his father would screw up everything. Andy, of course, seemed to have more brains than his father. That was the new format more or less."

The second Panda cartoon Lantz directed, *Knock, Knock!*, had more going for it than solid animation and good story. It represented another truly historical *first* in Lantz's distinguished career. Besides being a good cartoon, it marked the debut of Walter's foremost cartoon star, Woody Woodpecker. The film first opened in theaters on November 25, 1940, and induced a flurry of laughter from moviegoers all over.

Knock, Knock! is a truly fine cartoon that involves a marvelous conflict between brain and bird. The story opens with Andy asking his father if it's true that you can snatch a bird by putting salt on its tail. Just before Pop can answer, he hears a knock-knock-knocking sound. That continuous pounding sound is none other than Woody Woodpecker pecking away at the cottage roof. Eventually the bird bores a hole through the roof and reaches down to tweak Pop's nose. Then, with a wide grin, Woody says, "Guess who?" before issuing his first "ha-hah-ah-ha-ha" laugh on the screen. That prompts a chase unseen in cartoons in recent years. Pop grabs a rifle wanting to rid the world of this menacing bird. Andy tags along with a salt shaker, hoping to prove that the legendary salt myth does work. Once the chase winds down — with neither party apparently going to be successful in catching Woody — Andy catches the bird offguard and pours the entire shaker of salt on the bird's tail. Helplessly defeated, Woody can't move but does cry for help. Out of nowhere appear two other woodpeckers, one of whom tells Pop, "Confidentially, this guy's crazy." Moments later, the other two woodpeckers join in on the chorus of "ha-hah-hah-ha" laughs before hopping all over the place.

The cartoon received good reviews and brought tears of laughter to millions of theatergoers. A critic for *Showman's Trade Review* felt the cartoon was another solid addition to Lantz's Andy Panda series and would "entertain patrons, especially the kiddies."

Walter explains how Woody evolved: "My wife suggested that since I had animated animals like mice, rabbits and so forth, that maybe I should invent some kind of woodpecker character. I thought it was a good idea so I created Woody."

Lantz wasn't totally satisfied with Woody's first cartoon appearance, especially the drawing of the woodpecker. Woody was certainly more grotesque than any other cartoon character on the screen. Even Lantz agrees. "We weren't totally satisfied with Woody. He was one of the most grotesque looking characters I had ever seen. He had a very long bill, a short top knot, large yellow legs, and an all-blue body with a red vest. But over the years, we modified him," Lantz recalls. "That happens with a cartoon character. You look at the first Bugs Bunny, Mickey Mouse, or Donald Duck, and they didn't look anything like they do today. They've all gone through some changes, which is something you couldn't do with a live character."

Subsequent Woodys that Lantz directed included *Woody Woodpecker* (1941), which was the first cartoon in the series to use the character's name in the title of a cartoon. The film opens with Woody under observation by his fellow forest animals. They find the bird's looney behavior too much to bear, so they intimidate him into seeing a psychiatrist. Woody's visit doesn't result in his being committed but his doctor does wind up in an asylum, unable to put up with Woody's brash antics. Interestingly enough, the cartoon was originally to be called *The Cracked Nut*, which would have been a more appropriate title. In *The Screwdriver* (1941), Woody makes life miserable for a traffic cop as a careless driver, and battles a hunger-starved cat in *What's Cookin'?* (1941).

Veteran actor Mel Blanc supplied the voice for Woody in the first four or five cartoons. Later, Ben "Bugs" Hardaway was removed from the story department to replace Blanc, who had signed an exclusive contract to voice cartoons for Warner Brothers. Hardaway continued to act as a story man on Lantz cartoons in addition to his role as the voice of Woody.

In 1948, Hardaway was replaced when Lantz wanted a new artist to voice his woodpecker. Of those who auditioned on tape, the artist Lantz picked was Grace Stafford Lantz, his wife. She landed the job without Walter's knowing at first. Without informing her husband, Grace "tried out" as the voice of Woody. Walter was not present during the recording session and heard only the playback of each audition. After listening to some 50 taped auditions, Lantz was completely satisfied with his wife's and was surprised when he discovered whom he had hired. Certainly hiring Grace wasn't a mistake. She brought new life to Woody and made him seem chirpier than in earlier cartoons.

Lantz first employed his wife in the 1948 Woody Woodpecker cartoon, *Banquet Busters*. It was by her request that she didn't receive any voice credit in Woody cartoons until *Termites from Mars* was produced in 1952. Grace chose not to have her name listed because she didn't want children to become disillusioned if they knew a woman had voiced a woodpecker. As Lantz recalls, "It was proven later that this wasn't true. So we started giving her screen credit. And the reason I selected Gracie—having been in the theatre—was because she had very good diction. So when we speeded up the voice we didn't lose any of the diction in the dialogue, which was very important."

In addition to these cartoons, Lantz went on to direct three more Andy Panda cartoons in 1941 and two in 1942 before calling it quits as a director. He employed in his place such cartoon vets as James Culhane (who directed Lantz's favorite Woody cartoon, *The Barber of Seville*) and Dick Lundy (long a director at MGM) until the series' demise in 1949.

Lantz became primarily a cartoon producer, running the studio and spending time on creating new characters and story ideas. During the 1940s, he produced several new cartoon series, including Swing Symphonies (which were based on popular tunes of the day like "The Boogie Woogie Bugle Boy of Company B") and Musical Miniatures. Both series were usually billed as "Walter Lantz Cartune Specials." Walter continued in his new capacity as a producer right up into the 1950s. Throughout those years, Lantz had a reputable staff of well-seasoned cartoon directors—animators such as Alex Lovy, Dick Lundy, James Culhane, Don Patterson, Ray Patterson, Jack Hannah, Paul J. Smith, and Sid Marcus.

In 1951, Lantz returned to directing cartoons for reasons unclear. It is quite possible, knowing Lantz, that he missed the thrill of carrying the seed of an idea right through to completion. His first cartoon as a comeback director was *Wickety Wacket*, which has Woody playing croquet and disturbing a gopher who is sleeping in his home underneath the croquet lawn. In all, Lantz directed a total of five cartoons that year—all of them starring Woody

Woodpecker. Some others included *Slingshot 6 7/8*, in which Woody enters a shooting contest in a Western town and wins first prize with a slingshot as his weapon. In *Redwood Sap*, Woody forgets to save food for the winter and his begging induces no sympathy from the forest denizens. *Woody Woodpecker Polka*, a lively effort, has Woody crash a barn dance for free eats. Wally Walrus becomes his escort and the two stage a slapstick struggle over food.

Lantz decided to hang it up as a director after supervising just four cartoons in 1952. His first was *Born to Peck*, a film of flashbacks of Woody remembering the past when he was young, destructive, and sharp as a buzzard. Subsequent entries included *Stage Hoax*, in which Woody poses as a woman and hitches a stagecoach ride across the desert, and *Woodpecker in the Rough*, with Woody as a golf maniac.

Reducing himself to just a cartoon producer, Lantz left it up to his staff of directors to churn out new animated shorts. Walter didn't have much to worry about since his studio was running strong and his cartoons were still pulling in hefty box-office revenues. Woody was among the top ten moneymakers in the short subjects field, an honor he upheld for about a decade. But Lantz wasn't through creating new animated stars for theatrical distribution. It was as if each new year was another beginning, a new plateau to reach, a new territory to explore. Lantz had some other possibilities he wanted to explore — and explore them he did.

So it came as no surprise to moviegoers in 1952 when Lantz introduced a brand new character and his sixth cartoon series. The character was Chaplinesque; he scooted around street corners using Chaplin's one-legged stand, and at times was contagiously funny. Chilly Willy was his name, a character that soon became as popular as Woody Woodpecker. Chilly's first cartoon bore his own name, *Chilly Willy*, and was released on December 21, 1953. Paul J. Smith, whom Lantz describes as "a competent director and fantastic animator," was chosen to direct the pilot cartoon. The final results were so side-splitting that new cartoons were ordered and Chilly became a permanent screen star. Chilly went on to entertain moviegoers in about 35 more cartoons until the series was terminated in 1968. He was the second most successful cartoon star Lantz had invented, next to Woody Woodpecker.

Lantz soon discovered that his cartoons might have other outlets to screen in than theatres. In 1957, Walter developed the concept of a half-hour television series called *The Woody Woodpecker Show*. The show was first broadcast on ABC and was sponsored by Kellogg's for nine consecutive seasons. Each show was strung together by three theatrical cartoons and live footage of Lantz explaining how animated cartoons are made. The opening of each show combined cartoon and live footage of Woody and Lantz together, with his beloved woodpecker introducing him as "My boss, Walter Lantz."

Walter remembers the show with tremendous enthusiasm since it opened a flurry of offers from companies to produce Woody Woodpecker merchandise. The television show turned out to be another profitable venture for Lantz, one that was timely and entertaining for children and adult viewers. In discussing the series, Lantz's fondest memories are of the live segments he filmed on the process of cartoon animation. As he says, "It was a *first* for television. We showed the entire process of cartoon animation. The first segment was how I discovered Woody Woodpecker, and I made the first drawings of how Woody looked at the different stages. Every segment after that was five minutes showing every phase of cartoon production. The first was how Woody was created. Then, the next one showed how Andy Panda was created, and then we showed every phase: how a director worked on a storyboard, how the animation was done, inking and painting, sound, recording, and the voice artists. To my knowledge, it has never been done since!"

With the television show generating new revenue, Lantz continued to produce new cartoons for the theaters. By the 1960s, he trimmed the budgets of his cartoons and implemented limited animation, a style which used fewer cels per second. Having reduced his budgets, Lantz expanded on the number of cartoons he animated per season—now a total of 13. Woody Woodpecker remained his primary series, with Chilly Willy running a close second. Strewn among the package were additional cartoon series with such stars as the Beary Family, a cartoon adaptation of television's *The Life of Riley*, Inspector Willoughby, and Hickory, Dickory, and Doc. In addition, Lantz produced some public-service commercials with Woody. Because of his relatively high production, Lantz succeeded to become the single most active producer of theatrical cartoons up until 1973. It was then that his studio ceased production and Lantz laid off his staff.

Lantz found it was no longer feasible to produce cartoons for the theaters and expect to recoup production costs quickly. As Lantz says, "It sometimes took up to three years to realize your costs back. That was after publicity and distribution costs. There just wasn't any money left in theatrical cartoons. To produce them right today would cost about $90,000 a cartoon. When I saw that I couldn't do it anymore, that's when I decided to take a hiatus."

Although he's not animating new cartoons, Lantz doesn't want people to believe he's no longer in business. Each year, Universal Pictures reissues about 13 Lantz cartoons to 12,000 theatres in the United States, and in 72 countries around the world. Lantz says that some of the cartoon releases generate as much revenue today as the old ones did. In the meantime, Walter prepares new cartoon packages for television, supervises licensing of his cartoon characters, and lectures as colleges and animation festivals. Even *The Woody Woodpecker Show* has found new life in foreign television markets.

Recognizing his astonishing career, in 1980, the Motion Picture Academy of Arts and Science awarded Lantz with a Honorary Academy Award for his technical achievements in the field of cartoon animation. The award was rather fitting, especially since all Lantz wanted to do throughout his career was to entertain people. As Lantz recalls, "I was really very much surprised. In fact, I was so pleased that I did some animation of Woody—at my own expense—accepting the Oscar with me. It was just a great, great honor."

Lantz finds himself busy working on a second career. Besides minding his studio, Walter devotes much of his spare time to painting. His works, largely still lifes of his characters in landscapes, have been sold to art galleries in Hawaii and New York.

Looking back on his career, Lantz has no regrets—just fond memories of an industry that will never be the same. As he says, "I've had so many wonderful moments in this business, and the business has been very good to me. It's very hard to pick out one thing that's been great. But, you know, I've had my hits and misses on pictures. But I will say one thing, I've had more of my share of hits than misses."

Chapter 8

Dave Fleischer

Just mentioning the name Dave Fleischer stirs up some fond memories in the field of animated cartoons. Many remember the animated favorites he served up in the 1930s and 1940s. Others recall how he provided major innovations in animation and other achievements which have since gone unrivaled. Characters like Betty Boop, Popeye, Superman, and Gabby, were his primary cartoon stars. These and other series were produced at the Fleischer Studios, which Dave and his brother Max jointly ran.

On July 14, 1894, Dave became the fourth and second youngest son born to William and Amelia Fleischer. His parents emigrated to the United States from Austria, where Fleischer was born, in 1897, because of increasing persecution of European Jewry in that country.

The Fleischers made their new home on the same site where New York's Radio Music Hall stands today. Eventually William lost his lucrative position as tailor for B. Altman's, a lavish New York department store. Claiming unemployment was the Fleischer way of life for some time. This led to their moving from apartment to apartment until the rent was affordable.

Of the family there were five brothers, all of whom worked at the Fleischer Studios. The eldest was Charles, followed by Max, Joe, Dave, and Lou. They had one sister, Ethel. Dave was the least inspired of the brothers. He loathed school and found other interests than the subjects he was forced to learn. During his preteen years, Fleischer became upset because the public school he attended lacked one important but basic subject, an introduction to art. Art was one of the second great wonders of the world to Fleischer. He often incorporated his artistic ideas on paper for something as menial as his mother's shopping list. Rather than list the items by name only, Dave drew sketches that corresponded with the grocery product. Thus he penned circles for salt, dots for pepper, and squares for sugar. Everything Dave saw in life was completely visual; the ideas just spilled out of him.

His father took notice of Dave's knack for drawing and put him to work after he graduated from school. William had Dave draw designs of the latest fashions out of store windows and sold patterns of them to nearby clothing stores.

Through with his job, Dave went on to secure various odd jobs. His first was as usher of the Palace Theatre in New York. There he took great pride in his work, making sure that the brass was polished and the aisles were spotless. It not only furnished Dave with regular income but a chance to take notes while watching animated cartoons.

When Dave grew out of the job, he pursued something more creative. He went on to work for the Walker Engraving Company, where he began as an errand boy before moving his way up to the art department. Later, at age 18, he left the engraving firm to become a cutter at Pathé Films.

In the meantime, brother Max was exerting himself as an errand boy for the Brooklyn Daily Eagle. His life dream — sort of a local boy makes good ambition — was to become an artist for the Eagle. Four years later, Max made his way up to artist and his career in cartooning started to show promise.

There he became friends with John Randolph Bray, a senior artist for the Eagle and later a pioneer in cartoon animation. Bray stayed on not much longer; he wanted to pursue a career as a freelance cartoonist. He penned several popular strips for numerous comic weeklies, including "Puck," "Life," and "Judge." Max remained loyal to the Eagle a short time longer but then accepted a higher paying position as retoucher and photoengraver with a Boston commercial art studio. With the march of time, Max Fleischer lost all contact with Bray for about eight years.

One of Max's greatest interests was mechanics. It played an important role later in his career when he created several astounding technical innovations in the field of animation. Actually, historians have noted that Max Fleischer's interest in animation was likely inspired by his fascination with mechanics. He became so imbued with mechanics that he took on a prestigious job as art editor for Popular Science Monthly.

Learning various techniques of mechanics served as a springboard to a much heralded career in cartoon animation. It began shortly before the outbreak of World War I. Dave and Max had been unsatisfied up until that time with the results of other cartoonists' animated films. The one cartoon subject they took note of the most was Winsor McCay's Gertie the Trained Dinosaur. It was not, as many believe, the first cartoon but it was the first extensive piece of animation to receive critical acclaim. The outstanding response to McCay's cartoon inspired other artists to follow in his footsteps. The cartoon boom had begun.

Among the artists priming themselves for production of one-reel cartoons were the Fleischer brothers. When Dave was off his day shift at Pathé, he rushed to his brother's house to help finish inventing a revolutionary piece of machinery in cartoon animation: the Rotoscope. This device was a vertical lightboard that magnified onto a table a single frame of film. Max's idea was to trace live footage frame-by-frame to achieve lifelike motion. He was searching for fluid motion in animation, which was lacking in other cartoons. Dave and Max copied the actions of a live actor on film and made him into a cartoon character.

The actor selected to go before the camera was Dave. He wore a puffy sleeved clown suit with large white buttons and performed somersaults before the camera. The result was the birth of Koko the Clown, a character featured in a series of Out of the Inkwell cartoons.

Dave was actually Koko with some exaggerations in the sketchings before coming to the screen as one of the earliest cartoon marvels. The pilot film was well received by critics and encouraged the Fleischers to produce additional films. Dave let brother Max handle the business end of selling the project, since he continued to work full time as a cutter for Pathé Films.

One of the first studios Max approached was Paramount Pictures. The studio had been turning out a tremendous volume of cartoons produced by J.R. Bray. He was the same Bray that Fleischer had been associated with during his years on the *Brooklyn Eagle*. Unfortunately, Max's appointment to screen his pilot was with a man who knew very little about the potential of animated cartoons. His name was Adolph Zukor, president of Paramount Pictures. Fortunately Max had a chance to meet Bray, who told him that he had an exclusive contract to supply Paramount with short-subject material. So before Zukor had a sporting chance to judge Fleischer's cartoon proposal, Bray gave his opinion. He thought it was an ostentatious and inventive film and hired Max to produce one Inkwell cartoon a month.

Response to the new series was overwhelming. On April 21, 1919, a critic for the *New York Times* wrote: "One's first reflection after seeing this bit of work is, 'Why doesn't Mr. Fleischer do more?' After a deluge of pen-and-ink comedies in which the figures move with mechanical jerks with little or no wit to guide them, it is a treat to watch the smooth motion of Mr. Fleischer's figure and enjoy the cleverness that animates it." Months later that same reviewer said: "Mr. Fleischer's work by its wit of conception and skill of execution makes the general run of animated cartoons seem dull and crude."

Such raves were not uncommon for Fleischer cartoons, especially for the Inkwell series. Koko was a remarkable character; his fluid movement attracted favorable response but it was the novel idea of combining live footage with animation that saved these films. The stock opening of each film had Koko materialize out of a cartoonist's inkwell or pen. Unitl he was placed in some animated situation, Koko harrassed the animator constantly. Max was the animator; Dave continued to pose as Koko for the Rotoscope drawings.

One of the Fleischers' greatest challenges was coming up with a different opening each week. One week Koko was drawn in pieces—held together by a wire—which merged together when the string was pulled. Or ink came toppling out from an inkwell with this large blotch transforming into Koko. Another clever opener was Koko—instead of Fleischer—drawing the entire live setting and Max himself.

The Inkwell series was a proud achievement for the Fleischers, especially for Dave. As a youngster Dave wasn't one to pursue his ability as an artist as much as Max. He never took the matter of drawing too serious. Somehow over the years he changed his attitude and became a genius behind the screen.

Much of the Inkwell series' success goes to Dave. It was he who directed the most ingenious cartoons and invented clever gags that topped his competitors. Dave gained the edge in the way he directed the series and in how he handled his staff of animators. He gave them, in effect, creative freedom while animating scenes for a particular gag. Dave never stopped his animators from interjecting ideas of their own into a specific gag. Giving his staff that much free rein was, of course, unheard of at other studios.

Around the second to last season of Inkwell cartoons, in 1924, a new series was born to the screen: the Bouncing Ball cartoons. Animator Seymour Kneitel created the series, which was based on popular song titles of that day. Sing-along films were not a unique idea but became a great method to stimulate audience participation. Song slides showing lyrics of well-known tunes were a staple in theaters as far back as the 1890s. Either a live singer or a musician invited the audience to sing-along before the theatre organist began to play along.

The Fleischers' series was the first to bring movement to what was otherwise known as "a static presentation." Thus the beginning of sing-along films served as a means of two-way communication. It emphasized the meaning of the song — through its lyrics and music — and generated a positive response from the audience.

The first Song Car-Tune, *Oh, Mabel*, was animated by Dick Huemer and premiered at New York's Circle Theatre. Huemer recalls that the audience reaction was so strong that "the theatre manager had to rewind the film and run it again." The motion of the bouncing ball was achieved by photographing a Fleischer employee waving a stick over a line of lyrics. Attached to the end of the stick was a fluorescent ball the size of a golf ball. It stood out among the lyrics since they were white letters on a flexible black showcard.

Theatre organists provided the musical accompaniment for the Song Car-Tunes since sound hadn't been invented. One organist, Harry J. Jenkins, played for the series in Boston. In an article for *Theatre Organ Bombarde*, he recalls: "I played for many bouncing ball song films in Boston theatres between 1924 and 1927. Sometimes they had been used in other theatres before coming to mine, and arrived with some frames missing — something I didn't discover until rehearsal — if we had one. It was a puzzle to follow the ball as it bounced completely past two words to a third, at the expense of a couple of measures of music. Somehow we still managed and the audience sang along."

Some films featured Koko with his sidekick Fitz the dog. One of the more amusing Bouncing Ball cartoons is *In the Good Old Summertime* (1924). The film introduces Koko as a conductor of a musical orchestra, with Fitz at his side. The broad visual imagination of Dave Fleischer permeates this cartoon, especially when Koko grabs Fitz and shakes him violently into the shape of a tuning fork. Koko strikes his new tuning fork against the music stand and his orchestra begins to play. Some frames later, the tuning fork metamorphoses back to Fitz.

Even though the Song Car-Tunes had a unique sound of their own, Dave and Max had a burning desire to invent something even better. Dr. Lee DeForest, who was experimenting with talking pictures, produced in association with the Fleischers a series of synchronized sound films called "Phonofilms." The first two films didn't draw rave reviews nor did DeForest's sound invention.

But DeForest wasn't about to build from scratch and start all over. He devoted much of his time signing name performers to appear in his films, hoping that would increase their box-office value. Dave Fleischer proposed that DeForest incorporate his sound process with sing-along films. That actually seemed like the most appropriate format for the patented synchronized sound process DeForest had invented.

So as it turned out that—four years before Walt Disney's *Steamboat Willie* —the Fleischers produced a series of synchronized sound cartoons with DeForest. The first film, *My Old Kentucky Home*, emphasizes a marvelous blend of singing talent in the Metropolitan Quartet, with Jimmy Flora at the organ. Since the sound process was unrefined, the sound and the lips of characters were not synchronized—but the film came off strikingly deliberate, as precise as possible. Fleischer could at least look upon the first production as a beginning to a new revolution in movie cartooning. As always, Dave and Max were one step ahead of their competitors: one reason for their prolonged success.

The sing-along cartoons continued to reap modest rewards due to the addition of sound. But fast approaching it was the Inkwell series. These films didn't short-circuit until around 1929 when imaginative ideas were in as short supply as money to keep the series afloat. The cartoons produced in the late 1920s showed the same strengths and weaknesses as earlier cartoon entries. The films were either good or inherently bad on all counts.

It was between 1927 and 1929 that some titles began featuring less live footage and more cartoon animation. The blend of live action with animation hadn't lost appeal; rather, the Fleischers could no longer afford the luxury of combining the two media. That especially held true when sound cartoons came of age after Walt Disney's synchronized sound release, *Steamboat Willie* (1928). The film, like many of Fleischer's productions, revolutionized the cartoon industry. It put some studios out of business and prompted others to adapt to sound if they wanted to survive.

Because live action and animation were so expensive, the Fleischers found other means of showing off their ideas. They resorted instead to gimmicks, or one-laugh ideas. In *Koko's Earth Control*, for example, Fitz yanks the lever that bears the warning sign, "Danger/Beware—if this handle is pulled, the world will come to an end." The world doesn't exactly stop dead, but through a fantastic array of camera tricks, it goes berserk! Everyday actions of people walking and driving are accelerated to spin-wheeling speeds. Buildings slide to one side as the earth tilts. Pedestrians find themselves in a self-induced demonstration of slip and slide on the sidewalks. These are comical, mischievous moments carefully animated by Fleischer and his staff. Dave showed in cartoons like this one that imagination can sometimes be as entertaining as stock technical gimmicks like live action with animation—maybe better.

With the addition of sound to the Fleischers' cartoons in 1929, the studio took a stronger stand on venturing into new possibilities. Like their peers, the Fleischer brothers had run the gamut with silent cartoons. The studio's new direction seemed predetermined. Sound cartoons gave filmmakers and theatre exhibitors a new product and the business of animation a new breath of life. Every major cartoon studio, including the Fleischers, abandoned silent cartoons and centered their attention on dreaming up new films produced in sound.

The Fleischers were among the first to unveil their newest sound series (Disney, of course, beat everybody by introducing Mickey Mouse sound cartoons in 1928) to moviegoers and film exhibitors. The series drew tremendous attention in trade papers. Paramount went so far as to run a full-page advertisement promoting the series: "Paramount *Talkartoons* are something entirely new and entirely different from anything ever seen and heard before. For the first time cartoons will be actually talking pictures, not merely cartoons synchronized after their creation. By a special process, the cartoon figures will actually talk. The novelty value alone of *Talkartoons* will make them successful. But, in addition, they will tell complete stories and be brilliantly entertaining."

Notice that Paramount's ad calls the series "actually talking pictures," something that wasn't fully realized. The Fleischers went instead with the idea of synchronizing the dialogue and music in their films after the animation had been completed. Thus, not much emphasis was placed on precise lip movement and dialogue was kept to a minimum. Much like Paul Terry's *Terrytoons*, the crux of these Talkartoons were shaped around a ragtime musical score and there was very little emphasis on strong characterizations.

In order to promote the *newness* of this all-talking series, the Fleischers retired Koko the Clown and spent hours formulating cartoon stories that didn't fit into a specific formula. Changes were also made in the style of animation. Gone was the silent film technique of black-and-white line drawings in favor of full-animation cels and backgrounds. The change brought on additional expense since more animators had to be hired to command the heavy workload of animation. Another important addition was Lou Fleischer, who because of his musical knowledge was put in charge of supervising the music for the Fleischer cartoons. Since the studio didn't have a musical director, Lou Fleischer purchased the rights to existing Paramount records and used songs from them as musical soundtracks. Songs incorporated into their cartoons included "Mimi," "Isn't It Romantic," "Beyond the Blue Horizon," and "Love Me Tonight."

The dialogue for *Talkartoons* was what Dave Fleischer called "post-synched." In other words, Dave provided some metrical breakdown on the dialogue. An example would be the line, "I'm going to the store." The animators would take the line and animate the exact number of frames necessary for the precise lip movement of the character. After the scene was animated, a voice performer dubbed in the chosen line of dialogue. As Al Eugster, one of the Fleischers' animators, recalls: "The dialogue was very stilted because of the metrical breakdown." But the technique did have its advantages, since it offered the voice performers a chance to ad-lib under their breath, something that gave the Popeye cartoons tremendous magic.

Unlike rival directors of cartoon series, Dave Fleischer didn't have typewritten scripts for the *Talkartoon* series. Instead, he supplied a rough story idea and had the head animator lay it out, stage it, and break it up into scenes. Because scripts were never used, Fleischer had no control over the amount of footage that was animated. Showing that he wasn't a traditionalist, Fleischer didn't time his scenes to musical bar sheets like other cartoon directors. Timing scenes to musical bar sheets was supposedly a way of keeping the action well paced and animated with precision. Dave chose the unorthodox method of ad-libbing his way through eight-minutes and kept adding gags until he was satisfied. For the sake of accuracy, Fleischer did have two of his animators check over each scene and retime them.

Sometimes Dave became so gag-happy that he drove animators silly. In

The Peanut Vendor, for instance, a scene was already planned in which a monkey jumped from bar to bar to shake loose some fleas from his body. With the scene almost animated, Fleischer told animator Myron Waldman to hold off on finishing it because he wanted to insert another gag. The gag Dave dreamed up involved a flea falling from the monkey to the ground and being taken away by two fellow fleas on a stretcher. Fortunately, Waldman convinced Dave that there was no room for the gag because the scene was being animated to a recorded song.

Fleischer's brand of humor has been described as "broad, direct, and somewhat vulgar." Animator Shamus Culhane remembers that Dave's style of comedy was "just a reflection of his ethnic background. He had this very vigorous style that was earthy, crude, but honest." Culhane later added that animators had no problems adapting to Fleischer's humor because they responded by embellishing it with ideas of their own. Story conferences for *Talkartoons* lasted about an hour, with scripts usually focusing on a basic plot or subplot.

The third cartoon of the series, *Hot Dog*, resurrected the character Bimbo from the Inkwell series. Dave Fleischer was hoping that Bimbo could compete with such cartoon luminaries as Mickey Mouse, Bosko, and Oswald the Rabbit. The cartoon opens with Bimbo driving his automobile when, suddenly, he spots a girl roller skating. The girl is gorgeous, sporting large breasts and a shapely bathing beauty figure. Bimbo pulls alongside of her and tries to pick her up. The girl resists and Bimbo goes in hot pursuit after her. During his chase, he exceeds the speed limit and ends up being pulled over by a traffic cop. The entire scene results in Bimbo's appearing in court. He explains his testimony by playing a banjo and singing to the judge and courtroom jury. His ambitious exhibition results in beguiling the entire court—including the judge—to dance frenetically to the sounds of his banjo. As a result of his wild but entertaining session, Bimbo is set free without bail.

The cartoon, in addition to celebrating Bimbo's return to the screen, marked Lou Fleischer's introduction to his brother's cartoon studio. He supplied the musical soundtracks for the film and assisted in recording sound for each picture. Lou Fleischer was hired at a starting salary of $100 a week, but that soon changed to $125. Lou didn't complain because he realized that $100 a week was considered a sizeable amount during those Depression years.

After producing several more *Talkartoons* starring Bimbo, Dave decided to terminate Bimbo as the series' star. He found that Bimbo couldn't compete with studio rivals like Mickey Mouse or Oswald the Rabbit. To further complicate matters, Fleischer's animators never animated Bimbo the same for every cartoon. Sometimes he was drawn as a white dog, while other times he appeared as a black dog. Shamus Culhane cites this inconsistency as arising because Dave Fleischer "didn't want to be tied down to a certain way of drawing characters." Beside some changes in appearance, Bimbo's voice fluctuated to different levels in every cartoon. His voice was deeper than most of his cartoon contemporaries and more human and realistic than, let's say, Mickey Mouse.

But Bimbo's return to the animated film hardly compares to the most significant Talkartoon produced that same year. *Dizzy Dishes*, the sixth cartoon of the series, introduced a character who later became known as Betty Boop.

She wasn't as attractive in earlier Talkartoons as she was in later Fleischer cartoons. That was due mainly to her dog-like appearance. Betty was one of the screen's oddest-looking characters; she had long dog ears, large jowls (similar to Richard Nixon's), a button nose, and gave every indication that she was a dog. Grim Natwich, who later animated for Ub Iwerks and Walt Disney, invented Betty in the mold of singer Helen Kane (who was, incidentally, a Paramount star). Natwick has said that he first conceived Betty from looking at a song sheet with Kane on the cover. Grim took the basic features of Kane and blended them with his conception of a French poodle, thus giving cinemagoers their first glimpse of Betty Boop. Legend has it that animators had distinct problems in animating Betty because she didn't have a visible neck, her thighs were too wide, and her fingers were fat and frog-like. Fleischer's staff soon overcame these complications as the character went through periodic changes with each Talkartoon episode.

Because of certain changes, Betty began to figure more prominently in Fleischer cartoons around 1931. By then she had established herself as one of the screen's most eminent cartoon stars and was no longer considered "supporting material." Instead, Betty became a star of her own series and was supported in each adventure by Bimbo and Koko the Clown, who was brought out of retirement. Dave Fleischer was responsible for making Betty world renowned since he standardized her appearance and made her more feminine, removing the dog ears and dog nose. These modifications were quite apparent in the 1932 Talkartoon, *Any Rags*. It was in this cartoon that her dog ears were reduced to earrings. The loss of her dog features gave Betty a good deal of winsome qualities and a new status as a sex goddess.

However, historians have recorded the Talkartoon release, *Minnie the Moocher*, as the first in which Betty exhibits any real personality. The cartoon had additional historical value since it was the first Boop cartoon to feature a big name talent: Cab Calloway and his orchestra provided some exciting moments by appearing in the film. Calloway was rotoscoped as a ghost walrus who dances to the sounds of the orchestra. The scene appears later in the film when Betty—despondent over life at home—runs away and asks Bimbo to come with her. Their first stop is inside a cave for shelter. There they meet the singing walrus Calloway, whose ghostly presence turns them snowball white with fright. After the film, Betty became known world-wide as a Jewish princess and was compared to another sex symbol of the cinema, Mae West. Betty was in every sense of the word just adorable.

Calloway appeared in other Boop cartoons, including *Old Man of the Mountain* and *Snow White*. People like Calloway were induced to appear in Fleischer cartoons at a reduced rate, since Paramount promised to book their act in the company's theatre chain. Other stars who became frequent guests in Boop cartoons were Rubinoff the famous violinist, Don Redman and the Royal Samoans with Miri.

Dave Fleischer took advantage of Betty's tremendous sex appeal and made use of it in every cartoon. As a result, a good majority of the stories had sexual overtones to them. In one of her 1933 episodes, *Boop-Ooop-a-Doop*, Betty is propositioned by Boss, the proprietor of a local circus. This leads to a violent tussle between the ringmaster and Betty, who won't give in. During the film's final minutes, the ringmaster is subdued and Bimbo and Koko ask Betty if she's all right. She says, "Nope, he couldn't take my boop-oop-a-doop."

Another sex-oriented film was *Is My Palm Read?* In this cartoon adventure, Betty's sexual values are exploited when she visits a nearby palm reader, Professor Bimbo. He turns out the lights upon her entrance into his mind-reading room so that he can get a peek of Betty's silhouette—thanks mainly to her "see-through-skirt." In retrospect, these sexual themes were common and enjoyable teasers in Fleischer cartoons. Even dating back to Bimbo's return in *Hot Dog*, there was within the film a sexual innuendo. Using sex as a topic gave Betty Boop cartoons tremendous appeal in the 1930s, appeal which runs strong even today.

Betty was, of course, portrayed as a flirt and tease who managed to keep her sexual desires under control. Her image as a sexy playmate was toned down in the mid-1930s when stricter censorship laws were enforced against cartoons and live films which contained sexual implications. Because of the Hays Office, a movie censorship board then in operation, Betty underwent some substantial revisions. Gone was the garter, the short skirt, the décolletage that made her so unique. In its place was a more fully clothed Betty, a character stripped of her charm. Betty became a bachelor girl who showed no interest in men whatsoever.

Stricter film codes not only resulted in Betty's ultimate demise, but in the eventual house-cleaning of her supporting characters. Gone as well were the wonderful animals that populated her films, including Bimbo and Koko. Other cartoon characters were introduced, primarily those who had established themselves as comic strip stars. They included Carl Anderson's Henry, Jimmy Swinnerton's Little Jimmy, and Otto Soglow's The Little King (who starred in a series of cartoons for Van Beuren). None of them meshed as well with Betty, resulting in quick exits for most of them.

The best character to appear in post-Code Betty Boop's was Grampy, a sage old inventor whose profession inspired some truly remarkable gags from the Fleischer team. His film debut was *Betty Boop and Grampy* (1935), which has Grampy using his ingenuity to liven up a dull party. He later starred in *Grampy's Indoor Outing* (1936), a story that has Grampy quieting Junior's disappointment over not going to a rained-out carnival by turning the inside of his apartment into an amusement park! One of his last films was *Housecleaning Blues* (1937). Fleischer historian Leslie Cabarga believes that the Fleischers showed special interest in Grampy because he reflected their own fondness for mechanical tinkering.

The primary voice of Betty Boop was Mae Questel, who later became known as Aunt Bluebell in television margarine commercials. There were several other women who voiced Betty, including Margie Heinz, Kate Wright, Bonnie Poe, and Ann Rothschild.

Rothschild did the voice of Betty after the first cartoon, *Dizzy Dishes*, until Questel took over in the early thirties. Both women visually resembled Betty, which may have been the reason Fleischer hired them. He could use them for personal appearances and other promotional tours involving the character.

The Talkartoon series wasn't renamed until after the release of *Betty Boop Limited* in July, 1932. Naming the series after Betty was appropriate since she *was* the series!

Although Dave Fleischer continued to direct new Betty Boops, he thrived for new cartoon series ideas. Boop cartoons were rapidly becoming an old commodity, one that couldn't be a marketable item forever. Betty's role in the series had been reduced to minor appearances, with other subordinate characters receiving more time on the screen. It became a distressing situation for the Fleischer team.

Fortunately, another series had been under way, one that endured long after the Fleischers left Paramount. The series was the jocular adventures of Popeye the Sailor. Popeye first came into the cartoon world in 1919 when Elzie Segar, a world famous comic strip artist, first conceived the musclebound sailor in the classic strip, *Thimble Theatre*. Originally, Popeye was spotlighted as the character Ham Gravy opposite his stick-like girl friend, Olive Oyl. As the strip grew in popularity, Segar began to experiment more with the character. About a decade later, after giving Gravy a facelift, Segar introduced the character as Popeye in his strip on January 17, 1929.

Even then, Popeye displayed most of the same features that moviegoers became accustomed to in later cartoons: a gruff, straight-talking, hard-hitting sailor who didn't take guff from anybody. The sailor's first appearance was so well received that Segar made him a regular in the strip. In 1932, when Max Fleischer negotiated film rights to King Features' comic strip characters, he bought the rights to Popeye. Segar's strip had long been a favorite of Max's, thus prompting him to secure film rights to the strip. Max paid for the rights even though he thought Popeye was "a nutty little creature." As he later added: "But I thought I could do something with him."

Living up to his word, Fleischer assigned young Dave to direct the first cartoon to star Popeye, *Popeye the Sailor* (1933), which was actually a Betty Boop cartoon. It was Max's idea to feature Popeye as an *extra* to measure public reaction. However, Popeye's role became more than a cameo—he was the star! Betty Boop's part was incidental.

The film was undoubtedly one of the most memorable animated moments in film history. In the opening shot, a newspaper headline spins into the picture—complete with a front page picture of the sailor—and proclaims: "Popeye a movie star—The sailor with the sock accepts movie contracts!" Holding tight on the newspaper, the camera catches Popeye as he comes to life off the front page to immortalize for the first time his expository song, "I'm Popeye the Sailor Man." Throughout the ballad, Popeye shows off his man-of-steel strength. He does everything from sock an anchor into tiny remnants to punching a clock into a legion of smaller ones. At the scene's end, Popeye utters his first words: "Well, blow me down!"

The film dissolves to Olive Oyl waiting on a dock for her sailor to come home. Scores of sailors approach Olive, who promptly kicks them out of the scene. Even Bluto hopes to make time with Olive—but Popeye squelches his efforts.

Popeye restores order and takes Olive to a carnival. Bluto follows them, hoping to outdo Popeye at all the carnival games. In a later sequence, a hula dancing Betty Boop lures Popeye up on stage to dance with her. In the meantime, Bluto steals Olive and ties her to a railroad track. Hearing Olive's distress call—"Help, Popeye! Help!"—the free-swinging sailor comes to the rescue. He punches Bluto into a coffin and saves Olive from an oncoming locomotive. Afterwards, Popeye declares triumphantly, "I'm Popeye the Sailor Man … toot! toot!"

Limiting his appearance in the cartoon was most certainly a wise decision by Dave Fleischer. He obviously recalled past mistakes animators had made in transforming a comic strip character to film. Most of the characters weren't fully developed enough to star in films of their own. But Popeye was certainly ready.

Critics lauded him as a marvelous new addition to the Fleischer cartoon family, later resulting in their officially launching a Popeye cartoon series some months later. His first cartoon, *I Yam What I Yam*, was first shown to moviegoers on September 29, 1933.

Veteran screen actor William Costello was picked to voice Popeye (who went under the Pseudonym of Red Pepper Sam). His previous stage and film experience included a regular part as Gus Gorilla on the Betty Boop radio show. Despite a good sounding voice, Max didn't feel that Costello's was *muscular* enough; Dave and brother Lou felt otherwise, however, so Costello stayed.

The actor lost his job when he became impossible to handle. The inevitable popularity that had thrust Costello into the limelight blew up his ego beyond recall. Costello soon thought no matter how steep his demands, they should be met. Demanding a vacation during mid-production became his undoing. Max Fleischer fired him. A short time later, a search began for his replacement. Dave Fleischer has said the talent hunt was more difficult than he first anticipated. Little did Dave realize that Costello's successor was right under his nose.

There was an inbetweener in the cartoon department who imitated Popeye to the delight of his peers. His voice impression was so good that Fleischer set up an audition. Trying out as the sailor wasn't too difficult for Jack Mercer, the man most remembered as the voice of Popeye. He had every mannerism, nuance, and voice inflection down to perfection. Jack even inserted occasional mutterings between lines that Fleischer kept in the cartoons. Most of his under-the-breath ad-libs make the Popeye cartoons simply priceless to watch.

Mae Questel, long the voice of Betty Boop, provided the same charm in Olive Oyl. Her side squalling voice for the character, Questel says, was inspired by Zasu Pitts. Lines like, "Yoo-hoo. Popeye, Here I ya-a-yam!" gave Olive the same dumb-like charm of Gracie Allen.

The first day of taping, Mercer over-extended his vocal chords. Dave Fleischer treated his sore throat with candies and sodas but nothing worked and they wound up choosing the best takes for the cartoon. Fortunately, Mercer never experienced that problem again.

Popeye cartoons were constructed differently from Betty Boop's. Popeye cartoons had more of a story; Betty Boops consisted mostly of gags. In the Popeye series, sight gags were kept to a minimum and there was generally more dialogue in the films. By comparison, Boop cartoons employed very little dialogue and applied more music and short situations into the context of the story.

Dave Fleischer built the entire Popeye series around a minimum of stories as well. He had about five basic ideas that were reworked throughout Popeye's long theatrical run. Some basic plots included the supposed fickleness of women, especially Olive Oyl's.

In *Barnacle Bill*, Olive leaves Popeye for Barnacle Bill, whom she believes is a much tougher sailor. Popeye, of course, reacts violently to win back his sweetheart. The same applies in *Clean Shaven Man*. This time around Olive makes it clear she can only fall for a clean-shaven man. As a result, Popeye and Bluto battle it out to see who'll be the cleanest shaven of the two. While in the midst of battle, they spot Olive leaving a barber shop with another man, who has long hair and a beard!

Another winning formula was the "all that work for nothing" syndrome. In *Olive's Sweepstakes Ticket*, Popeye searches industriously for a first prize sweepstakes ticket Olive has carelessly lost. Regaining the ticket, Popeye learns that the coveted prize is nothing more than a caged parrot! Popeye goes to a similar trouble to help out Olive in *Females Is Fickle*. This time Olive sends him after her goldfish, who's fallen into the sea and can't swim. Popeye finally recovers the fish — but Olive feels he's lonely and sets him free!

Another recurring theme was "kindness to animals." In *Be Kind to Animals*, Popeye and Olive are shown feeding the birds in a park. They spot Bluto shamelessly whipping a horse, excluding no mean trick in the book: he even drinks the horse's trough dry. Turning livid with rage, Popeye comes to the rescue of the poor abused horse. He beats Bluto, straps him to the horse's harness, and whips him for good measure. The end provides a clever twist as Bluto finds himself the recipient of his own medicine.

Equally amusing is *Leave Well Enough Alone*. The film opens with Popeye buying all the animals from Olive's pet shop to set them free. But the animals find life so terrible on the outside that they return to the confines of their cages. All Popeye can say is, "Well, blow me down!"

There were also stories involving Bluto and Popeye lusting for another woman. Olive just wasn't good enough! In *Never Kick a Woman*, Popeye melts upon meeting a Mae West-like gym teacher. She's just what the doctor ordered! To win Popeye back, Olive gulps down a can of spinach and clobbers the buxom sexpot to parts unknown. A similar theme resulted in *Hospitaliky*. Bluto and Popeye try to severely injure themselves to wind up in the hospital under the care of nurse Olive Oyl (who Popeye describes as "just beautiful"). The boys try all sorts of suicidal attempts to guarantee them a free ambulance ride to the hospital — but nothing works. Finally, Popeye resorts to a trick unseen in previous cartoons. He feeds Bluto spinach so that Bluto can beat him up badly enough to warrant a trip to the hospital.

By the mid-thirties, Dave Fleischer continued to direct Popeye and focused his attentions on territories unexplored. His brother Max and studio technician John E. Burks had coinvented a three-dimensional process for animated cartoons. The process, which was originally filed for patent in 1933, was introduced a year later.

The machine responsible for producing the effect was built on a revolving turntable 12 feet in diameter, with elaborate miniature sets of various backgrounds constructed and placed near the back of the turntable. Completing the structure was a steel frame where cels were filmed with a deep background behind it, culminating in a tridimensional effect. Dave first introduced the Turntable process in a series of gentle fables called, *Color Classics*. The series pilot featured Betty Boop in a fairy-tale spoof entitled *Poor Cinderella* (1934). Because of Disney's tight patent on three-strip Technicolor, the earliest Color Classics were filmed in two-strip color (The cartoon, *Somewhere in Dreamland*, 1936, was the first to employ the full three-strip color process.) Of those critics who saw *Cinderella*, a reviewer for *Motion Picture Herald* wrote: "The use of color immeasurably enhances the effectiveness of the subject, and its origin should make the number especially appealing to youngsters."

The story goes that Max Fleischer adapted the idea of a fable series from Disney's *Silly Symphonies*. Max wasn't the first animator to emulate Disney. Other less competitive studio animators — like Ub Iwerks and Burt Gillett — tried to compete with kindred cartoon series. Max did a remarkable job in animating a bright, sentimental series that rivaled Disney. Dave's direction was razor-sharp and well paced. The secret to success was keeping the characters believable and the stories uncontrived. Most of Dave's cartoons personified suburban life — a formula he utilized in most of his films.

One of the most engaging efforts in the 1934 season was *Little Dutch Mill*. The story involves two Dutch children, Hans and Frieda, and their pet duck spying on a sinister miser. Catching the children, the miser ties them up and growls, "No one knows about my gold. I've kept my secret well. When I burn your tongues out, even you won't tell." The scene generates a tremendous amount of realism and empathy for the children. As expected, the miser's efforts to torch the children are thwarted by the townspeople who rescue Hans and Frieda. They seize the miser and sentence him to a bath, a haircut, and new clothes, which prompts him to remark, "Not that!" Although the ending surprises no one, the cartoon is brightly colored and keeps filmgoers on the edge of their seats.

Another solid production was *Christmas Comes But Once a Year*, which was released December 4, 1936. The cartoon opens on Christmas morning at an orphanage. The little urchins rise to find out what Santa Claus has brought them. Bright smiles and good cheer fill the room until the orphans' gifts begin to break. Outside, Grampy hears all the commotion and decides to rectify the situation. He notices the children are wallowing in their sorrow. Hoping to revive their good spirits, Grampy charges into the orphanage kitchen and throws everything in the room into one massive pile. Out of the assorted hardware, Grampy creates countless numbers of ingenious toys. Later, he dresses up like Santa Claus and delivers the new toys to the children. The cartoon bars nothing imaginative and makes the screen glimmer as the toys come to life — thanks in large part to the 3-D process.

Matching this superior cartoon is *Greedy Humpty Dumpty* (1936). Fleischer takes the colorful tale of Humpty Dumpty and gives it a full-blown treatment. Instead of being humble, Humpty reigns as a frugal ruler of Mother

Goose Land who likes to count his riches. Desiring more wealth, he gazes out his parlor window at the sun. The golden rays of the sun prompt Humpty to believe its core to be as solid as gold. Setting his designs on the sun, Humpty orders his makers to build a castle wall as high as the sun. Once completed, the King climbs to the planet and thrusts his axe into the surface. There he hopes to dig out the gold he believes exists. Rather than strike gold, Humpty's incision triggers an eruption of lightning bolts and explosions that send him toppling down to Earth. He cracks upon impact, and as the story goes, "All the king's horses and all the king's men couldn't put Humpty back together again." Nicely executed, the idea of turning Humpty into a money-monger proves to be good entertainment. Fleischer continued to produce similar fairy-tale spoofs until he discontinued the series in 1937.

With the 3-D process a success, the Fleischers decided to experiment even further with his technique. Max went on to produce a couple of experimental Popeye cartoons using the Turntable process. The first production, *Popeye the Sailor Meets Sinbad the Sailor* (1936), was the first of three two-reel Fleischer specials starring Popeye. Besides introducing Popeye featurettes, the cartoons marked the first Popeye cartoon. Most theaters treated them like features and made them the main attraction. Not bad for a 20-minute cartoon!

(Although Max Fleischer was the first to experiment with the three-dimensional process, animator Ub Iwerks conceived a similar technique — called "multiple animation" — which he spotlighted in the 1934 ComiColor cartoon, *The Headless Horseman*.)

Dave was commissioned to direct the three films, performing a superb job as usual. *Sinbad* is undoubtedly the best of the three. It is a clever, funny, and imaginative short that outdoes some of the best Popeye cartoons in terms of laughs. The animation is well drawn and the wide spectrum of rainbow colors complements the final product. The story concerns Bluto as Sinbad who lives on a remote island. Offshore, Bluto spots a ship heading towards the island with three passengers aboard: Popeye, Olive Oyl, and Wimpy. Bluto naturally focuses his attention on Olive and casts designs on making her a queen of the island. To fulfill his fantasy, Bluto orders his pet condor to destroy the vessel and bring back the girl. The condor proves successful in snatching Olive, but pays for it later when Popeye comes to the rescue. Popeye wards off a legion of animals who guard the island, making mincemeat of them and Bluto!

Critics lauded the cartoon as a marvelous, innovative creation. The process of Turntable animation was stunning to most critics. As a critic for the *Motion Picture Herald* said: "The veteran cartoon producer, Max Fleischer, herewith offers the first three-dimensional two-reeler in colors, his most ambitious effort and one which merits the attention of exhibitors as a decidedly original and completely entertaining subject.... One of the best of its kind."

Fleischer's brother Dave did an equally superb job the following year with his second Technicolor featurette, *Popeye Meets Ali Baba and His 40 Thieves* (1937). The cartoon received top-of-the-bill bookings around the country, and one newspaper ad Paramount ran showed Popeye proclaiming, "Gable and Taylor is just amachures. I yam the greatest lover in moovin' pitchers."

Little did film patrons realize that Popeye didn't make love in the film. It was just a clever ploy on the part of Paramount's promotional department to lure filmgoers to the theaters. Instead, the film was just another send-up showcasing the love-hate relationship between Bluto and Popeye, with Bluto in the role of Abul Hassan. Nonetheless, in terms of solid construction, the film results in some good laughs and clever gags.

Bluto, in the role of Abul Hassan, robs from the poor and gives to himself. He stores all of his stolen treasures in a secret cave. The cave door opens only to the command, "Open sesame!" Receiving news of the thieves' recent wrongdoings, coastguardsman Popeye pilots a seaplane to round up the mob and put them behind bars. Aiding him in his mission are Wimpy and Olive Oyl, who stows away just before takeoff. Once over Arabia, the plane crash-lands in the desert, leaving our three heroes stranded. They miraculously make it through the desert to a small desert town, which has just been vandalized (by whomelse but Bluto). Popeye pursues the crooks once they kidnap Olive moments later. Enraged, Popeye mounts a camel and heads off after Hassan and his tribe. Reaching their destination, the thieves enter the secret cave after reciting the magical words, "Open, sesame!" Left outside, Popeye makes a lame attempt at repeating the password, ordering, "Open says me!"

Meanwhile, Dave was having headaches of his own with the animation for his newest feature, *Gulliver's Travels*, with another problem being the script. Five writers and he wrote a screenplay loosely based on Jonathan Swift's tale — improvising with ideas of their own. Omitted were Gulliver's feud between the kings of Lilliput and Blefuscu, and his arrival in Lilliput. Although the characters were delightful, they didn't project any sentiment and empathy for Gulliver. Gabby, one of Fleischer's creations, was more obnoxious as the town crier than humorous — a problem that similarly plagued Daffy Duck at the outset of his career. Sam Parker acted out the role of Gulliver on film, which was retracted and animated. Some original plans had called for Popeye to star as Gulliver, which might have livened up the film.

Critics agreed the film's Christmas 1939 release with mixed reactions. A critic for the *Motion Picture Herald* wrote: "This synthesized version bothers very little with characterization and undertakes little or no temperamental or cultural differentiation between the Giant and the Lilliputians.... The picture is vividly challenging in Technicolor, which of course it needed very much to be, because without the benefit of range of the palette it would have been difficult indeed to create this spirit of make-believe."

Although *Gulliver* didn't receive high acclaim, Fleischer wasn't about to abstain from directing another cartoon feature. It just meant that he should have planned more carefully before springing into production. Most reasons Disney cartoon features become classics stem from careful planning. Some of his films took as much as four years to animate! Learning from his first mistake, Fleischer made vast improvements before directing his second feature — a much more solid one called *Mr. Bug* (1941). The film was later reissued as *Hoppity Goes to Town*.

Dave returned to his regular duties as a cartoon series director. By now in 1939, Betty Boop had retired from the screen and Popeye had become the studio's number-one breadwinner. His productions had been limited to directing

Popeye cartoons, until 1940, when he introduced a series of *Stone Age* cartoons. The series predates television's *The Flintstones*, in which modern mechanical devices become the focus of attention in prehistoric times. Another short-lived series Fleischer went on to direct was a series of *Gabby* cartoons. Fleischer believed that Gabby had some appeal, so he decided to test him in a series. It didn't work. One of the last series Fleischer created was *Animated Antics*, which featured lesser-known characters in predictable but hilarious mishaps.

With those failures behind him, Fleischer concentrated on directing two more cartoon specials. The first was *Raggedy Ann and Raggedy Andy* (1940), which was based on characters and stories by Johnny Gruelle. Another special produced with lesser success was a two-reel adaptation of Edgar Allan Poe's *The Raven* (1940).

The last series Fleischer directed was *Superman*. Paramount was aware of the tremendous following the comic strip superhero had gained over the years. Smelling a new opportunity, Paramount asked the Fleischers if they would animate a series of Superman cartoons. The Fleischers told Paramount that such an undertaking was just impossible. Like most film productions, the studio knew the bottom line here was *money*. So Paramount executives were willing to back the Fleischers with as much capital as necessary to animate the pilot cartoon. Believing he could dissuade them, Dave told Paramount it would cost around $100,000 to animate the cartoon. Paramount took Dave up on his offer and what resulted was the series' first release, *Superman*, on September 26, 1941. Fleischer contracted two actors from the radio version, Bud Collyer and Joan Alexander, to voice Clark Kent (alias Superman) and Lois Lane. The series continued with incredible success, long after Fleischer left Paramount in 1942.

Shortly after the release of *Terror on Midway*, the last Fleischer-produced Superman cartoon, Paramount decided to terminate its relationship with Max and Dave. Perhaps, expecting another Disney, the studio grew tired of pouring large sums of money into production that didn't profit them as much as they had expected. Still dependent on cartoon shorts, Paramount contracted three longtime studio employees — animators Seymour Kneitel, Isadore Sparber, and business manager Sam Buchwald — to run a new cartoon division under the name of Famous Studios (The Superman and Popeye series continued as primary productions under the new studio).

Although leaving Paramount came as a shock, Dave took it well and went on to land a job as a producer of cartoons for Columbia Pictures. The studio was not known for good quality cartoons, thus Fleischer quit in 1944. Later, Dave became a reliable gag writer for live action films at Universal Pictures, where he remained for fifteen years. His legendary efforts left Fleischer well known and revered when he died in 1979 after more than a decade of retirement.

Like most great cartoon animators, Dave never won an Oscar for his achievements, but through his fine talent won the hearts of millions of filmgoers everywhere.

Chapter 9

Other Directors

The Clampetts, the Joneses, the Frelengs, the Fleischers, and the Averys will always be chronicled as some of animation's most proficient cartoon directors. Unfortunately, in a field as wide ranging as animation, not every cartoon director has received proper recognition over the years. In an attempt to rectify this, following are brief discussions of the contributions other auteurs have made to cartoon animation.

The UPA studios turned out some marvelous cartoons because of proficient men like Pete Burness. Burness, a two-time Academy Award-winner, first started his career as an inbetweener for Van Beuren in 1933. Working up some profound experience, Pete went on to animate cartoons for Warner Brothers' director Robert McKimson in the late 1940s. A short time later, Burness found his niche in cartoons as a director of UPA's prize-winning Mr. Magoo series. Magoo became UPA's bread-and-butter product, despite the fact that fewer cels were used to animate them and budgets were skimpier than rival cartoon studios. Although others disagreed, Burness fought against changing Magoo into a softer, less crotchety personality. Some directors experimented with the idea, but Burness later contended: "I believed that his character would have been stronger if he had continued crotchety, even *nasty*." Two of Burness's cartoons — *When Magoo Flew* (1954) and *Magoo's Puddle Jumper* (1956) — won Academy Awards for the director.

Equally prominent in cartoon animation was director Jack Hannah. Hannah started out as an inbetweener and assistant to Norman Ferguson, who directed Walt Disney's Pluto cartoons. Later, Jack became a story man on Donald Duck cartoons, before joining the ranks of director in 1944. Since Donald had become one of his specialties, Hannah was mostly assigned to direct Donald Duck cartoons and assist Jack King, until the latter's retirement. One of his first creations was a team of mischievous chipmunks, Chip 'n' Dale. Two of his earliest cartoon standouts were *No Sail* (1945), which has Donald and Goofy lost at sea, and a simply hilarious Goofy sports reel, *Double Dribble* (1946).

Being stuck with one character had its disadvantages, as Hannah later revealed. "I got so damned tired of that duck's voice, I just could not stand having to work with it all the time."

Hannah later gained prominence for his invention of Humphrey and Ranger Willoughby, a park ranger-and-bear tandem. (Humphrey was first introduced in a Donald Duck cartoon, *Rugged Bear*, in 1953.) During the studio's lean years, Hannah was picked to supervise the production of new animation for Disney's television show. Then, in 1959, Hannah left Disney to finish his career with Walter Lantz directing Woody Woodpecker, Chilly Willy, Inspector Willoughby (who was modeled after Ranger Willoughby), and Doc cartoons.

Another director who worked for Disney was Burt Gillett. One of the last pioneer animators, in 1915, Gillett began animating The Katzenjammer Kids for Charles Bowers, and later on Mutt and Jeff cartoons. In between chores at the Barre/Bowers Studios, Burt found time to challenge other endeavors. In 1917, he worked on Krazy Kat cartoons for producer Gregory LaCava, before employing his talents on such cartoon series as Comics and Lampoons and Judge Rummy. After a brief stint on these productions, Gillett wound up as a staff animator on Max Fleischer's Out of the Inkwell series in 1923. Gillett continued to animate for Fleischer until he landed a job with Walt Disney Studios in 1928. Two years later, in 1930, Gillett was promoted to director and worked principally on Mickey Mouse and Silly Symphony cartoons. Two Symphony cartoons animated a year apart — Flowers and Trees (1932) and The Three Little Pigs (1933) — won Academy Awards. His first Oscar was for the first three-strip Technicolor cartoon, because of its rich designs and radiant animation.

Rapidly becoming a wanted man, Gillett took an offer to direct a series of cartoons for Van Beuren in 1933. Although the chance to direct a new series of independent cartoons didn't excite him, the salary offer did: a whopping weekly installment of $400. His first series, Toddle Tales, combined live action of children with animated characters telling stories that taught some deep moral. Only three films were produced for the series and it became Van Beuren's last black-and-white endeavor. Gillett next supervised a color series — first filmed in two-color process and then in three-strip Technicolor — called Rainbow Parades. The series alternated one-shot stories with cartoons featuring continuing characters. Of his Rainbow cartoons, Gillett's best were — ironically enough — his last two: Toonerville Trolley and Felix the Cat and the Goose That Laid the Golden Egg. In 1936, after meeting its quota of ten cartoons, Van Beuren shut its doors. Gillett returned for a brief Disney stint before going back as a director for Lantz in the 1940s. Gillett died in 1972.

John Hubley, a three-time Academy Award-winner, first came to Hollywood in 1935. There he became affiliated with Walt Disney Productions for a number of years, first as an animator on such productions as Snow White and the Seven Dwarfs and Dumbo, and as art director of Pinocchio and Bambi. Then, in 1943, he codirected with Paul Sommers a series of Professor Small and Mr. Tall cartoons for Columbia Pictures. When Columbia discontinued making cartoons, Hubley found employment as a director for UPA, a studio he cofounded. There he directed the studio's two stylized renditions of the Fox and Crow in The Magic Fluke (1949) and Robin Hoodlum (1949), which some consider his best. That same season, Hubley introduced UPA's newest creation, Mr. Magoo (who was inspired by W.C. Field's screen character), in Ragtime Bear (1949), a Jolly Frolics cartoon. Some other notable Magoos were Spellbound Hound (1950) and Fuddy Duddy Buddy (1951). But one of his top-notch cartoon spoofs was Rooty Toot Toot (1952), a stylized rendition of the Frankie and Johnny story, which won Hubley an Academy Award and became his last cartoon for UPA. Then, in 1955, John and his wife Faith organized their own cartoon production company, Storyboard. He went on to animate and produce such award-winning features *Moonbird* (1959), *The Hole* (1962), on which he shared producer credit with his wife, and *Herb Alpert and the Tijuana Brass Double Feature* (1966). Hubley's last productions were *Doonesbury*, an animated television special on the popular comic strip, and a cartoon feature based on Richard Adams' *Watership Down*. Hubley died during open heart surgery on February 23, 1977.

Another veteran animator and prize-winning director was Alex Lovy, who began his career as a staff animator for Van Beuren in 1933. Lovy remained at Van Beuren until he had a chance to direct cartoons for Walter Lantz in 1938, beginning with the Willie the Mouse series. One year later, in 1939, Lovy helped create one of Lantz's foremost cartoon stars, Andy Panda. The character was first shown to the public in a 1939 Lantz cartoon, *Life Begins for Andy Panda*, which Lovy directed. Lovy went on to supervise Andy Panda and Woody Woodpecker cartoons before he quit in 1948. Columbia Pictures signed him to direct some cartoons, before he returned to Lantz as a director in 1953. Upon his return, Lovy initiated the character Chilly Willy in a series of cartoons, starting with *Chilly Willy* (1953). Lovy continued to direct other Lantz cartoons until 1959. Then, he accepted a job as associate producer for Hanna-Barbera Productions, the largest single producer of Saturday morning television cartoons.

One cartoon tandem that had the same rampant chemistry of Hanna and Barbera were Hugh Harman and Rudolf Ising. Both had kindred beginnings in animation, starting out as animators for Walt Disney in 1922 on *Laugh-o-Grams* and *Alice in Cartoonland*. In 1929, they went on to animate *Oswald the Rabbit* cartoons for George Winkler, who took over for Disney temporarily. Disney had been the producer of the series, but lost controlling rights to it because of a contractual feud he had with producer Charles Mintz. When Walter Lantz pulled the series from Winkler, Harman and Ising were left jobless since Lantz brought in a new staff of animators. The cartoon tandem left Lantz in 1930 to produce cartoons independently. They went on to create Warner Brothers' first cartoon series, Bosko, and helped set up the studio's first cartoon department. The first official Bosko cartoon and first Looney Tunes was *Sinkin' in the Bathtub*, which was released in May 1930. (Harman and Ising had animated with Friz Freleng a commercial film, *Bosko—the Talk-Ink Kid*, prior to the first Looney Tunes cartoon. The film was never released.)

Realizing that one series wasn't enough, Harman and Ising banded together to create a musical cartoon series, Merrie Melodies. At that point, in 1931, Harman held on as director of Bosko, while Ising went on to supervise Merrie Melodies. Both continued to work separately from that point on. In 1933, with Warners' cartoons a success, Hugh and Rudy demanded more financial backing for these films. Their demands not met, Harman and Ising left Warners in 1933 to command a new cartoon division for MGM. They left Warners shaken—but not without taking Bosko with them. (They later produced a new series of Bosko cartoons for MGM, but not with the same success as the former series). MGM offered them double their Warner's budget to produce new color cartoons, the first being *Happy Harmonies*. Harman and Ising proceeded to churn out from eight to twelve cartoons a year. One character Ising introduced was Little Cheeser, a cute mouse who recalls the voice of Warners' Sniffles the Mouse. Ising went on to direct a series of Barney Bear cartoons through the early forties—films like *The Bear That Couldn't Sleep* (1939) and *The Bear and the Beavers* (1942). One of his single efforts, *The Milky Way* (1940), became Metro's first Academy Award–winning cartoon. Meanwhile, Harman had his share of hits, including *Peace on Earth* (1939), which was nominated for an Academy Award, and *The Mad Maestro* (1939). Later, in 1940, Ising spawned the first in a series of Tom and Jerry cartoons, starting with *Puss Gets the Boot*, which he directed. (The characters were created by animators Bill Hanna and Joseph Barbera.)

Unlike Harman and Ising, veteran cartoon director Jack Kinney had a fondness for fast pace and vigorous gags in his cartoons at Disney. In February, 1931, Kinney quit his job in the advertising department of a Los Angeles daily newspaper to become a cartoon apprentice at Walt Disney Studios. Although he could draw, animation was a new and complicated technique to him. His tireless efforts sprung him from the bottom rung up the ladder of success in no time. He became an animator, story sketch man, gag man, story director, and finally director. His first impressive work was *Bone Trouble* (1940), which some consider one of his best Pluto shorts. One of his films, *der Fuehrer's Face* (1943) starring Donald Duck, which he wrote and directed, won an Academy Award. Three others—*How to Play Football* (1949), *The Brave Engineer* (1950), and *Pigs Is Pigs* (1954)—were also nominated for Oscars. *Motormania*, which he wrote and directed in 1951, received an award from the National Safety Council. On some cartoons, Jack's brother Dick Kinney served as a writer. In the late 1950s, Kinney became a supervisor of production of new animation for Disney's television show. In 1958, the prize-winning director departed from Disney to direct a series of Mr. Magoo features for UPA, including *1000 Arabian Knights* (1959). He later opened his own studio in Hollywood, a firm his son now operates, and produced a new series of Popeye cartoons for television.

Kinney and Warner Brothers' cartoon director Robert McKimson had similar traits as directors: their fondness for slapdash humor. McKimson started his career in 1932 as an animator for Leon Schlesinger. In 1946, Schlesinger boosted McKimson up to the position of director. His first assignment was a Daffy Duck cartoon, *Daffy Doodles* (1946), which costars Porky Pig. McKimson didn't have that same deft sense of humor as his cartoon contemporaries—Bob Clampett and Friz Freleng. Nor did Robert employ a lot of burlesque in his characters or cartoons. McKimson was a cartoon director in his own world, a world that contained all the subtleties of life. As McKimson's career grew, so did his talent as one of animation's most respected cartoon directors. His credits are as prodigious as his peers: he created the cartoon characters of Foghorn Leghorn, Henry Hawk, and the Tasmanian Devil. Some of his best cartoons included *A Fractured Leghorn* (1950), Bugs Bunny's *French Rarebit* (1951), *The Honeymousers* (1958), a cartoon spoof of television's *The Honeymooners*, and *People Are Bunny* (1959). When Warner Brothers shut down its cartoon division in 1963, McKimson took a two year break before joining DePatie-Freleng Enterprises, where he remained active until his death in 1977.

Filmographies

Tex Avery

Warner Brothers

1936. "Golddiggers of '49" (with Porky, Beans/January 6/Looney Tunes), "Page Miss Glory" (March 7/Merrie Melodies), "The Blow-Out" (with Porky/April 4/Looney Tunes), "Plane Dippy" (with Porky/April 30/Looney Tunes), "I'd Love to Take Orders from You" (May 16/Merrie Melodies), "I Love to Singa" (July 18/Merrie Melodies), "Milk and Money" (with Porky/October 3/Looney Tunes), and "The Village Smithy" (with Porky/November 14/Looney Tunes).

1937. "Porky the Wrestler" (with Porky/January 9/Looney Tunes), "I Only Have Eyes for You" (March 6/Merrie Melodies), "Picador Porky" (with Porky/March 13/Looney Tunes), "Porky's Duck Hunt" (with Porky, Daffy/April 17/Looney Tunes), "Uncle Tom's Bungalow" (July 12/Merrie Melodies), "Egghead Rides Again" (with Egghead/July 17/Merrie Melodies), "A Sunbonnet Blue" (August 21/Merrie Melodies), "Porky's Garden" (with Porky/September 11/Looney Tunes), "I Wanna Be a Sailor" (September 25/Merrie Melodies), and "Little Red Walking Hood" (November 6/Merrie Melodies).

1938. "Sneezing Weasel" (March 12/Merrie Melodies), "Penguin Parade" (April 23/Merrie Melodies), "The Isle of Pongo Pongo" (with Egghead/May 28/Merrie Melodies), "Cinderella Meets Fella" (with Egghead/July 23/Merrie Melodies), "A Feud There Was" (with Egghead; first cartoon in which he was billed as Elmer Fudd/September 24/Merrie Melodies), "Johnny Smith and Poker Huntas" (with Egghead/October 22/Merrie Melodies), "Daffy Duck in Hollywood" (with Daffy/December 12/Merrie Melodies), and "Mice Will Play" (December 31/Merrie Melodies).

1939. "Hamateur Night" (with Egghead/January 28/Merrie Melodies), "A Day at the Zoo" (with Egghead/March 11/Merrie Melodies), "Thugs with Dirty Mugs" (May 6/Merrie Melodies), "Believe It or Else" (with Egghead/June 3/Merrie Melodies), "Dangerous Dan McFoo" (July 15/Merrie Melodies), "Detouring America" (A.A. nominee/August 25/Merrie Melodies), "Land of the Midnight Fun" (September 23/Merrie Melodies), "Fresh Fish" (November 4/Merrie Melodies), and "Screwball Football" (December 16/Merrie Melodies).

1940. "Early Worm Gets the Bird" (January 13/Merrie Melodies), "Cross Country Detours" (March 16/Merrie Melodies), "The Bear's Tale" (April 13/Merrie Melodies), "A Gander at Mother Goose" (May 25/Merrie Melodies), "Circus Today" (June 22/Merrie Melodies), "A Wild Hare" (with Bugs Bunny, Elmer Fudd/A.A. nominee/July 27/

Merrie Melodies), "Ceiling Hero" (August 24/Merrie Melodies), "Holiday Highlights" (October 12/Merrie Melodies), and "Of Fox and Hounds" (December 7/Merrie Melodies).

1941.   "The Haunted Mouse" (February 15/Looney Tunes), "The Crackpot Quail" (February 15/Merrie Melodies), "Tortoise Beats Hare" (with Bugs Bunny/March 15/ Merrie Melodies), "Porky's Preview" (with Porky/April 19/Looney Tunes), "Hollywood Steps Out" (A.A. nominee/May 24/Merrie Melodies), "The Heckling Hare" (with Bugs/ July 5/Merrie Melodies), "Aviation Vacation" (August 2/Merrie Melodies), "All This and Rabbit Stew" (with Bugs/September 13/Merrie Melodies), "The Bug Parade" (October 11/Merrie Melodies), and "The Cagey Canary" (November 22/Merrie Melodies).

1942.   "Aloha Hooey" (January 24/Merrie Melodies) and "Crazy Cruise" (February 28/Merrie Melodies).

Paramount Pictures (Speaking of Animals)

1941.   "Speaking of Animals Down on the Farm" (August 18), "Speaking of Animals in a Pet Shop" (September 5), and "Speaking of Animals in the Zoo" (October 31).

Metro-Goldwyn-Mayer

1942.   "Blitz Wolf" (August 22) and "The Early Bird Dood It" (August 29).

1943.   "Dumb Hounded" (with Droopy/March 20), "Red Hot Riding Hood" (May 8), "Who Killed Who?" (June 19), "One Ham's Family" (August 14), and "What's Buzzin' Buzzard" (November 27).

1944.   "Screwball Squirrel" (with Screwy Squirrel/April 1), "Batty Baseball" (April 22), "Happy Go Nutty" (with Screwy Squirrel/June 24), "Big Heel Watha" (with Screwy Squirrel/October 21).

1945.   "Screwy Truant" (with Screwy Squirrel/January 13), "The Shooting of Dan McGoo" (with Droopy/March 3), "Jerky Turkey" (April 7), "Swing Shift Cinderella" (August 25), and "Wild and Woolfy" (with Droopy/November 3).

1946.   "Lonesome Lenny" (with Screwy Squirrel/March 9), "The Hick Chick" (June 15), "Northwest Hounded Police" (with Droopy/August 13), and "Henpecked Hoboes" (with George and Junior/October 26).

1947.   "Hound Hunters" (with George and Junior/April 12), "Red Hot Rangers" (with George and Junior/May 31), "Uncle Tom's Cabana" (July 19), "Slap Happy Lion" (September 20), and "King-Size Canary" (December 6).

1948.   "What Price Fleadom" (March 20), "Little Tinker" (May 15), "Half-Pint Pygmy" (with George and Junior/August 17), "Lucky Ducky" (October 9), and "The Cat That Hated People" (November 12).

1949.   "Bad Luck Blackie" (January 22), "Senor Droopy" (with Droopy/April 9), "House of Tomorrow" (June 11), "Doggone Tired" (July 30), "Wags to Riches" (August 13), "Little Rural Red Riding Hood" (September 17), "Out-Foxed" (with Droopy/October 12), and "Counterfeit Cat" (with Spike/December 24).

1950.   "Ventriloquit Cat" (May 27), "The Cuckoo Clock" (June 10), "Garden Gopher" (with Spike/September 30), "The Chump Champ" (with Droopy/November 4), and "The Peachy Cobbler" (December 9).

1951. "Cock-a-Doodle Dog" (with Spike/February 10), "Daredevil Droopy" (with Droopy/March 31), "Droopy's Good Deed" (with Droopy/May 5), "Symphony in Slang" (June 16), "Car of Tomorrow" (September 22), and "Droopy's Double Trouble" (with Droopy, Drippy/November 17).

1952. "Magical Maestro" (February 9, "One Cab's Family" (May 17), "Rock-a-Bye Bear" (July 12).

1953. "Little Johnny Jet" (April 18), "T.V. of Tomorrow" (June 6), and "Three Little Pups" (with Droopy/December 26).

1954. "Drag-a-long Droopy" (with Droopy/February 20), "Billy Boy" (May 8), "Homesteader Droopy" (with Droopy/July 10), "Farm of Tomorrow" (September 18), "The Flea Circus" (November 6), and "Dixieland Droopy" (with Droopy/December 4/ CinemaScope).

1955. "Field and Scream" (April 30), "The First Bad Man" (September 30), "Deputy Droopy" (with Droopy/October 28), and "Cellbound" (codirected by Michael Lah/ November 25).

1956. "Millionaire Droopy" (with Droopy/September 24/CinemaScope).

1957. "Cat's Meow" (January 25).

Walter Lantz Productions

1954. "Crazy Mixed-Up Pup" (October 30).

1955. "I'm Cold" (with Chilly Willy/January 2), "The Legend of Rock-a-Bye Point" (with Chilly Willy/March 11), and "Sh-h-h-h-!!" (April 1).

Bob Clampett

Warner Brothers

1937. "When's Your Birthday?" (with Joe E. Brown/feature-film/Clampett directed prologue and epilogue cartoon sequences in color), "Porky's Badtime Story" (July 24), "Get Rich Quick Porky" (August 28), "Rover's Rival" (October 9), and "Porky's Hero Agency" (December 4).

1938. "Porky's Poppa" (January 15), "What Price Porky?" (February 26), "Porky's Five and Ten" (April 16), "Injun Trouble" (May 21), "Porky's Party" (June 25), "Porky and Daffy" (August 6), "Porky in Wackyland" (September 24), "Porky's Naughty Nephew" (October 15), "Porky in Egypt" (November 5), and "The Daffy Doc" (November 26).

1939. "The Lone Stranger and Porky" (January 7), "Porky's Tire Trouble" (February 18), "Porky's Movie Mystery" (March 11), "Chicken Jitters" (April 22), "Kris Kolumbus, Jr." (May 13), "Polar Pals" (June 3), "Scalp Trouble" (June 24), "Porky's Picnic" (July 15), "Wise Quacks" (August 5), "Porky's Hotel" (September 2), "Jeeper's Creepers" (September 23), "Naughty Neighbors" (October 7), "Pied Piper Porky" (November 4), and "The Film Fan" (December 16).

1940. "Porky's Last Stand" (January 6), "Africa Squeaks" (January 27), "Ali Baba Bound" (February 10), "Pilgrim Porky" (March 16), "Slap Happy Pappy" (April 13), "Porky's Poor Fish" (April 27), "The Chewin' Bruin" (June 8), "Patient Porky" (August 24), "Prehistoric Porky" (October 12), "The Sour Puss" (November 2), and "The Timid Toreador" (codirected by Norm McCabe/December 21).

1941. "Porky's Snooze Reel" (codirected by Norm McCabe/January 11), "Goofy Groceries" (March 29/first color Clampett cartoon), "Farm Frolics" (May 10), "A Coy Decoy" (June 7), "Meet John Doughboy" (July 5), "We, the Animals Squeak" (August 8), "The Henpecked Duck" (August 30), "Cagey Canary" (codirected by Tex Avery/November 22), "Wabbit Twouble" (December 20/Clampett's first Bugs Bunny cartoon; he is credited as Wobert Cwampett), and "Porky's Pooch" (December 27/introduces the character Charlie the Dog).

1942. "Crazy Cruise" (codirected by Tex Avery/March 14), "Horton Hatches the Egg" (April 11), "The Wacky Wabbit" (May 2), "Nutty News" (May 23), "The Wacky Blackout" (July 11), "Bugs Bunny Gets the Boid" (July 11/introduces Beaky, a bashful buzzard), "Eatin' on the Cuff" (August 22/Clampett's last black-and-white Looney Tune), "The Hep Cat" (October 3/Clampett's and Warner's first color Looney Tune), and "A Tale of Two Kitties" (November 21/the first Tweety cartoon).

1943. "Coal Black and de Sebben Dwarfs" (January 16), "Tortoise Wins by a Hare" (February 20), "Wise Quacking Duck" (May 1), "Tin Pan Alley Cats" (June 26), "Corny Concerto" (September 25/his best known film), "Falling Hare" (October 10), and "An Itch in Time" (December 4).

1944. "What's Cookin' Doc?" (January 8), "Tick Tock Tuckered" (April 8/remake of Clampett's first film, "Porky's Badtime Story"), "Russian Rhapsody" (May 20), "Hare Ribbin'" (June 24), "Slightly Daffy" (July 17/remake of "Scalp Trouble"), "Birdy and the Beast" (August 19), "Buckaroo Bugs" (August 26), and "The Old Grey Hare" (October 28).

1945. "Draftee Daffy" (January 27), "Gruesome Twosome" (June 9), "Wagon Heels" (July 28/remake of "Injun Trouble"), and "Bashful Buzzard" (April 15).

1946. "Book Revue" (January 5), "Baby Bottleneck" (March 16), "Kitty Kornered" (June 8), "The Great Piggy Bank Robbery" (July 20), "Bacall to Arms" (August 3), and "The Big Snooze" (October 5).

1947. (Note: The following were cartoon productions originally started by Clampett and finished by other directors after he left Warner Brothers.) "Goofy Gophers" (January 25/started by Clampett; finished by Art Davis) and "Tweetie Pie" (May 3/started by Clampett; finished by Friz Freleng).

1949. "Dough for the Do-Do" (September 3/Clampett's "Porky in Wackyland" redone in color by Friz Freleng).

Private Snafu.

A wartime training cartoon series that featured a dopey-looking army soldier (voiced by Mel Blanc) named Private Snafu.

1943. "Fighting Tools" (release date unknown).

1944. "Booby Traps" (release date unknown). (Another bond-selling film Clampett directed was *Any Bonds Today* (1942), a three-minute trailer starring Bugs Bunny, Elmer Fudd and Porky Pig.)

Republic Pictures

1947. "It's a Grand Old Nag" (with Charlie Horse and Hay-dy La Mare; produced in TruColor).

Beany and Cecil

(Note: Clampett went on to create and direct for television *Time for Beany*, in 1949, starting as 15-minute adventures. Then came 52 half-hour films to lengthen the format. Then, in 1959, he produced a theatrical animated test reel *Beany and Cecil Meet Billy the Squid*. United Artists bought the reel as well as an entire group of Beany and Cecil cartoons for theatrical distribution, as listed as follows.)

"Spots Off a Leopard," Invasion of Earth by Robots," "Cecil Meets the Singing Dinosaur," "Little Ace from Outer Space," "Super-Cecil," "The Wildman of Wildsville," "Davey Crickett," "Strange Objects," "The Capture of Tear-a-Long the Dotted Lion," "A Trip to the Schmoon," "Grime Doesn't Pay," "Beany's Buffalo Hunt," "The Monstrous Monster," "Tommy Hawk," "Yo Ho and a Bubble of Gum," "The Seventh Voyage of Singood," "Cecil Meets Cecelia," "The Capture of Thunderbolt the Wondercolt," "The Rat Race for Space," "Beany and the Boo Birds," "Beany and Cecil Meet Ping-Pong," "The Greatest Schmoe on Earth," "Beany and Cecil Meet Billy the Squid," "The Capture of the Dreaded Three-Headed Threep," "Beany and the Jackstalk," "The Humbug," "Custard's Last Stand," "Hero by Trade," "The Illegal Eagle Egg," "Cecil Gets Careless," "Sleeping Beauty and the Beast," "Never Eat Quackers in Bed," "Dishonest John Meets Cowboy Starr," "Beany's Beany Cap Copter," "The Indiscreet Squeet," "The Phantom of the Horse Opera," "20,000 Little Leaguers under the Sea," "Malice in Blunder-land," "Buffalo Billy," "The Dirty Birdy," "The Attack of the Man-Eater Skeeters," "Davey Crickett's Leading Lady Bug," "Rin-Tin-Can," "Vild Vast Vasteland," "The Invisible Man Has Butter-Fingers," "Here Comes the Schmoe Boat," "Tain't Cricket, Crickett," "Cecil Always Saves the Day," "Ain't I a Little Stinger," "The Warring 20's," "Beany and Cecil Meet the Invisible Man," "Ain't That a Cork in the Snorkel," "Makes a Sea Serpent Sore," "So What and the Seven Whatnots," "Cecil's Comical Strip," "Beany's Resid-Jewels," "Wot the Heck," "Dragon Train," "Ten Feet Tall and Wet," "Dirty Pool," "Thumb Fun," "Living Doll," Beanyland," "Beany Blows His Top," "Beany Flips His Lid," "The Fleastone Kop Kaper," "The Mad Isle of Madhattan," "The Hammy Awards," "Harecules and the Golden Fleecing," "Cheery Cheery Beany," "Nya Ha Ha," "The Singing Swinging Sea Serpent," "There Goes a Good Squid," "Ben Hare," "Hare Today, Gone Tomorrow," "Oil's Well That Ends Well," "There's No Such Thing as a Sea Serpent," and "D.J. the D.J."

Dave Fleischer

Bray Company

1915–1920. "Experiment No. 1," "Experiment No. 2," "Experiment No. 3," "The Clown's Pup" (with Koko/Out of the Inkwell), "Tantalizing Fly" (with Koko/Out of the Inkwell), "Slides" (with Koko/Out of the Inkwell), "Kangaroo" (with Koko/Out of the Inkwell), "The Chinaman" (with Koko/Out of the Inkwell), "The Circus" (with Koko/Out of the Inkwell), "The Ouija Board" (with Koko/Out of the Inkwell), "The Clown's Little Brother" (with Koko/Out of the Inkwell), "The Card Game" (with Koko/Out of the Inkwell), "Perpetual Motion" (with Koko/Out of the Inkwell), "The Restaurant" (with Koko/Out of the Inkwell), "Cartoonland" (with Koko/Out of the Inkwell), "The Automobile Ride" (with Koko/Out of the Inkwell), and "Circus" (with Koko/Out of the Inkwell).

1921. "The First Man to the Moon" (with Koko/Out of the Inkwell), "Modeling" (with Koko/Out of the Inkwell), "Fishing" (with Koko/Out of the Inkwell), "November" (with Koko/Out of the Inkwell), "Invisible Ink" (with Koko/Out of the Inkwell/December), and "The Hypnotist" (with Koko/Out of the Inkwell).

1922. "The Dancing Doll" (with Koko/Out of the Inkwell/January), "Mosquito" (with Koko/Out of the Inkwell/March), "Bubbles" (with Koko/Out of the Inkwell/April), "The Challenge" (with Koko/Out of the Inkwell), "Pay Day" (with Koko/Out of the Inkwell/July), "The Show" (with Koko/Out of the Inkwell/September), "Reunion" (with Koko/Out of the Inkwell/October), "Birthday" (with Koko/Out of the Inkwell/November), and "Jumping Beans" (with Koko/Out of the Inkwell/December).

1923. "Flies" (with Koko/Out of the Inkwell/January), "Surprise" (with Koko/Out of the Inkwell/March), "Puzzle" (with Koko/Out of the Inkwell/April), "Trapped" (with Koko/Out of the Inkwell/May), "The Battle" (with Koko/Out of the Inkwell/July), "False Alarm" (with Koko/Out of the Inkwell/August), "Bedtime" (with Koko/Out of the Inkwell), "The Contest" (with Koko/Out of the Inkwell), "The Fortune Teller" (with Koko/Out of the Inkwell), "Laundry" (with Koko/Out of the Inkwell), and "Shadows" (with Koko/Out of the Inkwell).

1924. "Goodbye My Lady Love" (released with sound/Song Cartune/June), "Mother, Mother, Mother Pin a Rose on Me" (released with sound/Song Cartune/June), "Come Take a Trip in My Airship" (released with sound/Song Cartune/June), "Vaudeville" (with Koko/Out of the Inkwell/November), "Vacation" (with Koko/Out of the Inkwell/November), "League of Nations" (with Koko/Out of the Inkwell/November), "The Cure" (with Koko/Out of the Inkwell/December), "A Trip to Mars" (with Koko/Out of the Inkwell), "Sparring Partner" (with Koko/Out of the Inkwell), "Oh Mabel" (Song Cartune), "The Runaway" (with Koko/Out of the Inkwell), "The Masquerade" (with Koko/Out of the Inkwell), "Ko-Ko in 1999" (with Koko/Out of the Inkwell), and "Ko-Ko the Hot Shot" (with Koko/Out of the Inkwell).

1925. "Cartoon Factory" (with Koko/Out of the Inkwell), "Mother Goose Land" (with Koko/Out of the Inkwell), "Big Chief Ko-Ko" (with Koko/Out of the Inkwell), "Ko-Ko in Toyland" (with Koko/Out of the Inkwell), "I Love Lassie" (Song Cartune), "The Storm" (with Koko/Out of the Inkwell), "Ko-Ko the Barber" (with Koko/Out of the Inkwell), "Suwanee River" (Song Cartune), "Ko-Ko Trains 'Em" (with Koko/Out of the Inkwell), "Daisy Bell" (Song Cartune), "Ko-Ko Celebrates the Fourth" (with Koko/Out of the Inkwell), "Ko-Ko Sees Spooks" (with Koko/Out of the Inkwell), "Old Folks at Home" (Song Cartune), "Ko-Ko Nuts" (with Koko/Out of the Inkwell/September 5), "My Bonnie" (Song Cartune/September 12), "Ko-Ko on the Run" (with Koko/Out of the Inkwell/September 26), "Nutcracker Suite" (Song Cartune), "Ta-Ra-Ra-Boom-Dee-Aye" (Song Cartune), "Ko-Ko Eats" (with Koko/Out of the Inkwell), "Dixie" (Song Cartune), "Ko-Ko Packs Up" (with Koko/Out of the Inkwell/October 17), "Ko-Ko's Thanksgiving" (with Koko/Out of the Inkwell), and "Sailing Sailing" (Song Cartune).

1926. "My Old Kentucky Home" (released with sound/Song Cartune/January), "Ko-Ko Steps Out" (with Koko/Out of the Inkwell/January), "Darling Nellie Gray" (released with sound/Song Cartune/February), "Ko-Ko's Paradise" (with Koko/Out of the Inkwell/February), "Ko-Ko Baffles the Bulls" (with Koko/Out of the Inkwell/March), "Has Anybody Here Seen Kelly" (released with sound/Song Cartune/March), "It's the Cats" (with Koko/Out of the Inkwell/May), and "Tramp, Tramp, Tramp the Boys Are Marching" (Song Cartune/May).

1924–1926 (undated Song Cartunes).

"Dear Old Pal," "When the Midnight Choo-Choo Comes to Alabam," "Coming Through the Rye," "Yaka-Hula-Hicka-Ooola," "Oh, Suzanna," "My Wife's Gone to the Country," "Trail of the Lonesome Pine,"

"Margie," "Annie Laurie," "Pack Up Your Troubles," "Oh, How I Hate to Get Up in the Morning," and "East Side, West Side."

1927. "Ko-Ko Makes 'Em Laugh" (with Koko/Inkwell Imps), "Ko-Ko Plays Pool" (with Koko/Inkwell Imps/August 6), "Ko-Ko's Kane" (with Koko/Inkwell Imps/August 20), "Ko-Ko the Knight" (with Koko/Inkwell Imps/September 3), "Ko-Ko Hops Off" (with Koko/Inkwell Imps/September 17), "Sweet Adeline" (released with sound/Song Cartune/June), "Toot! Toot!" (with Koko/Out of the Inkwell/July), "Old Black Joe" (released with sound/Song Cartune/July), "By the Light of the Silvery Moon" (released with sound/Song Cartune/August), "Ko-Ko in the Fade-Away" (with Koko/Out of the Inkwell/September), "In the Good Old Summertime" (Song Cartune), "Oh You Beautiful Doll" (Song Cartune), "Ko-Ko at the Circus" (with Koko/Out of the Inkwell), "Ko-Ko Gets Egg-cited" (with Koko/Out of the Inkwell), "Ko-Ko Hot After It" (with Koko/Out of the Inkwell), "Ko-Ko Kidnapped" (with Koko/Out of the Inkwell), "Ko-Ko the Convict" (with Koko/Out of the Inkwell), "Ko-Ko the Kop" (with Koko/Inkwell Imps/October 1), "Ko-Ko Explores" (with Koko/Inkwell Imps/October 15), "Ko-Ko Chops Suey" (with Koko/Inkwell Imps/October 29), "Ko-Ko's Klock" (with Koko/Inkwell IMps/November 12), "Ko-Ko Kicks" (with Koko/Inkwell Imps/November 26), "Ko-Ko's Queen" (with Koko/Out of the Inkwell/December), "Ko-Ko's Quest" (with Koko/Inkwell Imps/December 10), "Ko-Ko the Kid" (with Koko/Inkwell Imps/December 24), "Ko-Ko Back Tracks" (with Koko/Inkwell Imps), and "Ko-Ko Needles the Boss" (with Koko/Inkwell Imps).

1928. "Ko-Ko's Kink" (with Koko/Inkwell Imps/January 7), "Ko-Ko's Kozy Korner" (with Koko/Inkwell Imps/January 21), "Ko-Ko's Germ Jam" (with Koko/Inkwell Imps/February 4), "Ko-Ko's Bawth" (with Koko/Inkwell Imps/February 18), "Ko-Ko Smokes" (with Koko/Inkwell Imps/March 3), "Ko-Ko's Tattoo" (with Koko/Inkwell Im-March 17), "Ko-Ko's Earth Control" (with Koko/Inkwell Imps/March 31), "Ko-Ko's Hot Dog" (with Koko/Inkwell Imps/April 14), "Ko-Ko's Haunted House" (with Koko/Inkwell Imps/April 28), "Ko-Ko Lamps Aladdin" (with Koko/Inkwell Imps/May 12), "Ko-Ko Squeals" (with Koko/Inkwell Imps/May 26), "Ko-Ko's Field Daze" (with Koko/Inkwell Imps/June 9), "Ko-Ko Goes Over" (with Koko/Inkwell Imps/June 23), "Ko-Ko's Catch" (with Koko/Inkwell Imps/July 7), "Ko-Ko's War Dogs" (with Koko/Inkwell Imps/July 21), "Ko-Ko's Chase" (with Koko/Inkwell Imps/August 11), "Ko-Ko Heaves Ho" (with Koko/Inkwell Imps/August 25), "Ko-Ko's Big Pull" (with Koko/Inkwell Imps/September 7), "Ko-Ko Cleans Up" (with Koko/Inkwell Imps/September 21), "Ko-Ko's Paradise" (with Koko/Inkwell Imps/October 8), "Ko-Ko's Dog Gone" (with Koko/Inkwell Imps/October 22), "Ko-Ko in the Rough" (with Koko/Inkwell Imps/November 3), "Ko-Ko's Magic" (with Koko/Inkwell Imps/November 16), "Ko-Ko on the Track" (with Koko/Inkwell Imps/December 4), "Ko-Ko's Act" (with Koko/Inkwell Imps/December 17), and "Ko-Ko's Courtship" (with Koko/Inkwell Imps/December 28).

1929 (silent releases). "No Eyes Today" (with Koko/Inkwell Imps/January 11), "Noise Annoys Ko-Ko" (with Koko/January 25/Inkwell Imps), "Ko-Ko Beats Time" (with Koko/Inkwell Imps/February 8), "Ko-Ko's Reward" (with Koko/Inkwell Im-February 23), "Ko-Ko's Hot Ink" (with Koko/Inkwell Imps/March 8), "Ko-Ko's Crib" (with Koko/Inkwell Imps/March 23), "Ko-Ko's Saxaphonies" (with Koko/Inkwell Imps/April 5), "Ko-Ko's Knock-Down" (with Koko/Inkwell Imps/April 19), "Ko-Ko's Signals" (with Koko/Inkwell Imps/May 3), "Ko-Ko's Conquest" (with Koko/Inkwell Imps/May 31), "Ko-Ko's Focus" (with Koko/Inkwell Imps/May 17), "Ko-Ko's Harem Scarem" (with Koko/Inkwell Imps/June 14), "Ko-Ko's Big Sale" (with Koko/Inkwell Imps/June 28), "Ko-Ko's Hypnotism" (with Koko/Inkwell Imps/July 12), and "Chemical Ko-Ko" (with Koko/Inkwell Imps/July 26).

1929 (talkies). "The Sidewalks of New York" (Screen Song/February 5), "Yankee Doodle Boy" (Screen Song/March 1), "Old Black Joe" (Screen Song/April 5), "Ye Olde

Melodies" (Screen Song/May 3), "Daisy Bell" (Screen Song/May 31), "Mother Pine a Rose on Me" (Screen Song/July 6), "Dixie" (Screen Song/August 17), "Goodbye My Lady Love" (Screen Song/August 31), "Chinatown My Chinatown" (Screen Song/August 29), "My Pony Boy" (Screen Song/September 13), "Smiles" (Screen Song/September 27), "Oh, You Beautiful Doll" (Screen Song/October 14), "Noah's Lark" (Talkartoon/October 25), "After the Ball" (Screen Song/November 8), "Put on Your Old Gray Bonnet" (Screen Song/November 22), "Accordion Joe" (Talkartoon/December 12), and "I've Got Rings on My Fingers" (Screen Song/December 17).

1930.   "Bedelia" (Screen Song/January 3), "Marriage Wows" (Talkartoon/January 8), "In the Shade of the Old Apple Tree" (Screen Song/January 16), "I'm Afraid to Come Home in the Dark" (Screen Song/January 30), "Radio Riot" (Talkartoon/February 13), "Prisoner's Song" (Screen Song/March 1), "Hot Dog" (Talkartoon/March 29), "I'm Forever Blowing Bubbles" (Screen Song/March 15), "La Paloma" (Screen Song/April 12), "Yes! We Have No Bananas" (Screen Song/April 26), "Fire Bugs" (Talkartoon/May 9), "Come Take a Trip in My Airship" (Screen Song/May 23), "In the Good Old Summertime" (Screen Song/June 6), "Wise Flies" (Talkartoon/July 18), "A Hot Time in the Old Town Tonight" (Screen Song/August 1), "Dizzy Dishes" (with Betty Boop/Talkartoon/August 9), "The Glow Worm" (Screen Song/August 18), "Barnacle Bill the Sailor" (Talkartoon/August 30), "The Stein Song" (with Rudy Vallee/Screen Song/September 6), "Swing, You Sinners" (Talkartoon/September 24), "Strike Up the Band" (Screen Song/September 26), "The Grand Uproar" (Talkartoon/October 4), "My Gal Sal" (Screen Song/October 18), "Sky Scraping" (Talkartoon/November 1), "Mariutch" (Screen Song/November·15), "Up to Mars" (Talkartoon/November 22), "On a Sunday Afternoon" (Screen Song/November 29), "Row, Row, Row" (Screen Song/December 20), and "Mysterious Mouse" (Talkartoon/December 27).

1931.   "Please Go 'Way and Let Me Sleep" (Screen Song/January 10), "The Ace of Spades" (Talkartoon/January 17), "By the Beautiful Sea" (Screen Song/January 24), "Tree Saps" (Talkartoon/February 21), "Teacher's Pest" (Talkartoon/February 7), "I Wonder Who's Kissing Her Now" (Screen Song/February 14), "I'd Climb the Highest Mountain" (Screen Song/March 7), "The Cow's Husband" (Talkartoon/March 14), "Somebody Stole My Gal" (Screen Song/March 20), "The Bum Bandit" (Talkartoon/April 4), "Any Little Girl That's a Nice Little Girl" (Screen Song/April 18), "The Male Man" (Talkartoon/April 25), "Twenty Legs Under the Sea" (Talkartoon/June 6), "Alexander's Ragtime Band" (Screen Song/May 9), "Silly Scandals" (with Betty Boop/Talkartoon/May 23), "And the Green Grass Grew All Around" (Screen Song/May 30), "My Wife's Gone to the Country" (Screen Song/May 31), "The Herring Murder Case" (Talkartoon/June 26), "That Old Gang of Mine" (Screen Song/July 11), "Bimbo's Initiation" (with Betty Boop/Talkartoon/July 24), "Betty Co-Ed" (with Rudy Vallee/Screen Song/August 1), "Bimbo's Express" (with Betty Boop/Talkartoon/August 22), "Mr. Gallagher and Mr. Shean" (Screen Song/August 29), "You're Driving Me Crazy" (Screen Song/September 19), "Minding the Baby" (with Betty Boop/Talkartoon/September 26), "Little Annie Rooney" (Screen Song/October 10), "In the Shade of the Old Apple Sauce" (Talkartoon/October 16), "Kitty from Kansas City" (with Rudy Vallee/Screen Song/November 1), "Mask-a-Raid" (with Betty Boop/Talkartoon/November 7), "By the Light of the Silvery Moon" (Screen Song/November 14), "Jack and the Beanstalk" (with Betty Boop/Talkartoon/November 21), "My Baby Cares for Me" (Screen Song/December 5), "Dizzy Red Riding Hood" (with Betty Boop/Talkartoon/December 12), and "Russian Lullaby" (with Arthur Tracy/Screen Song/December 26).

1932.   "Any Rags" (with Betty Boop/Talkartoon/January 2), "Sweet Jenny Lee" (Screen Song/January 9), "Boop-Oop-a-Doop" (with Betty Boop/Talkartoon/January 16), "Show Me the Way to Go Home" (Screen Song/January 30), "The Robot" (Talkartoon/February 5), "When the Red Red Robin Comes Bob Bob Bobbin' Along" (Screen Song/February 19), "Wait Till the Sun Shines, Nellie" (Screen Song/March 4), "Minnie the Moocher" (with Betty Boop, Cab Calloway and his orchestra/Talkartoon/March 11), "Swim or Sink" (with Betty Boop/Talkartoon/March 11), "Crazy Town" (with Betty Boop/Talkartoon/March 25), "Just One More Chance" (Screen Song/April 1), "The Dancing Fool" (with Betty Boop/Talkartoon/April 8), "Oh! How I Hate to Get Up in the Morning" (Screen Song/April 22), "Chess Nuts" (Talkartoon/April 13), "A Hunting We Will Go" (with Betty Boop/Talkartoon/April 29), "Shine on Harvest Moon" (Screen Song/May 6), "Let Me Call You Sweetheart" (with Ethel Merman/Screen Song/May 20), "Hide and Seek" (Talkartoon/May 26), "Admission Free" (with Betty Boop/Talkartoon/June 10), "I Ain't Got Nobody" (with the Mills Brothers/Screen Song/June 17), "The Betty Boop Limited" (with Betty Boop/Talkartoon/July 1), "You Try Somebody Else" (with Ethel Merman/Screen Song/July 29), "Rudy Vallee Melodies" (with Betty Boop/Screen Song/August 5), "Stopping the Show" (with Betty Boop/August 12), "Betty Boop Bizzy Bee" (with Betty Boop/August 19), "Down Among the Sugar Cane" (with Lillian Roth/Screen Song/August 26), "Betty Boop, M.D." (with Betty Boop/September 2), "Just Gigolo" (with Irene Bordini/Screen Song/September 9), "Betty Boop's Bamboo Isle" (with Betty Boop, the Royal Samoans and Miri/September 23), "School Days" (with Gus Edwards/Screen Song/September 30), "Betty Boop's Ups and Downs" (with Betty Boop/October 14), "Romantic Melodies" (with Arthur Tracy/Screen Song/October 21), "Betty Boop for President" (with Betty Boop/November 4), "When It's Sleepy Time Down South" (with the Boswell Sisters/Screen Song/November 11), "I'll Be Glad When You're Dead You Rascal You" (with Betty Boop, Louis Armstrong/November 25), "Sing a Song" (with James Melton/Screen Song/December 2), "Betty Boop's Museum" (with Betty Boop/December 16), and "Time on My Hands" (with Ethel Merman/Screen Song/December 23).

1933. "Betty Boop's Ker-Choo" (with Betty Boop/January 6), "Dinah" (with the Mills Brothers/Screen Song/January 13), "Betty Boop's Crazy Inventions" (with Betty Boop/January 27), "Ain't She Sweet" (with Lillian Roth/Screen Song/February 3), "Is My Palm Red" (with Betty Boop/February 17), "Reaching for the Moon" (with Arthur Tracy/Screen Song/February 24), "Betty Boop's Penthouse" (with Betty Boop/March 10), "Aloha Oe" (with the Royal Samoans/Screen Song/March 17), "Snow White" (with Betty Boop, Cab Calloway/March 31), "Popular Melodies" (with Arthur Tracy/Screen Song/April 7), "Betty Boop's Birthday Party" (with Betty Boop/April 21), "The Peanut Vendor" (with Armida/Screen Song/April 28), "Betty Boop's May Party" (with Betty Boop/May 12), "Song Shopping" (with Ethel Merman and Johnny Green/Screen Song/May 19), "Betty Boop's Big Boss" (with Betty Boop/June 2), "Boilesk" (with the Watson Sisters/Screen Song/June 9), "Mother Goose Land" (with Betty Boop/June 23), "Sing, Sisters, Sing!" (with the Three X Sisters/Screen Song/June 30), "Popeye the Sailor" (with Popeye, Betty Boop/July 14), "Down by the Old Mill Stream" (with the Funny Bones/Screen Song/July 21), "The Old Man of the Mountain" (with Betty Boop, Cab Calloway/August 4), "Stoopnocracy" (with Colonel Stoopnagle and Budd/Screen Song/August 18), "I Heard" (with Betty Boop, Don Redman/September 1), "When Yuba Plays the Rumba on the Tuba" (with the Mills Brothers/Screen Song/September 15), "I Yam What I Yam" (with Popeye/September 29), "Boo, Boo, Theme Song" (with the Funny Bones/Screen Song/October 3), "Morning Noon and Night" (with Betty Boop, Rubinoff/October 6), "Blow Me Down" (with Popeye/October 27), "Betty Boop's Halloween Party" (with Betty Boop/November 3), "I Like Mountain Music" (with the Eton Boys/Screen Song/November 10), "I Eats My Spinach" (with Popeye/November 17), "Parade of the Wooden Soldiers" (with Betty Boop, Rubinoff/December 1), "Season's Greetinks" (with Popeye/December 17), "Sing, Babies, Sing" (with Baby Rose Marie/Screen Song/December 15), and "Wild Elephinks" (with Popeye/December 29).

1934. "She Wronged Him Right" (with Betty Boop/January 5), "Keeps Rainin' All the Time" (with Gertrude Niesen/Screen Song/January 12), "Sock-a-Bye Baby" (with Popeye/January 19), "Red Hot Mama" (with Betty Boop/February 2), "Let's All Sing Like the Birdies Sing" (with Reis and Dunn/Screen Song/February 9), "Let's You and Him

Fight" (with Popeye/February 16), "Ha! Ha! Ha!" (with Betty Boop/March 2), "Tune Up and Sing" (with Lanny Ross/Screen Song/March 9), "The Man on the Flying Trapeze" (with Popeye/March 16), "Betty in Blunderland" (with Betty Boop/April 6), "Lazy Bones" (with Borrah Minevitch and his Harmonica Rascals/Screen Song/April 13), "Can You Take It" (with Popeye/April 27), "Betty Boop's Rise to Fame" (with Betty Boop/May 18), "This Little Piggie Went to Market" (with Singin' Sam/Screen Song/May 25), "Shoein' Horses" (with Popeye/June 1), "Betty Boop's Trial" (with Betty Boop/June 15), "She Reminds Me of You" (with the Eton Boys/Screen Song/June 22), "Strong to the Finich" (with Popeye/June 29), "Betty Boop's Lifeguard" (with Betty Boop/July 13), "Love Thy Neighbor" (with Mary Small/Screen Song/July 20), "Shiver Me Timbers" (with Popeye/July 27), "Poor Cinderella" (Color Classic/first in color/August 3), "There's Something About a Soldier" (with Betty Boop/August 17), "Axe Me Another" (with Popeye/August 30), "Betty Boop's Little Pal" (with Betty Boop/September 21), "A Dream Walking" (with Popeye/September 28), "Betty Boop's Prize Show" (with Betty Boop/October 19), "The Two-Alarm Fire" (with Popeye/October 26), "Little Dutch Mill" (Color Classic/October 26), "Keep in Style" (with Betty Boop/November 16), "The Dance Contest" (with Popeye/November 23), "When My Ship Comes In" (with Betty Boop/December 21), and "We Aim to Please" (with Popeye/December 28).

1935. "An Elephant Never Forgets" (Color Classic/January 2), "Baby Be Good" (with Betty Boop/January 18), "Beware of Barnacle Bill" (with Popeye/January 25), "Taking the Blame" (with Betty Boop/February 15), "Be Kind to Animals" (with Popeye/February 22), "The Song of the Birds" (Color Classic/February 27), "Stop That Noise" (with Betty Boop/March 15), "Pleased to Meet Cha!" (with Popeye/March 22), "Swat the Fly" (with Betty Boop/April 19), "The Hyp-nut-tist" (with Popeye/April 26), "The Kids in the Shop" (Color Classic/May 19), "No! No! A Thousand Times No!" (with Betty Boop/May 24), "Choose Your Weppins" (with Popeye/May 31), "A Little Soap and Water" (with Betty Boop/June 21), "For Better or Worser" (with Popeye/June 28), "Dancing on the Moon" (Color Classic/July 12), "A Language All My Own" (with Betty Boop/July 19), "Dizzy Divers" (with Popeye/July 26), "Betty Boop and Grampy" (with Betty Boop/August 16), "You Gotta Be a Football Hero" (with Popeye/August 30), "Time for Love" (Color Classic/September 6), "I Wished on the Moon" (with Abe Lyman and orchestra/Screen Song/September 20), "Judge for a Day" (with Betty Boop/September 20), "King of the Mardi Gras" (with Popeye/September 27), "Making Stars" (with Betty Boop/October 18), "Adventures of Popeye" (with Popeye/October 25), "Musical Memories" (Color Classic/November 8), "The Spinach Overture" (with Popeye/December 7), "Betty Boop, with Henry, the Funniest Living American" (with Betty Boop/December 22), and "It's Easy to Remember" (with Richard Himber and orchestra/Screen Song/December 29).

1936. "Vim, Vigor and Vitaliky" (with Popeye/January 3), "Somewhere in Dreamland" (Color Classic/January 17), "No Other One" (with Hal Kemp and orchestra/Screen Song/January 24), "Little Nobody" (with Betty Boop/January 27), "Betty Boop and the Little King" (with Betty Boop/January 31), "A Clean Shaven Man" (with Popeye/February 7), "Not Now" (with Betty Boop/February 28), "Brotherly Love" (with Popeye/March 6), "The Little Stranger" (Color Classic/March 13), "Betty Boop and Little Jimmy" (with Betty Boop/March 27), "I Feel Like a Feather in the Breeze" (with Jack Denny and orchestra/Screen Song/March 27), "I-Ski Love-Ski You-Ski" (with Popeye/April 3), "We Did It" (with Betty Boop/April 24), "Bridge Ahoy" (with Popeye/May 1), "What, No Spinach?" (with Popeye/May 7), "The Cowweb Hotel" (Color Classic/May 15), "A Song a Day" (with Betty Boop/May 22), "I Don't Want to Make History" (with Vincent Lopez and orchestra/Screen Song/May 22), "More Pep" (with Betty Boop/June 19), "I Wanna Be a Lifeguard" (with Popeye/June 26), "Greedy Humpty Dumpty" (Color Classic/July 10), "You're Not Built That Way" (with Betty Boop/July 17), "Let's Get Movin'" (with Popeye/July 24), "The Hills of Wyomin'" (with the Westerners/Screen Song/July 31), "Happy You and Merry Me" (with Betty Boop/August 21), "Never Kick a Woman" (with Popeye/August 28), "Training Pigeons" (with Betty Boop/September 18), "I Can't Escape from You" (with Joe Reichman and orchestra/Screen Song/September 25), "Little Swee' Pea" (with Popeye/September 25), "Play Safe" (Color Classic/October 16), "Grampy's Indoor Outing" (with Betty Boop/October 16), "Hold the Wire" (with Popeye/October 23), "Be Human" (with Betty Boop/November 20), "The Spinach Roadster" (with Popeye/ November 26), "Talking Through My Heart" (with Dick Stabile and orchestra/Screen Song/November 27), "Popeye the Sailor Meets Sinbad the Sailor" (with Popeye/3-reel special in color/November 27), "Christmas Comes But Once a Year" (Color Classic/ December 4), "Making Friends" (with Betty Boop/December 18), and "I'm in the Army Now" (with Popeye/December 25).

1937. "House Cleaning Blues" (with Betty Boop/January 15), "The Paneless Window Washer" (with Popeye/January 22), "Never Should Have Told You" (with Nat Brandywine and orchestra/Screen Song/January 29), "Whoops! I'm a Cowboy" (with Betty Boop/February 12), "Bunny Mooning" (Color Classic/February 12), "Organ Grinder's Swing" (with Popeye/February 19), "The Hot Air Salesman" (with Betty Boop/March 12), "My Artistical Temperature" (with Popeye/March 19), "Twilight on the Trail" (with the Westerners/Screen Song/March 26), "Pudgy Takes a Bow-Wow" (with Betty Boop/ April 9), "Hospitaliky" (with Popeye/April 16), "Chicken a la King" (Color Classic/April 16), "Pudgy Picks a Fight" (with Betty Boop/May 14), "The Twisker Pitcher" (with Popeye/May 21), "Please Keep Me in Your Dreams" (with Henry King and orchestra/ Screen Song/May 28), "The Impractical Joker" (with Betty Boop/June 18), "Morning, Noon and Nightclub" (with Popeye/June 18), "A Car-Tune Portrait" (Color Classic/ June 26), "Lost and Foundry" (with Popeye/July 16), "Ding Dong Doggie" (with Betty Boop/July 23), "You Came to My Rescue" (with Shep Fields and orchestra/Screen Song/ July 30), "I Never Changes My Altitude" (with Popeye/August 20), "Peeping Penguins" (Color Classic/August 26), "The Candid Candidate" (with Betty Boop/August 27), "I Like Babies and Infinks" (with Popeye/September 18), "Service with a Smile" (with Betty Boop/September 23), "Whispers in the Dark" (with Gus Arnheim and orchestra/Screen Song/September 24), "The Football Toucher Downer" (with Popeye/October 15), "The New Deal Show" (with Betty Boop/October 22), "Educated Fish" (A.A. nominee/ Color Classic/October 29), "Proteck the Weakerist" (with Popeye/November 19), "The Foxy Hunter" (with Betty Boop/November 26), "Magic on Broadway" (with Jay Freeman and orchestra/Screen Song/November 26), "Popeye the Sailor Meets Ali Baba's Forty Thieves" (with Popeye/2-reel special in color/November 26), "Fowl Play" (with Popeye/ December 17), "Zula Hula" (with Betty Boop/December 24), and "Little Lamby" (Color Classic/December 31).

1938. "Let's Celebrake" (with Popeye/January 21), "Riding the Rails" (with Betty Boop/January 28), "You Took the Words Right Out of My Heart" (with Jerry Blaine and orchestra/Screen Song/January 28), "Learn Polikness" (with Popeye/February 18), "Be Up to Date" (with Betty Boop/February 25), "The Tears of an Onion" (Color Classic/February 26), "The House Builder Upper" (with Popeye/March 18), "Honest Love and True" (with Betty Boop/March 25), "Thanks for the Memory" (with Bert Block and his orchestra/Screen Song/March 25), "Out of the Inkwell" (with Betty Boop/April 22), "Big Chief Ugh-Amugh-Ugh" (with Popeye/April 25), "Hold It!" (Color Classic/April 29), "Swing School" (with Betty Boop/May 27), "You Leave Me Breathless" (with Jimmy Dorsey and orchestra/Screen Song/May 27), "I Yam Love Sick" (with Popeye/May 29), "Plumbing Is a Pipe" (with Popeye/June 17), "Hunky and Spunky" (A.A. nominee/Color Classic/June 24), "Pudgy and the Lost Kitten" (with Betty Boop/June 24), "The Jeep" (with Popeye/July 15), "Buzzy Boop" (with Betty Boop/July 29), "Beside a Moonlit Stream" (with Frank Dailey and orchestra/Screen Song/July 29), "Pudgy the Watchman" (with Betty Boop/August 12), "Bulldozing the Bull" (with Popeye/August 19), "All's Fair at the Fair" (Color Classic/August 26), "Buzzy Boop at the Concert" (with Betty Boop/ September 16), "Mutiny Ain't Nice" (with Popeye/September 23), "Sally Swing" (with Betty Boop/October 14), "Goonland" (with Popeye/October 21), "The Playful Polar Bears" (Color Classic/October 28), "A Date to Skate" (with Popeye/November 18), "On with the New" (with Betty Boop/December 2), "Pudgy in Thrills and Chills" (with Betty Boop/December 23), and "Cops Is Always Right" (with Popeye/December 29).

1939. "Always Kickin'" (Color Classic/January 26), "My Friend the Monkey" (with Betty Boop/January 27), "Customers Wanted" (with Popeye/January 27), "So Does an Automobile" (with Betty Boop/March 31), "Aladdin and His Wonderful Lamp" (with Popeye/2-reel special in color/April 7), "Small Fry" (Color Classic/April 21), "Leave Well Enough Alone" (with Popeye/April 28), "Musical Mountaineers" (with Betty Boop/May 12), "Wotta Nightmare" (with Popeye/May 19), "The Scared Crows" (with Betty Boop/June 9), "Ghosks Is the Bunk" (with Popeye/June 14), "Barnyard Brat" (Color Classic/June 30), "Rhythm on the Reservation" (with Betty Boop/July 7), "Hello, How Am I" (with Popeye/July 14), "It's the Natural Thing to Do" (with Popeye/July 30), "Yip, Yip, Yippy" (August 11/officially released as a Betty Boop cartoon, but she does not appear), "The Fresh Vegetable Mystery" (Color Classic/September 29), "Never Sock a Baby" (with Popeye/November 3), and "Gulliver's Travels" (feature-length cartoon/December 22).

1940. "Shakespearian Spinach" (with Popeye/January 19), "Way Back When a Triangle Had Its Points" (Stone Age/January 26), "Little Lambkin" (Color Classic/February 2), "Way Back When a Nightclub Was a Stick" (Stone Age/March 15), "Ants in the Plants" (Color Classic/March 15), "Stealin' Ain't Honest" (with Popeye/March 22), "Me Feelin's Is Hurt" (with Popeye/April 12), "Granite Hotel" (Stone Age/April 26), "A Kick in Time" (Color Classic/May 17), "Onion Pacific" (with Popeye/May 24), "The Foul Ball Player" (Stone Age/May 24), "Wimmen Is a Myskery" (with Popeye/June 7), "The Ugly Dino" (Stone Age/June 14), "Nurse Mates" (with Popeye/June 20), "Wedding Belts" (Stone Age/July 5), "Fightin' Pals" (with Popeye/July 12), "Snubbed by a Snob" (Color Classic/July 19), "Way Back When a Razzberry Was a Fruit" (Stone Age/July 26), "Doing Impossikible Stunts" (with Popeye/August 2), "The Fulla Bluff Man" (Stone Age/August 9), "Wimmin Hadn't Oughta Drive" (with Popeye/August 16), "You Can't Shoe a Horsefly" (Color Classic/August 23), "Puttin' on the Act" (with Popeye/August 30), "Springtime in the Rock Age" (Stone Age/August 30), "Pedagogical Institution (College to You)" (Stone Age/September 13), "Popeye Meets William Tell" (with Popeye/September 20), "The Dandy Lion" (Animated Antics/September 20), "Way Back When Women Had Their Weigh" (Stone Age/September 26), "My Pop, My Pop" (with Popeye/October 18), "King for a Day" (with Gabby/October 18), "Sneak, Snoop and Snitch" (Animated Antics/October 25), "The Constable" (with Gabby/November 15), "With Poopdeck Pappy" (with Popeye/November 15), "Mommy Loves Puppy" (Animated Antics/November 29), "Popeye Presents Eugene the Jeep" (with Popeye/December 13), and "Bring Himself Back Alive" (Animated Antics/December 20).

1941. "Problem Pappy" (with Popeye/January 10), "All's Well" (with Gabby January 17), "Quiet! Please" (with Popeye/February 7), "Zero, the Hound" (Animated Antics/February 14), "Two for the Zoo" (with Gabby/February 21), "Olive's Sweepstakes Ticket" (with Popeye/March 7), "Twinkletoes Gets the Bird" (Animated Antics/March 14), "Flies Ain't Human" (with Popeye/April 4), "Swing Cleaning" (with Gabby/April 11), "Raggedy Ann and Raggedy Andy" (2-reel special/April 11), "Sneak, Snoop and Snitch in Triple Trouble" (Animated Antics/May 9), "Popeye Meets Rip Van Winkle" (with Popeye/May 9), "Olive's Birthday Presink" (with Popeye/June 13), "Fire Cheese" (with Gabby/June 20), "Twinkletoes—Where He Goes Nobody Knows" (Animated Antics/June 27), "Child Psykolojiky" (with Popeye/July 11), "Copy Cat" (Animated Antics/July 18), "Gabby Goes Fishing" (with Gabby/July 18), "The Wizard of Ants" (Animated Antics/August 8), "Pest Pilot" (with Popeye/August 8), "It's a Hap-Hap-Happy Day" (with Gabby/August 15), "Vitamin Hay" (Color Classic/August 22), "Twinkletoes in Hat Stuff" (Animated Antics/August 29), "I'll Never Crow Again" (with Popeye/September 19), "Superman" (A.A. nominee/with Superman/September 26), "The Mighty Navy" (with Popeye/November 14), "The Mechanical Monster" (with Superman/November 21), "Nix on Hypnotricks" (with Popeye/December 19), and "Mr. Bug Goes to Town" (a.k.a. "Hoppity Goes to Town"/feature-length cartoon/December 4).

1942. "Billion Dollar Limited" (with Superman/January 9), "Kickin' the Conga 'Round" (with Popeye/January 17), "Blunder Below" (with Popeye/February 13), "The Arctic Giant" (with Superman/February 26), "Fleets of Stren'th" (with Popeye/March 13), "The Bulleteers" (with Superman/March 26), "The Raven" (2-reel special/April 3), "Pip-Eye, Pup-Eye, Poop-Eye, and Peep-Eye" (with Popeye/April 10), "The Magnetic Telescope" (with Superman/April 24), "Olive Oyl and Water Don't Mix" (with Popeye/May 8), "Many Tanks" (with Popeye/May 15), "Electric Earthquake" (with Superman/May 15), "Baby Wants a Bottleship" (with Popeye/July 3), "Volcano" (with Superman/July 10), and "Terror on the Midway" (with Superman/August 30).

Friz Freleng

Warner Brothers

1932. "Ride Him, Bosko" (codirected by Hugh Harman/September 17/Looney Tunes).

1933. "Bosko in Dutch" (codirected by Hugh Harman/January 14/Looney Tunes), "Bosko in Person" (February 11/Looney Tunes), "Beau Bosko" (codirected by Hugh Harman/July 1/Looney Tunes), and "Bosko's Picture Show" (codirected by Hugh Harman/August 26/Looney Tunes).

1934. "Buddy the Gob" (January 13/Looney Tunes), "Buddy and Towser" (February 24/Looney Tunes), "Buddy's Trolley Troubles" (May 5/Looney Tunes), "Beauty and the Beast" (April 14/first Cinecolor Merrie Melodies), "Goin' to Heaven on a Mule" (May 19/Merrie Melodies), "How Do I Know It's Sunday?" (June 9/Merrie Melodies), "Why Do I Dream Those Dreams?" (June 30/Merrie Melodies), "The Girl at the Ironing Board" (September 15/Merrie Melodies), "The Miller's Daughter" (September 8/Merrie Melodies), "Shake Your Powder Puff" (September 29/Merrie Melodies), "Those Beautiful Dames" (November 10/Merrie Melodies), and "Pop Goes My Heart" (December 8/Merrie Melodies).

1935. "Mr. and Mrs. Is the Name" (January 19/Merrie Melodies), "Country Boy" (February 9/Merrie Melodies), "I Haven't Got a Hat" (March 2/first Porky Pig cartoon/Merrie Melodies), "Along Flirtation Walk" (April 6/Merrie Melodies), "My Green Fedora" (May 4/Merrie Melodies), "Into Your Dance" (June 8/Merrie Melodies), "The Country Mouse" (July 13/Merrie Melodies), "Merrie Old Soul" (August 17/Merrie Melodies), "The Lady in Red" (September 21/Merrie Melodies), "Little Dutch Plate" (October 19/Merrie Melodies), "Billboard Frolics" (November 9/Merrie Melodies), and "Flowers for Madame" (November 30/Merrie Melodies).

1936. "I Want to Play House" (January 18/Merrie Melodies), "The Cat Came Back" (February 8/Merrie Melodies), "I'm a Big Shot Now" (April 11/Merrie Melodies), "When I Yoo-Hoo" (June 27/Merrie Melodies), "Sunday Go to Meetin' Time" (August 8/Merrie Melodies), "At Your Service Madame" (August 29/Merrie Melodies), "Boulevardier from the Bronx" (October 10/Merrie Melodies), and "Coocoonut Grove" (November 28/Merrie Melodies).

1937. "He Was Her Man" (January 2/Merrie Melodies), "Pigs Is Pigs" (January 30/Merrie Melodies), "The Fella with the Fiddle" (March 27/Merrie Melodies), "She Was an Acrobat's Daughter" (April 10/Merrie Melodies), "Clean Pastures" (May 22/Merrie

Melodies), "Streamlined Greta Green" (June 19/Merrie Melodies), "Sweet Sioux" (July 3/ Merrie Melodies), "Plenty of Money and You" (July 31/Merrie Melodies), "Dog Daze" (September 18/Merrie Melodies), "The Lyin' Mouse (October 16/Merrie Melodies), and "September in the Rain" (December 18/Merrie Melodies).

1938. "My Little Buckaroo" (January 29/Merrie Melodies), "Jungle Jitters" (February 19/Merrie Melodies), and "A Star Is Hatched" (April 2/Merrie Melodies).

MGM's Captain and the Kids

1938. "Poultry Pirates" (April 16) and "Pygmy Hunt" (August 6).

Warner Brothers

1940. "You Ought to Be in Pictures" (with Porky, Daffy/April 18/Looney Tunes), "Porky's Baseball Broadcast" (July 6/Looney Tunes), "Confederate Honey" (March 30/ Merrie Melodies), "Hardship of Miles Standish" (April 27/Merrie Melodies), "Little Blabbermouse" (July 6/Merrie Melodies), "Calling Dr. Porky" (September 21/Looney Tunes), "Porky's Hired Hand" (November 30/Looney Tunes), "Malibu Beach Party" (September 14/Merrie Melodies), and "Shop, Look, and Listen" (December 21/Merrie Melodies).

1941. "The Fighting 69½" (January 18/Merrie Melodies), "The Cat's Tale" (March 1/Merrie Melodies), "Porky's Bear Facts" (March 29/Looney Tunes), "Trial of Mr. Wolf" (April 26/Merrie Melodies), "Hiawatha's Rabbit Hunt" (with Bugs Bunny/June 7/ Merrie Melodies), "The Wacky Worm" (June 21/Merrie Melodies), "Sport Chumpions" (August 16/Merrie Melodies), "Notes to You" (with Porky Pig/September 20/Looney Tunes), "Rookie Review" (October 25/Merrie Melodies), and "Rhapsody in Rivets" (December 6/A.A. nominee/Merrie Melodies).

1942. "Porky's Pastry Pirates" (January 17/Looney Tunes), "The Wabbit Who Came to Supper" (with Elmer, Bugs Bunny/March 28/Merrie Melodies), "Saps in Chaps" (April 11/Looney Tunes), "Lights Fantastic" (May 23/Merrie Melodies), "Double Chaser" (June 27/Merrie Melodies), "Foney Fables" (August 1/Merrie Melodies), "Fresh Hare" (with Bugs Bunny, Elmer/August 22/Merrie Melodies), "The Sheepish Wolf" (October 17/Merrie Melodies), "The Hare Brained Hypnotist" (with Bugs Bunny, Elmer/ October 31/Merrie Melodies), and "Ding Dong Daddy" (December 5/Merrie Melodies).

1943. "Pigs in a Polka" (with Porky/February 6/Merrie Melodies), "Fifth Column Mouse" (March 6/Merrie Melodies), "Greetings Bait!" (May 15/Merrie Melodies), "Jack Wabbit and the Beanstalk" (with Bugs Bunny/June 12/Merrie Melodies), "Hiss and Make Up" (September 11/Merrie Melodies), and "Daffy the Commando" (with Daffy Duck/ November 20/Looney Tunes).

1944. "Little Red Riding Rabbit" (with Bugs Bunny/January 1/Merrie Melodies), "Meatless Flyday" (January 29/Merrie Melodies), "Bugs Bunny Nips the Nips" (April 22/ Merrie Melodies), "Duck Soup to Nuts" (with Porky, Daffy/May 27/Looney Tunes), "Hare Force" (with Bugs Bunny/July 22/Merrie Melodies), "Goldilocks and the Jivin' Bears" (September 2/Merrie Melodies), and "Stage Door Cartoon" (with Bugs, Elmer/ December 30/Merrie Melodies).

1945. "Herr Meets Hare" (with Bugs/January 13/Merrie Melodies), "Life with Feathers" (with Sylvester the Cat/March 24/Merrie Melodies), "Hare Trigger" (with Bugs, Yosemite Sam/May 5/Merrie Melodies), "Ain't That Ducky" (with Daffy/May 19/Looney Tunes), and "Peck Up Your Troubles" (with Sylvester/October 20/Merrie Melodies).

1946. "Holiday for Shoestrings" (February 23/Merrie Melodies), "Baseball Bugs" (with Bugs/February 2/Looney Tunes), "Hollywood Daffy" (with Daffy/June 22/ Merrie Melodies), "Of Thee I Sting" (August 17/Merrie Melodies), "Racketeer Rabbit" (with Bugs, Peter Lorre, Edward G. Robinson/September 14/Looney Tunes), and "Rhapsody Rabbit" (with Bugs/November 9/Merrie Melodies).

1947. "Gay Anties" (February 15/Merrie Melodies), "A Hare Grows in Manhattan" (with Bugs/March 22/Merrie Melodies), "Tweetie Pie" (with Sylvester/May 3/A.A. winner), "Rabbit Transit" (with Bugs/May 10/Looney Tunes), "Along Came Daffy" (with Daffy/June 14/Looney Tunes), and "Slick Hare" (with Elmer, Bugs/November 1/Merrie Melodies).

1948. "Back Alley Oproar" (with Elmer, Sylvester/March 27/Merrie Melodies), "I Taw a Puttytat" (with Tweety, Sylvester/April 2/Merrie Melodies), "Buccaneer Bunny" (with Bugs, Yosemite Sam/May 8/Looney Tunes), "Bugs Bunny Rides Again" (with Bugs, Yosemite Sam/June 12/Merrie Melodies), "Hare Splitter" (with Bugs/September 25/ Merrie Melodies), and "Kit for Cat" (with Elmer, Sylvester/November 6/Looney Tunes).

1949. "Wise Quackers" (with Daffy, Elmer/January 1/Looney Tunes), "Hare-Do" (with Bugs, Elmer/January 15/Merrie Melodies), "High Diving Hare" (with Bugs, Yosemite Sam/April 30/Looney Tunes), "Curtain Razor" (May 21/Looney Tunes), "Mouse Mazura" (June 11/Merrie Melodies), "Bad Ol' Puttytat" (with Tweety, Sylvester/ July 23/Merrie Melodies), "Dough for the Do-Do" (codirected by Bob Clampett/ September 3/Merrie Melodies), "Each Dawn I Crow" (September 24/Merrie Melodies), "Knights Must Fall" (with Bugs/July 16/Merrie Melodies), and "Which Is Witch?" (December 3/Looney Tunes).

1950. "Home Tweet Home" (with Tweety, Sylvester/January 4/Merrie Melodies), "Mutiny on the Bunny" (with Bugs/February 11/Looney Tunes), "The Lion's Busy" (February 18/Looney Tunes), "Big House Bunny" (with Bugs, Yosemite Sam/April 22/ Merrie Melodies), "His Bitter Half" (May 20/Merrie Melodies), "All Abir-r-r-d" (with Tweety, Sylvester/June 24/Looney Tunes), "Golden Yeggs" (with Daffy/August 5/ Merrie Melodies), "Bunker Hill Bunny" (with Bugs, Yosemite Sam/September 23/ Merrie Melodies), "Canary Row" (with Tweety, Sylvester/October 7/Merrie Melodies), and "Stooge for a Mouse" (October 21/Merrie Melodies).

1951. "Canned Feud" (February 3/Looney Tunes), "Rabbit Every Monday" (with Bugs, Yosemite Sam/February 10/Looney Tunes), "Putty Tat Trouble" (with Tweety, Sylvester/February 24/Looney Tunes), "A Bone for a Bone" (with the Goofy Gophers/ April 7/Looney Tunes), "Fair-Haired Hare" (with Bugs, Yosemite Sam/April 14/Looney Tunes), "Room and Bird" (with Tweety, Sylvester/June 2/Merrie Melodies), "His Hare Raising Tale" (with Bugs/August 11/Looney Tunes), "Tweety's S.O.S." (with Tweety, Sylvester/September 22/Merrie Melodies), "Ballot Box Bunny" (with Bugs, Yosemite Sam/October 6/Merrie Melodies), and "Tweet Tweet Tweety" (with Tweety, Sylvester/ December 15/Looney Tunes).

1952. "Gift Wrapped" (February 16/Looney Tunes), "Foxy by Proxy" (with Bugs/ February 23/Merrie Melodies), "14 Carrot Rabbit" (with Bugs, Yosemite Sam/March 15/ Looney Tunes), "Little Red Rodent Hood" (May 3/Merrie Melodies), "Ain't She Tweet" (with Tweety, Sylvester/June 21/Looney Tunes), "Cracked Quack" (with Daffy/July 5/ Merrie Melodies), "Bird in a Guilty Cage" (with Tweety, Sylvester/August 30/Looney Tunes), "Tree for Two" (October 18/Merrie Melodies), and "Hare Lift" (with Bugs, Yosemite Sam/December 20/Looney Tunes).

1953. "Snow Business" (January 17/Looney Tunes), "A Mouse Divided" (with Sylvester/January 31/Merrie Melodies), "Fowl Weather" (with Tweety, Sylvester/

April 4/Merrie Melodies), "Southern Fried Rabbit" (with Bugs, Yosemite Sam/May 2/ Looney Tunes), "Ant Pasted" (with Elmer/May 9/Looney Tunes), "Hare Trimmed" (with Bugs, Yosemite Sam/June 20/Merrie Melodies), "Tom-Tom Tomcat" (June 27/Merrie Melodies), "A Street Car Named Sylvester" (with Sylvester/September 9/Looney Tunes), "Catty Cornered" (October 31/Merrie Melodies), and "Robot Rabbit" (with Bugs, Elmer/ December 12/Looney Tunes).

1954. "Dog Pounded" (January 2/Looney Tunes), "Captain Hareblower" (with Bugs, Yosemite Sam/January 16/Merrie Melodies), "I Gopher You" (with the Goofy Gophers/January 30/Merrie Melodies), "Bugs and Thugs" (with Bugs/March 13/Looney Tunes), "Dr. Jerkyl's Hide" (with Bugs/May 8/Looney Tunes), "Muzzle Tough" (June 26/Merrie Melodies), "Satan's Waitin'" (August 7/Looney Tunes), "Yankee Doodle Bugs" (with Bugs, Nephew Clyde/August 28/Looney Tunes), "Goo Goo Goliath" (September 18/Merrie Melodies), and "By Word of Mouse" (October 2/Looney Tunes).

1955. "Pizzicato Pussycat" (with Tweety, Sylvester/January 1/Merrie Melodies), "Pests for Guests" (with Elmer, Goofy Gophers/January 29/Merrie Melodies), "Stork Naked" (with Daffy/Feb. 26/Merrie Molodies), "Sahara Hare" (with Bugs, Yosemite Sam/ March 26/Looney Tunes), "Sandy Claws" (with Tweety, Sylvester/April 2/Looney Tunes), "Tweety's Circus" (with Tweety, Sylvester/June 4/Merrie Melodies), "Lumber Jerks" (with Goofy Gophers/June 25/Looney Tunes), "This Is a Life?" (with Bugs, Daffy/ July 9/Merrie Melodies), "A Kiddie's Kitty" (August 20/Merrie Melodies), "Hyde and Hare" (with Bugs/August 27/Looney Tunes), "Speedy Gonzales" (with Sylvester/ September 17/Merrie Melodies), "Red Riding Hoodwinked" (with Tweety, Sylvester/ October 29/Looney Tunes), "Roman Legion-Hare" (with Bugs/November 12/Looney Tunes), "Heir Conditioned" (with Sylvester, Elmer/November 26/Looney Tunes), and "Pappy's Puppy" (December 17/Merrie Melodies).

1956. "Tweet and Sour" (with Tweety, Sylvester/March 24/Looney Tunes), "Rabbitson Crusoe" (with Bugs, Yosemite Sam/April 28/Looney Tunes), "Tree Cornered Tweety" (with Tweety, Sylvester/May 19/Merrie Melodies), "Napoleon Bunny-Part" (with Bugs/June 16/Merrie Melodies), "Tugboat Granny" (with Tweety, Sylvester/June 23/Merrie Melodies), "A Star Is Bored" (with Bugs, Daffy/September 15/Looney Tunes), "Yankee Dood It" (with Elmer, Sylvester/October 13/Merrie Melodies), and "Two Crows from Tacos" (November 24/Merrie Melodies).

1957. "The Three Little Bops" (January 5/Looney Tunes), "Tweet Zoo" (with Tweety, Sylvester/January 12/Merrie Melodies), "Tweety and the Beanstalk" (with Tweety, Sylvester/March 16/Merrie Melodies), "Piker's Peak" (with Bugs, Yosemite Sam/May 25/Looney Tunes), "Birds Anonymous" (with Tweety, Sylvester/August 10/ A.A. winner/Merrie Melodies), "Bugsy and Mugsy" (with Bugs, Rocky, Mugsy/August 31/Looney Tunes), "Greey for Tweety" (with Tweety, Sylvester/September 28/Looney Tunes), "Show Biz Bugs" (with Bugs, Daffy/November 2/Looney Tunes), and "Gonzales' Tamales" (with Speedy Gonzales/November 30/Looney Tunes).

1958. "Hare-Less Wolf" (with Bugs/February 1/Merrie Melodies), "A Pizza Tweety Pie" (with Tweety, Sylvester/February 22/Looney Tunes), "A Waggily Tale" (April 26/ Looney Tunes), "Knighty Knight Bugs" (with Bugs, Yosemite Sam/August 23/A.A. winner/Looney Tunes), and "A Bird in a Bonnet" (with Tweety, Sylvester/September 27/ Looney Tunes).

1959. "Trick or Tweet" (with Tweety, Sylvester/March 21/Merrie Melodies), "Apes of Wrath" (with Bugs/April 18/Merrie Melodies), "Mexicali Shmoes" (with Speedy Gonzales/July 4/Looney Tunes), "Tweet and Lovely" (with Tweety, Sylvester/July 18/Merrie Melodies), "Wild and Woolly Hare" (with Bugs, Yosemite Sam/August 1/Looney Tunes), "Here Today, Gone Tamale" (with Speedy Gonzales/August 29/Looney Tunes), and "Tweet Dreams" (with Tweety, Sylvester/December 5/Looney Tunes).

1960. "West of Pesos" (with Speedy Gonzales/January 23/Merrie Melodies), "Horse Hare" (with Bugs, Yosemite Sam/February 13/Looney Tunes), "Goldimouse and the Three Cats" (March 19/Looney Tunes), "Person to Bunny" (with Bugs, Daffy, Elmer/April 2/ Merrie Melodies), "Hyde and Go Tweet" (with Tweety, Sylvester/May 14/Merrie Melodies), "Mouse and Garden" (July 16/Looney Tunes), "Trip for Tat" (with Tweety, Sylvester/October 29/Merrie Melodies), "Lighter Than Hare" (with Bugs, Yosemite Sam/ December 17/Merrie Melodies).

1961. "Prince Violent" (September 2/Merrie Melodies), "What's My Lion?" (with Elmer/October 21/Looney Tunes), and "The Last Hungry Cat" (with Tweety, Sylvester/ December 2/Merrie Melodies).

1962. "Crow's Feat" (April 21/Merrie Melodies), "Mexican Boarders" (with Speedy Gonzales, Slowpoke, Rodriguez, Sylvester/May 12/Looney Tunes), "Honey's Money" (with Yosemite Sam/September 1/Merrie Melodies), "The Jet Cage" (with Tweety, Sylvester/September 22/Looney Tunes), and "Shishkabugs" (with Bugs, Yosemite Sam/ December 8/Looney Tunes).

De Patie–Freleng Enterprises

1963. "Devil Feud Cake" (February 9/Merrie Melodies), "Mexican Cat Dance" (with Speedy Gonzales, Sylvester/April 20/Merrie Melodies), "Chili Weather" (August 17/ Merrie Melodies), "The Unmentionables" (September 7/Looney Tunes), and "Claws in the Lease" (with Tweety, Sylvester, Sylvester Jr./November 9/Merrie Melodies).

1964. "Nuts and Volts" (with Speedy Gonzales, Sylvester/April 25/Looney Tunes).

Pink Panther

"The Pink Phink" (December 18).

Hanna and Barbera

Metro-Goldwyn-Mayer

(Following is a listing of all Tom and Jerry cartoons unless noted otherwise.)

1940. "Puss Gets the Boot" (first Tom and Jerry cartoon/February 10), "Swing Social" (Special/May 18), and "Gallopin' Gals" (Special/October 26).

1941. "Goose Goes South" (Special/April 26), "The Midnight Snack" (July 19/re: February 27, 1948), "Officer Pooch" (Special/September 6), and "The Night Before Christmas" (December 3).

1942. "The Fraidy Cat" (May 10), "Puss 'n' Toots" (May 30), "The Bowling Alley Cat" (July 18), and "Fine Feathered Friend" (October 10/re: January 1, 1949).

1943. "Sufferin' Cats" (January 16/re: June 4, 1949), "Lonesome Mouse" (May 2/re: November 26, 1949), "Yankee Doodle Mouse" (A.A. winner/June 26), "War Dogs" (Special/October 9), and "Baby Puss" (December 25).

1944. "Zoot Cat" (February 15), "Million Dollar Cat" (May 16/re: May 6, 1954), "Bodyguard" (July 22), "Puttin' on the Dog" (October 28/re: October 20, 1951), and "Mouse Trouble" (A.A. winner/December 23/re: December 12, 1951/originally "Cat Nipped" and "Kitty Foiled").

1945. "The Mouse Comes to Dinner (May 5/re: January 19, 1952/originally "Mouse to Dinner"), "Mouse in Manhattan" (July 7/originally "Manhattan Serenade"), "Tee for Two" (July 21), "Flirty Birdy" (September 22/re: July 4, 1953/originally "Love Boids"), and "Quiet Please!" (A.A. winner/December 12).

1946. "Springtime for Thomas" (March 30), "The Milky Waif" (May 18), "Trap Happy" (June 29/re: March 6, 1954), and "Solid Serenade" (August 31).

1947. "Cat Fishin'" (February 12/re: October 30, 1954), "Part-Time Pal" (March 15/ originally "Fair Weather Friend"), "The Cat's Concerto" (A.A. winner/April 10), "Dr. Jekyll and Mr. Mouse" (June 14), "Salt Water Tabby" (July 12), "A Mouse in the House" (August 30), and "Invisible Mouse" (September 24).

1948. "Kitty Foiled" (May 1), "Truce Hurts" (July 17), "Old Rockin' Chair Tom" (September 18), "Professor Tom" (October 30), and "Mouse Cleaning" (December 11).

1949. "Polka Dot Puss" (February 26/re: September 28, 1956), "Little Orphan" (A.A. winner/April 30), "Heavenly Puss" (July 7/re: October 26, 1956), "The Cat and Mermouse" (September 3), "Love That Pup" (October 1), "Jerry's Diary" (October 22), and "Tennis Chumps" (December 10).

1950. "Little Quacker" (January 7), "Saturday Evening Puss" (January 14/originally "Party Cat"), "Texas Tom" (March 11), "Jerry and the Lion" (April 8/originally "Hold That Lion"), "Safety Second" (July 1/originally "F'r Safety Sake"), "Tom and Jerry in the Hollywood Bowl" (September 16), "Cue Ball Cat" (October 19), and "Framed Cat" (October 21).

1951. "Casanova Cat" (January 16), "Jerry and the Goldfish" (March 3), "Jerry's Cousin" (April 7/originally "City Cousin" and "Muscles Mouse"), "Sleepy Time Tom" (May 26), "His Mouse Friday" (July 7), "Flying Cat" (August 28), "Slicked-Up Pup (September 8), "Nit-Witty Kitty" (October 6), and "Cat Napping" (December 8).

1952. "Duck Doctor" (January 10), "Little Runaway" (January 31), "The Two Mouseketeers" (A.A. winner/March 15), "Smitten Kitten" (April 12), "Triplet Trouble" (June 21), "Fit to Be Tied" (July 26), "Push-Button Kitty" (September 6, "Dog House" (October 3), and "Cruise Cat" (October 18).

1953. "Jerry and Jumbo" (January 22), "Posse Cat" (February 6), "Puppy Tale" (March 19), "Johann Mouse" (A.A. winner/March 14), "That's My Pup" (May 28), "Just Ducky" (September 5), "Two Little Indians" (October 17), and "Life with Tom" (November 4).

1954. "Hick-Cup Pup" (April 17/originally "Tyke Takes a Nap"), "Little School Mouse" (May 29), "Mouse for Sale" (June 28), "Mice Follies" (July 1), "Baby Butch" (August 14), "Neapolitan Mouse" (October 2), "Downhearted Duckling" (November 13), "Pet Peeve" (November 20), "Touché Pusse Cat" (December 18/re: May 21, 1955).

1955. (Hanna and Barbera shared dual roles as director and producer in the following cartoons up until 1957.) "Flying Sorceress" (January 27), "The Egg and Jerry" (March 23/remake of "Hatch Up Your Troubles"), "Muscle Beach Tom" (June 28), "Down Beat Bear" (September 12), "Blue Cat Blues" (October 3), "Make Mine Freedom" (Special/

December 2), "Barbecue Brawl" (December 7), "Tom's Photo Finish" (December 14), and "Happy Go Lucky" (December 31/originally "One Quack Mind").

1956. "Busy Buddies" (January 22), "Tops with Pops" (February 2/remake of "Love That Pup"), "Mucho Mouse" (February 9), "Give and Tyke" (with Spike and Tyke/March 29), "Feedin' the Kiddie" (June 7/remake of "Little Orphan"), "Scat Cats" (with Spike and Tyke/July 26), "Robin Hoodwinked" (December 31), "Tot Watchers" (December 31), and "The Vanishing Duck" (December 31).

1957. "Royal Cat Nap" (March 7).

William Hanna alone

1938. "Blue Monday" (with the Captain and the Kids/April 2) and "What a Lion" (with the Captain and the Kids/July 16).

Ub Iwerks

Walt Disney Studios

(Released through Pat Powers Celebrity Pictures)

Silly Symphony Cartoons

1929. "Hell's Bells" and "Springtime" (no release dates available).

Columbia Pictures release

1930. "Summer" (January 6), "Autumn" (February 13), and "Arctic Antics" (June 5).

Pat Powers' Celebrity Pictures

(Released through Metro-Goldwyn-Mayer)

Flip the Frog

1930. "Fiddlesticks" (Cinecolor/August 16), "Flying Fists" (September 6), "The Village Barber" (September 27), "Little Orphan" (release date unavailable), "Cuckoo Murder Case" (October 18), and "Puddle Pranks" (release date unavailable).

1931. "The Village Smithie" (January 31), "The Soup Song" (January 31), "Laughing Gas" (March 14), "Ragtime Romeo" (May 2), "The New Car" (July 25), "Movie Mad" (August 29), "The Village Specialist" (September 12), "Jail Birds" (September 26), "Africa Squeaks" (October 17), and "Spooks" (December 21).

1932. "The Milkman" (February 20), "What a Life!" (March 26), "Fire! Fire!" (March 5), "School Days" (May 14), "Puppy Love" (April 30), "Bully" (June 18), "The Office Boy" (July 16), "Room Runners" (August 13), "Circus" (August 27), "Stormy Seas" (August 22), "Goal Rush" (release date unavailable), "Phoney Express" (release date unavailable), "The Music Lesson" (October 29), "Nurse Maid" (November 26), and "Funny Face" (December 24).

1933. "Cuckoo the Magician" (January 21), "Flip's Lunch Room" (April 3), "Techno-Cracked" (Cinecolor/May 8), "Bulloney" (May 30), "Chinaman's Chance" (June 24), "Pale-Face" (August 12), and "Soda Squirt" (October 12).

Willie Whopper

1933. "Play Ball" (September 16), "Spite Fright" (October 14), "Stratos-Fear" (November 11), and "Davy Jones" (Cinecolor/December 9).

1934. "Hell's Fire" (Cinecolor/January 6), "Robin Hood Jr." (February 5), "Insultin' the Sultan" (April 14), "Reducing Creme" (May 19), "Rasslin' Round" (June 1), "Cave Man" (July 6), "Jungle Jitters" (July 24), "Good Scout" (September 1), and "Viva Willie" (September 20).

ComiColor Cartoons:

1933. "Jack and the Beanstalk."

1934. "The Little Red Hen" (February 16), "The Brave Tin Soldier" (April 7), "Puss 'n' Boots" (May 17), "The Queen of Hearts" (June 25), "Aladdin and the Wonderful Lamp" (August 10), "The Headless Horseman" (October 1), "The Valiant Tailor" (October 29), "Don Quixote" (November 26), and "Jack Frost" (December 24).

1935. "Little Black Sambo" (February 6), "Bremen Town Musicians" (March 6), "Old Mother Hubbard" (April 3), "Mary's Little Lamb" (May 1), "Summertime" (June 15), "Sinbad the Sailor" (July 30), "The Three Bears" (August 30), "Balloon Land" (September 30), "Simple Simon" (November 15), and "Humpty Dumpty" (December 30).

1936. "Ali Baba" (January 30), "Tom Thumb" (March 30), "Dick Whittington's Cat" (May 30), "Little Boy Blue" (July 30), and "Happy Days" (September 30).

Warner Brothers

1937. "Porky and Gabby" (May 15/Looney Tunes) and "Porky's Super Service" (July 3/Looney Tunes).

Columbia Pictures (Color Rhapsody Cartoons)

1937. "Skeleton Frolics" (with Scrappy/January 29), "Scrappy's Trip to Mars" (February 14), "Merry Mannequins" (with Scrappy/March 19), and "Foxy Pup" (with Scrappy/May 21).

1938. "Horses on the Merry-Go-Round" (with Scrappy/February 17), "Showtime" (with Scrappy/April 13), "The Frog Pond" (August 12), and "Midnight Frolics" (with Scrappy/November 3).

1939. "The Gorilla Hunt" (with Scrappy/February 24), "Nells Yells" (with Scrappy/June 30), and "Crop Chasers" (September 22).

1940. "Blackboard Revue" (March 15), "Ye Olde Swap Shoppe" (June 28), and "Wise Owl" (December 6).

Chuck Jones

Warner Brothers

1938. "The Night Watchman" (November 19/Merrie Melodies).

1939. "Dog Gone Modern" (January 14/Merrie Melodies), "Robin Hood Makes Good" (February 11/Merrie Melodies), "Presto Change-O" (with Bugs Bunny/March 25/Merrie Melodies), "Daffy Duck and the Dinosaur" (with Daffy Duck/April 22/Merrie Melodies), "Naughty But Mice" (with Sniffles/May 20/Merrie Melodies), "Old Glory" (with Porky Pig/July 1/Merrie Melodies), "Snow Man's Land" (July 29/Merrie Melodies), "Little Brother Rat" (with Sniffles/September 2/Merrie Melodies), "The Little Lion Hunter" (with Inki/October 7/Merrie Melodies), "The Good Egg" (October 21/Merrie Melodies), "Sniffles the Bookworm" (with Sniffles/December 2/Merrie Melodies), and "The Curious Puppy" (December 30/Merrie Melodies).

1940. "Mighty Hunters" (with Canyon Kiddies/January 27/Merrie Melodies), "Elmer's Candid Camera" (with Elmer Fudd, Bugs Bunny/March 2/Merrie Melodies), "Sniffles Takes a Trip" (with Sniffles/May 11/Merrie Melodies), "Tom Thumb in Trouble" (June 8/Merrie Melodies), "The Egg Collector" (with Sniffles/July 20/Merrie Melodies), "Ghost Wanted" (August 10/Merrie Melodies), "Stage Fright" (September 28/Merrie Melodies), "Good Night Elmer" (with Elmer Fudd/October 26/Merrie Melodies), and "Bedtime for Sniffles" (with Sniffles/November 23/Merrie Melodies).

1941. "Elmer's Pet Rabbit" (with Bugs Bunny, Elmer Fudd/January 4/Merrie Melodies), "Sniffles Bells the Cat" (with Sniffles/February 1/Merrie Melodies), "Joe Glow, the Firefly" (March 8/Looney Tunes), "Toy Trouble" (with Sniffles/April 12/Merrie Melodies), "Porky's Ant" (with Porky Pig/May 10/Looney Tunes), "Porky's Prize Pony" (with Porky Pig/June 21/Looney Tunes), "Inki and the Lion" (with Inki/July 19/Merrie Melodies), "Snow Time for Comedy" (August 30/Merrie Melodies), "The Brave Little Bat" (with Sniffles/September 27/Merrie Melodies), and "Porky's Midnight Matinee" (with Porky Pig/November 22/Looney Tunes).

1942. "The Bird Came C.O.D." (with Conrad Cat/January 17/Merrie Melodies), "Conrad the Sailor" (with Conrad Cat/February 14/Merrie Melodies), "Porky's Cafe" (with Porky Pig/February 21/Looney Tunes), "Dog Tired" (April 25/Merrie Melodies), "The Draft Horse" (May 9/Merrie Melodies), "Hold the Lion, Please" (with Bugs Bunny/June 6/Merrie Melodies), "The Squawkin' Hawk" (with Henry Hawk/August 1/Merrie Melodies), "Fox Pop" (August 29/Merrie Melodies), "The Dover Boys" (September 19/Merrie Melodies), "My Favorite Duck" (with Daffy Duck, Porky Pig/December 5/Looney Tunes), and "Case of the Missing Hare" (with Bugs Bunny/December 12/Merrie Melodies).

1943. "To Duck or Not to Duck" (with Daffy Duck, Elmer Fudd/January 9/Looney Tunes), "Flop Goes the Weasel" (February 20/Merrie Melodies), "Super Rabbit" (with Bugs Bunny/April 3/Merrie Melodies), "The Unbearable Bear" (with Sniffles/April 17/Merrie Melodies), "The Aristo Cat" (with Hubie and Bertie/June 12/Merrie Melodies), "Wackiki Wabbit" (with Bugs Bunny/July 3/Merrie Melodies), "Fin 'n' Catty" (October 9/Merrie Melodies), and "Inki and the Minah Bird" (with Inki/November 6/Merrie Melodies).

1944. "Tom Turk and Daffy" (with Daffy Duck/February 12/Looney Tunes), "Bugs Bunny and the Three Bears" (with Bugs Bunny/February 26/Merrie Melodies), "The

Weakly Reporter" (March 25/Merrie Melodies), "Angel Puss" (June 3/Looney Tunes), "From Hand to Mouse" (August 5/Looney Tunes), and "Lost and Foundling" (with Sniffles/September 30/Merrie Melodies).

1945. "Odor-Able Kitty" (with Pepe LePew/January 5/Looney Tunes), "Trap Happy Porky" (with Porky Pig/February 24/Looney Tunes), "Hare Conditioned" (with Bugs Bunny/August 11/Looney Tunes), "Fresh Airedale" (August 25/Merrie Melodies), and "Hare Tonic" (with Bugs Bunny, Elmer Fudd/November 10/Looney Tunes).

1946. "Quentin Quail" (March 2/Merrie Melodies), "Hush My Mouse" (May 4/ Looney Tunes), "Hair Raising Hare" (with Bugs Bunny/May 25/Merrie Melodies), "The Eager Beaver" (July 13/Merrie Melodies), "Fair and Wormer" (September 28/Merrie Melodies), and "Roughly Squeaking" (with Hubie and Bertie/November 28/Looney Tunes).

1947. "Scent-Imental Over You" (with Pepe LePew/May 8/Looney Tunes), "Inki at the Circus" (with Inki/June 21/Merrie Melodies), "A Pest in the House" (with Daffy Duck, Elmer Fudd/August 2/Merrie Melodies), and "House Hunting Mice" (with Hubie and Bertie/September 6/Looney Tunes).

1948.   "A Feather in His Hare" (with Bugs Bunny/February 7/Looney Tunes), "Mississippi Hare" (with Bugs Bunny/February 26/Looney Tunes), "What's Brewin', Bruin?" (with Three Bears/February 28/Looney Tunes), "Rabbit Punch" (with Bugs Bun-April 10/Merrie Melodies), "Haredevil Hare" (with Bugs Bunny/July 24/Looney Tunes), "You Were Never Duckier" (with Daffy Duck/August 7/Merrie Melodies), "Daffy Dilly" (with Daffy Duck/October 30/Merrie Melodies), "My Bunny Lies Over the Sea" (with Bugs Bunny/December 4/Merrie Melodies), and "Scaredy Cat" (with Porky Pig, Sylvester/December 18/Merrie Melodies).

1949.   "Awful Orphan" (with Charlie Dog, Porky Pig/January 29/Merrie Melodies), "Mouse Wreckers" (with Hubie, Bertie, and Claude Cat/April 23/A.A. nominee/Looney Tunes), "The Bee-Deviled Bruin" (with Three Bears/May 14/Merrie Melodies), "Long-Haired Hare" (with Bugs Bunny/June 25/Looney Tunes), "Often an Orphan" (with Charlie Dog/August 13/Looney Tunes), "Fast and Furry-ous" (with Roadrunner/Looney Tunes/September 16), "Frigid Hare" (with Bugs Bunny/October 7/Merrie Melodies), "For Scent-Imental Reasons" (with Pepe LePew/November 12/A.A. winner/Looney Tunes), "Bear Feat" (with Three Bears/December 10/Looney Tunes), and "Rabbit Hood" (with Bugs Bunny/December 24/Merrie Melodies).

1950.   "The Scarlet Pumpernickel" (with Daffy Duck and an All-Star Cast/March 4/ Looney Tunes), "Homeless Hare" (with Bugs Bunny/March 11/Merrie Melodies), "The Hypo-Chondri-Cat" (with Claude Cat, Hubie, and Bertie/April 15/Merrie Melodies), "8 Ball Bunny" (with Bugs Bunny/July 8/Looney Tunes), "Dog Gone South" (with Charlie Dog/August 26/Merrie Melodies), "The Ducksters" (with Daffy Duck/September 2/ Looney Tunes), "Caveman Inki" (with Inki/November 25/Looney Tunes), "Rabbit of Seville" (with Bugs Bunny, Elmer Fudd/December 16/Looney Tunes), and "Two's a Crowd" (with Claude Cat/December 30/Looney Tunes).

1951.   "Bunny Hugged" (with Bugs Bunny/March 10/Merrie Melodies), "Scent-Imental Romeo" (with Pepe LePew/March 24/Merrie Melodies), "A Hound for Trouble" (with Charlie Dog/April 28/Looney Tunes), "Rabbit Fire" (with Bugs Bunny, Daffy Duck, Elmer Fudd/May 9/Looney Tunes), "Chow Hound" (June 16/Looney Tunes), "Wearing the Grin" (with Porky Pig/July 28/Looney Tunes), "A Bear for Punishment" (with Three Bears/October 20/Looney Tunes), and "Drip-Along Daffy" (with Porky Pig, Daffy Duck/November 17/Merrie Melodies).

1952. "Operation: Rabbit" (with Bugs Bunny, Wile E. Coyote/January 19/Looney Tunes), "Feed the Kitty" (with Marc Anthony/February 2/Merrie Melodies), "Little Beau Pepe" (with Pepe LePew/February 9/Merrie Melodies), "Water, Water Every Hare" (with Bugs Bunny/April 19/Looney Tunes), "Beep Beep" (with the Road Runner/May 24/Looney Tunes), "Going! Going! Gosh" (with the Road Runner/August 23/Merrie Melodies), "Mouse Warming" (with Hubie and Bertie/September 8/Looney Tunes), "Rabbit Seasoning" (with Bugs Bunny, Daffy Duck, and Elmer Fudd/September 20/ Merrie Melodies), and "Terrier Stricken" (with Claude Cat/November 29/Merrie Melodies).

1953. "Don't Give Up the Sheep" (with Wolf and Sheepdog/January 3/Looney Tunes), "Forward March Hare" (with Bugs Bunny/February 14/Looney Tunes), "Kiss Me Cat" (with Marc Anthony/February 21/Looney Tunes), "Duck Amuck" (with Daffy Duck/February 28/Merrie Melodies), "Much Ado About Nutting" (May 23/Merrie Melodies), "Wild Over You" (July 11/Looney Tunes), "Duck Dodgers and the 24½ Century" (with Daffy Duck, Porky Pig/July 25/Merrie Melodies), "Bully for Bugs" (with Bugs Bunny/August 9/Looney Tunes), "Zipping Along" (with the Road Runner/September 19/ Merrie Melodies), "Duck, Rabbit, Duck" (with Bugs Bunny/Daffy Duck, Elmer Fudd/ October 3/Merrie Melodies), and "Punch Trunk" (December 19/Looney Tunes).

1954. "Feline Frame-Up" (with Claude Cat, Marc Anthony/February 13/Looney Tunes), "No Barking" (with Claude Cat/February 27/Merrie Melodies), "The Cat's Bah" (with Pepe LePew/March 20/Looney Tunes), "Claws for Alarm" (with Porky Pig, Sylvester/May 22/Looney Tunes), "Bewitched Bunny" (with Bugs Bunny/July 24/Looney Tunes), "Stop, Look, and Hasten!" (with the Road Runner/August 14/Merrie Melodies), "From A to Z-Z-Z" (with Ralph Phillips/October 16/A.A. nominee/Looney Tunes), "Lumber Jack Rabbit" (with Bugs Bunny/November 13/3-D/Looney Tunes), "My Little Duckaroo" (with Daffy Duck/November 27/Merrie Melodies), "Sheep Ahoy" (with Wolf and Sheepdog/December 11/Merrie Melodies), and "Baby Buggy Bunny" (with Bugs Bunny/December 18/Merrie Melodies).

1955. "Beanstalk Bunny" (with Bugs Bunny, Daffy Duck, Elmer Fudd/February 12/Merrie Melodies), "Ready, Set, Zoom" (with the Road Runner/April 30/Looney Tunes), "Past Perfumance" (with Pepe LePew/May 21/Merrie Melodies), "Rabbit Rampage" (with Bugs Bunny, Elmer Fudd/June 11/Looney Tunes), "Double or Mutton" (with Wolf and Sheepdog/July 23/Looney Tunes), "Jumpin' Jupiter" (with Porky Pig, Sylvester/August 6/Merrie Melodies), "Knight-Mare Hare" (with Bugs Bunny/October 1/Merrie Melodies), "Two Scents Worth" (with Pepe LePew/October 15/Merrie Melodies), "Guided Muscle" (with the Road Runner/December 10/Looney Tunes), and "One Froggy Evening" (December 31/Merrie Melodies).

1956. "Bugs Bonnets" (with Bugs Bunny, Elmer Fudd/January 14/Merrie Melodies), "Broomstick Bunny" (with Bugs Bunny/February 25/Looney Tunes), "Rocket Squad" (with Daffy Duck, Porky Pig/March 10/Merrie Melodies), "Heaven Scent" (with Pepe LePew/March 31/Merrie Melodies), "Gee Whiz-z-z-z" (with the Road Runner/May 15/ Looney Tunes), "Barbary Coast Bunny" (with Bugs Bunny/July 21/Looney Tunes), "Rocket Bye Baby" (August 4/Merrie Melodies), "Deduce You Say" (with Daffy Duck, Porky Pig/September 29/Looney Tunes), "There They Go-Go-Go" (with the Road Runner/November 10/Looney Tunes), and "To Hare Is Human" (with Bugs Bunny, Wile E. Coyote/December 15/Merrie Melodies).

1957. "Scrambled Aches" (with the Road Runner/January 26/Looney Tunes), "Ali Baba Bunny" (with Bugs Bunny, Daffy Duck/February 9/Merrie Melodies), "Go Fly a Kite" (February 16/Looney Tunes), "Boyhood Daze" (with Ralph Phillips/April 20/ Merrie Melodies), "Steal Wool" (with Wolf and Sheepdog/June 8/Looney Tunes), "What's Opera, Doc?" (with Bugs Bunny, Elmer Fudd/July 6/Merrie Melodies), "Zoom and Bored" (with the Road Runner/September 14/Looney Tunes), and "Touche and Go" (with Pepe LePew/October 12/Merrie Melodies).

1958. "Robin Hood Daffy" (with Daffy Duck/March 8/Merrie Melodies), "Hare-Way to the Stars" (with Bugs Bunny/March 29/Looney Tunes), "Whoa, Be Gone" (with the Road Runner/April 12/Merrie Melodies), "To Itch His Own" (June 28/Merrie Melodies), "Hook, Line and Stinker" (with the Road Runner/October 11/Looney Tunes), "Hip, Hip-Hurry!" (with the Road Runner/December 6/Merrie Melodies), and "Cat Feud" (December 20/Merrie Melodies).

1959. "Baton Bunny" (with Bugs Bunny/January 10/Looney Tunes), "Hot Rod and Reel" (with the Road Runner/May 9/Looney Tunes), "Really Scent" (with Pepe LePew/June 27/Merrie Melodies), and "Wild About Hurry" (with the Road Runner/October 10/Merrie Melodies).

1960. "Fastest with the Mostest" (with the Road Runner/January 9/Looney Tunes), "Who Scent You?" (with Pepe LePew/April 23/Looney Tunes), "Rabbit's Feat" (with Bugs Bunny, Wile E. Coyote/June 4/Looney Tunes), "Ready Woolen and Able" (with Wolf and Sheepdog/July 30/Merrie Melodies), "Hopalong Casualty" (with the Roadrunner/October 8/Merrie Melodies), and "High Note" (December 3/Looney Tunes).

1961. "Zip 'n' Snort" (with the Road Runner/January 21/Merrie Melodies), "The Mouse on 57th Street" (February 25/Merrie Melodies), "The Abominable Snow Rabbit" (with Bugs Bunny, Daffy Duck/May 20/Looney Tunes), "Lickety Splat" (with the Road Runner/June 3/Looney Tunes), "A Scent of the Matterhorn" (with Pepe LePew/June 24/Looney Tunes), "Compressed Hare" (with Bugs Bunny/July 29/Merrie Melodies), "Beep Prepared" (with the Road Runner/November 11/A.A. nominee/Merrie Melodies), and "Nelly's Folly" (with Nellie, the Giraffe/December 30/A.A. nominee/Merrie Melodies).

1962. "A Sheep in the Deep" (with Wolf and Sheepdog/February 10/Merrie Melodies), "Zoom at the Top" (with the Road Runner/June 30/Merrie Melodies), "Louvre Come Back to Me" (with Pepe LePew/August 18/Looney Tunes), and "Martian Thru Georgia" (with Bugs Bunny/December 27/Merrie Melodies).

1963. "I Was a Teenage Thumb" (January 19/Merrie Melodies), "Now Hear This" (April 27/A.A. nominee/Looney Tunes), "Woolen Under Where" (with Wolf and Sheep-dog/May 11/Merrie Melodies), "Hare-Breadth Hurry" (with Bugs, Wile E. Coyote/June 8/Looney Tunes), "Mad As a Mars Hare" (with Bugs Bunny/October 19/Merrie Melodies), "Transylvania 6-500" (with Bugs Bunny/November 30/Merrie Melodies), and "To Beep or Not to Beep" (with the Road Runner/December 28/Merrie Melodies).

1964. "War and Pieces" (with the Road Runner/June 6/Looney Tunes).

At MGM

(In 1963, Jones left Warner Brothers to form Sib-Tower 12 Productions, a company which produced a new series of Tom and Jerry cartoons for Metro, with Jones directing. Following is a complete list of Tom and Jerry cartoons unless otherwise indicated.)

1963. "Penthouse Mouse."

1964. "The Cat Above and the Mouse Below," "Is There a Doctor in the Mouse," "Much Ado About Mousing," "Snowbody Loves Me," and "Unshrinkable Jerry Mouse."

1965. "The Dot and the Line (Chuck Jones Special/A.A. winner), "Ah Sweet Mouse-Story of Life," "Tom-ic Energy," "Bad Day at Cat Rock," "Brothers Carry Mouse

Off," "Haunted Mouse," "I'm Just Wild About Jerry," "On Feline Bondage," "Year of the Mouse," and "Cat's Me-Ouch."

1966. "Duel Personality," "Jerry Jerry Quite Contrary," and "Love Me, Love My Mouse" (with Ben Washam codirecting).

1967. "The Bear That Wasn't (Chuck Jones Special) and "The Cat Duplicat."

Walter Lantz

(Following is a complete listing of silent and sound theatrical cartoons directed by Walter Lantz. Silent cartoons release dates are listed as available.)

Bray Company

1924. "Col. Heeza Liar's Forbidden Fruit," "African Jungle," "Col. Heeza Liar's Ancestors," "Sky Pilot," "Col. Heeza Liar's Vacation," "Col Heeza Liar's Knighthood," "Horse Play" (with Col. Heeza Liar), "The Magic Lamp" (with Dinky Doodle/September 15), "The Giant Killer" (with Dinky Doodle/October 15), and "The Pied Piper" (with Dinky Doodle/December 1).

1925. "Little Red Riding Hood" (with Dinky Doodle/January 1), "Lyin' Tamer" (with Col. Heeza Liar), "The House That Dinky Built" (with Dinky Doodle/February 1), "Cinderella" (with Dinky Doodle/March 1), "Peter Pan Handled" (with Dinky Doodle/April 26), "Magic Carpet" (with Dinky Doodle/May 24), "Robinson Crusoe" (with Dinky Doodle/June 21), "Three Bears" (with Dinky Doodle/July 19), "Just Spooks" (with Dinky Doodle/September 13), "Dinky Doodle in the Circus" (November 29), and "Dinky Doodle in the Restaurant" (December 27).

1926. "Dinky Doodle in Lost and Found" (February 19), "Dinky Doodle in Uncle Tom's Cabin" (February 21), "Dinky Doodle in the Arctic" (March 21), "Dinky Doodle in Egypt" (April 8), "Dinky Doodle in the Wild West" (May 12), "The Pelican's Bill" (Unnatural History/May 30), "Dinky Doodle's Bed Time Story" (June 6), "Cat's Whiskers" (Unnatural History/June 20), "Dinky Doodle and the Little Orphan" (July 4), "The Mule's Disposition" (Unnatural History/July 8), "The Pig's Curly Tail" (Unnatural History/August 15), "Dinky Doodle in the Army" (August 29), "For the Love 'o' Pete" (with Pete the Pup), "Pete's Haunted House" (with Pete the Pup/October 2), "Pete's Party" (with Pete the Pup/October 26), and "The Tail of the Monkey" (Unnatural History/December 29).

1927. "Dog Gone It" (with Pete the Pup/January 4), "Cat's Nine Lives" (Unnatural History/January 15), "Hyena's Laugh" (Unnatural History/January 18), "Puppy Express" (with Pete the Pup/February 4), "Petering Out" (with Pete the Pup/February 16), "S'matter, Pete?" (with Pete the Pup/March 15), "Lunch Hound" (with Pete the Pup/April 8), and "Jingle Bells" (with Pete the Pup/April 26).

Universal Pictures

(Note: Lantz left Bray and became a gag writer for Mack Sennett and animated shots in 1928 for Universal Pictures' "Andy Gump" series. That explains the two-year gap between productions until Lantz started animating and directing Oswald the Rabbit cartoons, in 1929, for Universal Pictures.)

1929. "Ozzie of the Circus" (with Oswald/January 5), "Stage Stunt" (with Oswald/ May 13), "Stripes and Stars" (with Oswald/May 27), "Wicked West" (with Oswald/ June 10), "Nuts and Jolts" (with Oswald/June 24), "Ice Man's Luck" (with Oswald/July 8), "Weary Willies" (with Oswald/July 22), "Jungle Jingles" (with Oswald/July 22), "Saucy Sausages" (with Oswald/July 31), "Race Riot" (with Oswald/September 2), "Oil's Well" (with Oswald/September 16), "Permanent Wave" (with Oswald/September 29), "Cold Turkey" (with Oswald/October 15), "Amature Nite" (with Oswald/November 11), "Hurdy Gurdy" (with Oswald/November 24), and "Nutty Notes" (with Oswald/December 29).

1930. "Chile Con Carmen" (with Oswald/February 3), "Kisses and Kurses" (with Oswald/February 17), "Broadway Folly" (with Oswald/March 3), "Bowery Bimboes" (with Oswald/originally "Bowling Bimboes"/March 17), "Tramping Tramps" (with Oswald/March 31), "The Hash Shop" (with Oswald/originally "The Hash House"/April 4), "The Prison Panic" (with Oswald/April 27), "Hot for Hollywood" (with Oswald/ originally "Hollywood"/May 19), "Hell's Heels" (with Oswald/Lantz/June 2), "My Pal Paul" (with Oswald/June 16), "Not So Quiet" (with Oswald/July 7), "Spooks" (with Oswald/July 21), "Hen Fruit" (with Oswald/originally "Henpecked"/August 11), "Cold Feet" (with Oswald/August 13), "Snappy Salesman" (with Oswald/August 18), "The Singing Sap" (with Oswald/September 15), "The Detective" (with Oswald/September 22), "The Fowl Ball" (with Oswald/October 13), "The Navy" (with Oswald/November 3), "Mexico" (with Oswald/November 17), "Africa" (with Oswald/December 1), "Alaska" (with Oswald/December 15), and "Mars" (with Oswald/December 29).

1931. "China" (with Oswald/cd: Nolan/January 12), "College" (with Oswald/cd: Nolan/January 26), "Shipwrecked" (with Oswald/cd: Nolan/February 18), "The Farmer" (with Oswald/cd: Nolan/March 23), "The Fireman" (with Oswald/cd: Nolan/April 6), "Sunny South" (with Oswald/cd: Nolan/April 20), "The Country School" (with Oswald/ cd: Nolan/May 5), "The Band Master" (with Oswald/cd: Nolan/May 18), "North Woods" (with Oswald/cd: Nolan/June 29), "The Stone Age" (with Oswald/cd: Nolan/ July 13), "Radio Rhythm" (with Oswald/cd: Nolan/July 27), "Kentucky Bells" (with Oswald/originally "Horse Race"/cd: Nolan/September 2), "Hot Feet" (with Oswald/cd: Nolan/September 14), "The Hunter" (with Oswald/cd: Nolan/October 12), "Wonderland" (with Oswald/cd: Nolan/October 26), "The Hare Mail" (with Oswald/cd: Nolan/ November 30), "The Fisherman" (with Oswald/cd: Nolan/December 7), and "The Clown" (with Oswald/cd: Nolan/December 21).

1932. "Mechanical Man" (with Oswald/cd: Nolan/January 4), "Grandma's Pet" (with Oswald/cd: Nolan/January 18), "Wins Out" (with Oswald/cd: Nolan/March 14), "Beau and Arrows" (with Oswald/cd: Nolan/March 28), "Making Good" (with Oswald/ cd: Nolan/April 11), "Let's Eat" (with Oswald/originally "Foiled"/cd: Nolan/April 25), "The Winged Horse" (with Oswald/cd: Nolan/May 9), "To the Rescue" (with Oswald/cd: Nolan/May 23), "Cat Nipped" (with Oswald/cd: Nolan/May 23), "A Wet Knight" (with Oswald/cd: Nolan/June 20), "A Jungle Jumble" (with Oswald/cd: Nolan/July 4), "Day Nurse" (with Oswald/cd: Nolan/August 1), "The Athlete" (with Pooch the Pup/cd: Nolan/August 29), "The Busy Barber" (with Oswald/cd: Nolan/September 12), "The Butcher Boy" (with Pooch the Pup/cd: Nolan/September 26), "Carnival Capers" (with Oswald/cd: Nolan/October 10), "The Crowd Snores" (with Pooch the Pup/cd: Nolan/ October 24), "The Underdog" (with Pooch the Pup/cd: Nolan/November 7), "Wild and Woolly" (with Oswald/cd: Nolan/November 21), "Cats and Dogs" (with Pooch the Pup/ cd: Nolan/December 5), and "The Teacher's Pests" (with Oswald/cd: Nolan/December 19).

1933. "Merry Dog" (with Pooch the Pup/cd: Nolan/January 2), "The Plumber" (with Oswald/cd: Nolan/January 16), "The Terrible Troubador" (with Pooch the Pup/ cd: Nolan/February 13), "The Shriek" (with Oswald/cd: Nolan/February 27), "The Lumber Chumps" (with Pooch the Pup/cd: Nolan/March 13), "Going to Blazes" (with

Oswald/cd: Nolan/April 10), "Beau Beste" (with Oswald/cd: Nolan/May 22), "Nature's Workshop" (with Pooch the Pup/cd: Nolan/June 5), "Ham and Eggs" (with Oswald/cd: Nolan/June 19), "Pin Feathers" (with Pooch the Pup/cd: Nolan/July 3), "Confidence" (with Oswald/cd: Nolan/July 31), "Hot and Cold" (with Pooch the Pup/cd: Nolan/August 14), "King Klunk" (with Pooch the Pup/cd: Nolan/September 4), "Five and Dime" (with Oswald/cd: Nolan/September 18), "She Done Him Right" (with Pooch the Pup/cd: Nolan/September 25), "The Zoo" (with Oswald/cd: Nolan/November 6), "The Merry Old Soul" (with Oswald/cd: Nolan/November 27), and "Parking Space" (with Oswald/cd: Nolan/December 18).

1934. "Chicken Reel" (with Oswald/cd: Nolan/January 1), "The Candy House" (with Oswald/cd: Nolan/January 15), "The Country Fair" (with Oswald/cd: Nolan/February 5), "The Toy Shoppe" (with Oswald/cd: Nolan/February 19), "Wolf! Wolf!" (with Oswald/cd: Nolan/April 2), "The Ginger Bread Boy" (with Oswald/cd: Nolan/April 26), "Annie Moved Away" (with Oswald/cd: Nolan/April 30), "Goldielocks and the Three Bears" (with Oswald/cd: Nolan/May 14), "The Wax Works" (with Oswald/cd: Nolan/June 25), "William Tell" (with Oswald/cd: Nolan/July 9), "Chris Columbus, Jr." (with Oswald/July 23), "The Dizzy Dwarf" (with Oswald/cd: Nolan/August 6), "Ye Happy Pilgrims" (with Oswald/September 3), "Jolly Little Elves" (Cartune Classic/Cinecolor/A.A. nominee/October 1), "The Sky Larks" (with Oswald/October 22), "Spring in the Park" (with Oswald/November 12), and "Toyland Premiere" (Cartune Classic/Cinecolor/December 10).

1935. "Robinson Crusoe Isle" (with Oswald/January 7), "The Hillbilly" (with Oswald/originally "Hill Billies"/February 1), "Two Little Lambs" (with Oswald/March 11), "Do a Good Deed" (with Oswald/March 25), "Candy Land" (Cartune Classic/Cinecolor/April 22), "Elmer, the Great Dane" (with Oswald/April 29), "Springtime Serenade" (Cartune Classics/Cinecolor/May 27), "Towne Hall Follies" (with Oswald/June 3), "At Your Service" (with Oswald/July 8), "Three Lazy Mice" (Cartune Classics/Cinecolor/July 15), "Bronco Buster" (with Oswald/August 5), "Amateur Broadcast" (with Oswald/August 26), "The Quail Hunt" (with Oswald/Cinecolor/September 23), "The Fox and the Rabbit" (Cartune Classic/Cinecolor/September 30), "Monkey Wretches" (with Oswald/November 11), "The Case of the Lost Sheep" (with Oswald/December 9), and "Doctor Oswald" (with Oswald/December 30).

1936. "Soft Ball Game" (with Oswald/January 27), "Alaska Sweepstakes" (with Oswald/February 17), "Slumberland Express" (with Oswald/March 7), "Beauty Shoppe" (with Oswald/March 30), "Barnyard Five" (with Oswald/April 20), "Fun House" (with Oswald/May 4), "Farming Fools" (with Oswald/May 25), "Battle Royal" (with Oswald/June 22), "Music Hath Charms" (with Oswald/September 7), "Kiddie Review" (with Oswald/September 21), "Beach Combers" (with Oswald/October 5), "Night Life of the Bugs" (with Oswald/October 9), "The Puppet Show" (with Oswald/November 2), "Unpopular Mechanic" (with Oswald/November 6), "Turkey Dinner" (with Meany, Miny, and Moe/November 30), "Gopher Trouble" (with Oswald/November 30), and "Knights for a Day" (with Meany, Miny, and Moe/December 25).

1937. "The Golfers" (with Meany, Miny, and Moe/January 11), "House of Magic" (with Meany, Miny, and Moe/February 8), "Everybody Sings" (with Oswald/February 22), "The Big Race" (with Meany, Miny, and Moe/March 3), "Duck Hunt" (with Oswald/March 8), "Lumber Camp" (with Meany, Miny, and Moe/March 15), "The Birthday Party" (with Oswald/March 29), "Steel Workers" (with Meany, Miny, and Moe/April 26), "Trailer Thrills" (with Oswald/May 3), "The Stevedores" (with Meany, Miny, and Moe/April 26), "The Wily Weasel" (with Oswald/June 7), "Country Store" (with Meany, Miny, and Moe/July 5), "The Playful Pup" (with Oswald/July 12), "Fireman's Picnic" (with Meany, Miny, and Moe/August 16), "Rest Resort" (with Meany, Miny, and Moe/August 23), "Ostrich Feathers" (with Meany, Miny, and Moe/September 6), "Air Express" (with

Meany, Miny, and Moe/September 20), "Lovesick" (with Oswald/October 4), "The Keeper of the Lions" (with Oswald/October 18), "The Mechanical Handy Man" (with Oswald/November 8), "Football Fever" (with Oswald/November 13), "The Mysterious Jug" (with Oswald/November 29), and "The Dumb Cluck" (with Oswald/December 20).

1938.   "Yokel Boy Makes Good" (with Oswald/February 21).

(Lantz reduced himself to primarily a cartoon producer who directed some cartoons during intervals away from the job in the 1940s and 1950s. All films were in color starting in 1940.)

1940.   "Crazy House" (with Andy Panda/September 23), "Knock, Knock" (with Andy Panda; Woody Woodpecker's debut/November 25), and "Syncopated Sioux" (Walter Lantz Cartune Special/December 30).

1941.   "Fair Today" (Walter Lantz Cartune Special/February 24), "Scrub Me Mama with a Boogie Beat" (Walter Lantz Cartune Special/March 28), "Hysterical High Spots in American History" (Walter Lantz Cartune Special/March 31), "Dizzy Kitty" (with Andy Panda/May 26), "Salt Water Daffy" (Walter Lantz Cartune Special/June 9), "Woody Woodpecker" (with Woody Woodpecker/originally "The Cracked Nut"/July 7), "The Screwdriver" (with Woody Woodpecker/August 11), "The Boogie Woogie Bugle Boy of Company B" (Walter Lantz Cartune Special/A.A. nominee/September 1), "Man's Best Friend" (Walter Lantz Cartune Special/October 20), "Pantry Panic" (with Woody Wood-pecker/originally "What's Cookin?"/November 24), and "$21.00 a Day Once a Month" (Swing Symphonies/December 1).

1942.   "Hollywood Matador" (with Woody Woodpecker/February 9), "The Hams That Couldn't Be Cured" (Swing Symphonies/March 4), "Mother Goose on the Loose" (Walter Lantz Cartune Special/April 13), and "Goodbye Mr. Moth" (with Andy Panda/May 11).

1951.   "Wicket Wacky" (with Woody Woodpecker/May 28), "Slingshot 6⅞" (with Woody Woodpecker/July 23), "Redwood Sap" (with Woody Woodpecker/October 1), "Woody Woodpecker Polka" (with Woody Woodpecker/October 29), and "Destination Meatball" (with Woody Woodpecker/December 24).

1952.   "Born to Peck" (with Woody Woodpecker/February 25), "Stage Hoax" (with Woody Woodpecker/April 21), "Woodpecker in the Rough" (with Woody Woodpecker/July 14), "Scalp Treatment" (with Woody Woodpecker/September 8), and "The Great Who Dood It" (with Woody Woodpecker/October 20).

Index

W

Y

Bob Clampett's Porky Pig breaking out of a
Warner Bros. cartoon title ending, saying
"Th-th-that's all, f-f-folks!" © *Warner Bros.*